Chicken Soup for the Soul.

Believe in Angels

Room 706 B

3-25 2022

Chicken Soup for the Soul: Believe in Angels
101 Inspirational Stories of Hope, Miracles and Answered Prayers
Amy Newmark

Published by Chicken Soup for the Soul, LLC www.chickensoup.com
Copyright ©2022 by Chicken Soup for the Soul, LLC. All Rights Reserved.

The publisher gratefully acknowledges the many publishers and individuals who
granted Chicken Soup for the Soul permission to reprint the cited material.

Front cover photo of buildings courtesy of iStockphoto.com/petekarici (©petekarici),
photo of man courtesy of iStockphoto.com/Maxiphoto (©Maxiphoto)
Back cover and interior images of feathers courtesy of iStockphoto.com/Gluiki (©Gluiki)
Photo of Amy Newmark courtesy of Susan Morrow at SwickPix

Cover and Interior by Daniel Zaccari

Publisher's Cataloging-In-Publication Data
(Prepared by The Donohue Group, Inc.)

Names: Newmark, Amy, compiler.
Title: Chicken soup for the soul : believe in angels : 101
    inspirational stories of hope, miracles and answered prayers /
    [compiled by] Amy Newmark.
Other Titles: Believe in angels : 101 inspirational stories of hope,
    miracles and answered prayers
Description: [Cos Cob, Connecticut] : Chicken Soup for the Soul,
    LLC, [2022]
Identifiers: ISBN 9781611590869 (print) | ISBN 9781611593242 (ebook)
Subjects: LCSH: Angels--Literary collections. | Angels--Anecdotes. |
    Miracles--Literary collections. | Miracles--Anecdotes. | Prayer--
    Literary collections. | Prayer--Anecdotes. | LCGFT: Anecdotes.
Classification: LCC BL477 .C453 2021 (print) | LCC BL477 (ebook) |
    DDC 202/.15/02--dc23

Library of Congress Control Number: 2021948080

PRINTED IN THE UNITED STATES OF AMERICA
on acid∞free paper

28 27 26 25 24 23 22   01 02 03 04 05 06 07 08 09 10 11

3-25-2022

Chicken Soup
for the Soul®

Room
706
B

Believe
in
Angels

101 Inspirational
Stories of Hope, Miracles
and Answered Prayers

3-25-2022

Amy Newmark

CSS

Chicken Soup for the Soul, LLC
Cos Cob, CT

Changing lives one story at a time®
www.chickensoup.com

Table of Contents

❶
~Divine Messengers~

❷
~Angels in Disguise~

3

~Messages from Heaven~

4

~Guardians and Protectors~

5

~Answered Prayers~

❻

~Touched by an Angel~

❼

~Hope and Faith in Action~

❽

~Comfort from Beyond~

❾

~How Did That Happen?~

⑩

~Miraculous Connections~

Divine Messengers

Momentous Advice

Angels assist us in connecting with a powerful
yet gentle force, which encourages us to
live life to its fullest.
~Denise Linn

T he rain hadn't stopped for several days. The cold wind chilled my bones as I let in the babysitter at 6:30 A.M.

It was the last week of my six-month probationary period as a financial consultant trainee for a large insurance company. I'd had only two small sales, which was way below the average. I'd received a call the night before from my sales manager who demanded I arrive for a private meeting at 8:00 A.M. instead of my normal 10:00 A.M. arrival time. Plus, I was told I'd need my car, so I had to leave extra early due to the traffic issues on the Long Island Expressway.

I was sure I'd be fired, and I wondered why the manager couldn't have just told me over the phone. The extra cost of an early morning babysitter and parking in Manhattan threw a wrench in my budget, and it was only the fifth of the month.

I'd taken this job out of desperation after my husband announced one morning that he no longer wanted to be married. He left me to take care of our seven-year-old son alone. This new job was my first attempt at a career, a way to support my son and myself.

That morning, I didn't take time for breakfast or even a swig of coffee. I disliked driving on the Long Island Expressway during rush hour, especially in the rain. But here I was barreling down the highway in a deluge.

About thirty minutes into my drive, I saw someone standing on the side of the road. I pulled onto the small shoulder and stopped a few feet beyond the person. I jumped out of my car and asked if they needed a ride. Then I stopped in my tracks.

I stared at the person, but I couldn't tell if it was a male or a female. It was someone old with a withered face, stringy gray hair, and mud-spattered overalls that stopped at the ankles. The person stood barefoot in the cold rain. I told the stranger to get in my car.

The person took a few steps toward me and offered a hand for me to shake. As I reached out, I inhaled the most putrid smell, like dead, rotting animals. I let go of the handshake and took a step backward.

As I did, the person said, "Remember, you're a good person. Say 'yes' in your meeting this morning."

I stood frozen in shock. My mind searched for a reason why this total stranger would know I had a meeting. I pointed to my car and said, "Get in, please."

"No," the person said.

I was drenched and turned around to walk back to the driver's side of my car, but I stopped after taking two steps. I turned back toward the person to insist they get in, but no one was there.

I walked to the side of the road, only about four steps, and looked both ways. No one. There were no trees or bushes around that someone could hide behind. I looked all around the car, and there was nothing. No one.

I jumped back into my car and noticed I had mud on my right hand from shaking hands. I washed up when I reached my office. Then I went into the meeting.

I apologized to my manager for my poor sales performance and asked if there was a way I could make it up. I needed to keep this job.

The sales manager smiled and told me to relax. He said he wasn't going to fire me. At least, not now. He'd spoken to both of my customers and had never had people compliment one of his staff so much. Both said I was a nice person and went the extra mile for them.

Out of nowhere, the manager invited me into an exclusive training group. I'd be away for intensive training for a month, and then I would work longer hours with a personal trainer and mentor. The training would last a year, and I'd receive a high salary and higher commissions on sales. Plus, he handed me an extra bonus check to help cover my additional childcare expenses.

I recalled the words that mysterious stranger had said to me: "Say 'yes' in your meeting this morning."

I heard myself say, "Yes, of course."

I was shocked because I had no idea how I'd work out the month away.

That sales training helped me excel in sales and marketing for several companies and provided a strong foundation for my own business.

That odd conversation with a stranger in a deluge had changed my life. It took me a long time to understand that I'd met, shook hands, and spoken with an angel.

I still get a bit nauseated when I think of the overpowering smell from the stranger. But the handshake was firm, and the words were exactly what I needed to hear. Without those words, I would have instinctively declined that training offer, and my career would have ended that day.

At one of the lowest points in my life—during a cold, fall rainstorm on the treacherous Long Island Expressway—my life was transformed. And while the training was rigorous, and there were many moments when I wanted to quit because it all seemed too hard, the words of that angel gave me the staying power and confidence that I needed.

— Bluedolphin Crow —

Strangers in the Night

You should never feel alone there's always
someone to turn to, it is the Guardian Angel
who is watching over you.
~K. Sue

One Sunday afternoon, I felt remarkably listless and tired, so I decided to lie down for a nap. My husband thought this most unusual of me as I was normally tending to the children, cooking, gardening or puttering around with some artistic project. He felt my forehead and took my temperature. Sure enough, I had a high fever. He made arrangements with his mom to stay with the kids, who were five and seven years old at the time, and we went to the hospital.

After triage, it was determined there was a good chance I had pneumonia, and I was admitted for a brief stay. My fever was high enough that the doctor put me on an antibiotic IV drip. The plan was for an overnight stay and then to be released in the morning.

Well, things did not go as planned....

I remember feeling so out of control. I had kids to get ready for school the next morning, lunches to make, a family to take care of. But I also remember how tired I was and how all I wanted to do was sleep. I had to surrender to the medical professionals assigned to my care.

A couple of days passed, but I did not feel any better. Doctors came by. The nurses checked my vitals every morning and night. The best part of my day was when my husband visited. His visits always lifted my spirits.

On the third day in the hospital, I began feeling extremely uncomfortable. With no appetite or energy, I slept most of the day. That night, I remember waking up because I felt a presence in the room. I was lying on my left side and slowly rolled over onto my back.

At the foot of my bed stood two women in nun's black habits. One stood about a foot taller than the other. They did not speak; they just stood there motionless. I remember thinking, *Why would two nurses come to check on me in the middle of the night?* I quickly dismissed that thought and said to them, "I'm not doing so well tonight." They looked at me and then turned their gaze to the IV on the right of my bed, almost as if they were pointing to it with their eyes. I rolled over onto my left side and went back to sleep.

The next morning, I attempted to eat a little breakfast and decided to turn on the hospital television that my husband had rented for me during my stay. Scrolling through the channels, I landed on *The Montel Williams Show*. He had psychic Sylvia Browne as his guest, and they were discussing guardian angels.

Not long after the show ended, my husband called. We chatted about the kids, and I began telling him about the two nurses dressed in black who had come to check on me in the middle of the night. He was confused. Two nurses? Dressed in black? The more I talked to him about it, the more I realized how crazy it sounded. Then I recalled the *Montel* episode I had just watched. We both began to feel that something really strange had taken place that night. I told him that they had stared at my IV, which had to mean something.

When the doctor came by during his rounds later that morning, I let him know that I had had a rough night and had not slept well. He looked at the IV bag and checked my chart. I think he realized that I was not responding to the antibiotics he had prescribed for me.

That night was crucial. The doctor had apparently told my husband that morning after his rounds that the situation was quite dire. It wasn't until he decided to change my antibiotics that my situation improved, and I began responding and healing from the pneumonia. I was released the next day.

I'm not sure what happened in the middle of that night. Was I visited by two guardian angels? Did they manifest as nuns because of my Catholic upbringing? Were they there to let me know that the problem was in the IV bag I was hooked up to? The experience certainly had me baffled. I seemed to have more questions than answers. However, what I do know is that I will be forever grateful for this divine intervention. The day I left the hospital, I took with me a renewed sense of faith and the belief that angels are always present in our lives.

— Lydia Jackson —

Perfect Timing

Pay attention to your dreams — God's angels often
speak directly to our hearts when we are asleep.
~Eileen Elias Freeman,
The Angels' Little Instruction Book

My manuscript was finally done, but two nights later I had a vivid dream of feverishly working on it once again to make a November publishing date. I heard a gentle voice say, "Get up and write this down."

I opened one eye. It was still dark. I groaned and rolled over to go back to sleep. Then I felt someone, or something, lightly shake me. At first, I thought my subconscious was working overtime, but my subconscious had never done this before.

The voice commanded, "Get up and write this down. Do it now."

I sat up and swung my legs out of bed. I padded softly out of the room, careful not to wake my husband. Once in my office, I woke up my sleeping computer.

I recalled my dream, visualizing the changes made to a few paragraphs and additions to the text. It seemed I'd been perfecting the story for months, but now my fingers flew across the keyboard before I forgot the revisions I was supposed to make. At the same time, thinking about making those edits made my stomach churn because it meant it was time to send my work to the publisher. Afraid of rejection, I was stalling, and I knew it. But the dream seemed so real and the voice so insistent.

The story was near and dear to my heart and, at times, emotionally wrenching for me to write. Although a work of fiction, *Sheltering Angels* paralleled events in my own life, including my younger brother's devastating death. It took me years to work through my grief. In laying it all out on paper, I relived every heart-wrenching detail.

My writing-group friends and editor all told me, "Your experience and how you dealt with it may help someone else." Intellectually, I knew that to be true.

I completed the changes shown to me in the dream. After reading it aloud, I realized that the story sounded better. The manuscript was finished. While still at the keyboard, I e-mailed a publisher that I had used for my previous novel. Writing a professional introduction to my work, I attached the manuscript and hit Send. The book was out of my hands. Feeling a sense of relief, I went back to the bedroom where my husband was still sleeping. I showered and dressed and went to the kitchen for breakfast. Later, with a cup of coffee in hand, I returned to the computer to check my e-mails.

My eyes widened because I had had a reply from my publisher within one hour of sending my manuscript. Never had an answer come so quickly or at that hour. Wally, the owner of the small publishing company, acknowledged the receipt of my work and said, "Your e-mail could not have come at a better time. I'm getting ready for a virtual meeting with all my editors about what books we will put forward in the future. Since you are an established author with us, I'm adding *Sheltering Angels* to my pile. I'll have an answer for you in a day or two."

Sheltering Angels entered into the publishing process two days later. Its debut happened exactly on the day I dreamed. In hindsight, it's perfectly clear to me why the voice was so insistent.

— Nancy Emmick Panko —

Mystical Owl Quartet

If you're not okay, you might as well not pretend you are,
especially since life has a way of holding us down
until we utter that magic word: help!
That's when angels rush to your side.
~Glennon Doyle Melton

What do owls and the mystical algorithm of the universe have in common? Spiritually, owls symbolize death in the form of life transitions or change. Seemingly, four of them must symbolize a *very big* change, right? In May 2015, I moved from Maine to San Francisco with a new boyfriend, leaving behind everything and everyone for a Big Western Adventure. After the road trip, but still in the honeymoon phase, we landed in California, rented a house and bought furniture. During the nesting phase, I was alerted to the fact that I didn't know him all that well. A series of lies and unexpected circumstances prompted me to take the truck and drive far away in a fury of tears and disbelief. Flight was my natural instinct at the time.

One incredibly long day of driving later, I arrived at a friend's house. Like Yellowstone's Old Faithful, I vented in exasperation until I was out of steam. He thought I was being dramatic but was supportive nonetheless. After wearing out my welcome, I headed back "home" to face reality. Halfway there, I pulled off the I-5 into the desert east of Pinnacles National Park. Mid-May in the valley is warm — long days without a wisp of a cloud anywhere. Pulling over to stretch my legs and untack the damp shirt from the small of my back, I savored the golden light and temperature reprieve offered by dusk. For the first time in several days, the hornet's nest in my head quieted down. No doubt, the mindless drive on I-5 in an old truck without air-conditioning or radio had something to do with it. Tugging on my shirt, I hopped back onto the old bench seat, anxious to get where I was going with daylight remaining.

For thirteen slow miles, I drove into the desert moonscape on what was originally a stagecoach route used by early pioneers doing business at a nearby silver mine. Sand lapped the edge of the narrow, thin pavement, threatening to hide the road if the wind continued. Past rolling hills and cows grazing on what appeared to be sand, I eventually rolled past a falling-down farmhouse into a hot-spring resort promising solace and spring water with healing properties. Being in the middle of nowhere made me feel safe and untraceable — invisible even.

As dusk transitioned to dark, I built a nest in the back of the truck, inflated my sleeping pad, and arranged my pillow and nightclothes. I checked the batteries in my headlamp and deployed my toiletry bag to the tailgate for the nighttime ritual of lotions, potions, and teeth brushing. Other guests seemed to be tucked in already, so I slipped into my towel and tiptoed over to the hot springs. I chose a tub facing west. The profile of a ridge was illuminated with the very last sliver of orange sunlight. For a long while, I sat in that warm, sulphury water, wondering what went wrong. How had I so poorly misjudged my new boyfriend's character? What kind of lesson was the Universe trying to teach me? As the stars began piercing the sky, the paradox of soaking in self-pity and healing water was not lost on me.

Thoroughly relaxed from the heat of the springs, I returned to the truck, crawled into my nest and fell immediately to sleep. Waking at dawn, I sat up to push the truck-cab window open over the tailgate. The morning light had a filtered quality that made the desert look warm and velvety. Inspired, I grabbed my camera to shoot a few frames of the old farmhouse.

On my way there, a pine grove harboring two tent sites posed a distraction. A dark-haired woman standing outside the grove greeted me, with a Chihuahua in one arm and coffee cup in the other. We exchanged pleasantries as I observed the remaining teaspoon of coffee hypnotically rolling back and forth in the bottom of her tin cup. She explained that we were on Native American healing ground, and she was studying shamanism.

Torn by the parallel desire to hear more of her story or to capture the farmhouse in dreamy, morning light, I chose the farmhouse and excused myself. In parting, my acquaintance said, "The world is going to change, and women are going to be the ones who do it."

Nodding in agreement and contemplation, I thanked her for the chat and walked toward my subject. I captured several frames, admiring the juxtaposition of the lonely farmhouse in a desert oasis.

Feeling the need to get on the road, I headed for my bag on the tailgate, swapping the camera for toiletries. I simultaneously brushed my teeth and stowed things for the drive home. A moment after getting back on the road I looped back to thank the lady for the profound conversation and to ask if she'd like to keep in touch.

I didn't see her where we had previously stood, so I hopped out and walked to the pines. There was no vehicle there, and I realized there hadn't been one twenty minutes prior. Maybe she had parked in the shade somewhere. Nearing the grove, I still didn't sense her presence. No hiss of a propane stove or rustling of a Chihuahua in the pine needles. It was dark in the grove compared to the blue-sky morning outside. I walked in, pupils dilating quickly. No one was there. No dark-haired woman, no Chihuahua, no sign of a camper at all. Not a tent. Not a cooler. Nothing.

The clearing was small in circumference, with a radius of less than thirty feet in any direction from where I was standing. Wondering where the lady might be, the hairs on my arms stood at attention as I gazed upward into the pine canopy. On a branch directly above me sat four owls perched in a line. Spooked, I took a deep breath as my feet moved my body backward out of the pine grove.

No lady. Four owls.

I hustled to the truck and onto the old stagecoach road, subconsciously holding my breath for much of the drive back. Certain that the apparition wasn't imaginary, I puzzled over the encounter. It didn't feel like a haunting but rather a mystical messenger delivering a riddle.

Approaching the highway, I regained cell service and was startled by message alerts ding-ding-dinging on the seat beside me. Pulling over, I found a flood of messages from friends and loved ones whom I hadn't heard from in months. Feeling buoyed, I reconciled that my relationship had died, but my Big Western Adventure was just beginning.

Had the Universe sent a messenger previewing lessons I would encounter? Had she existed in that moment, in that desert oasis, to help me recognize and trust inner guidance on a higher level? Surrendering to my intuition, I started paying attention to these signs and seeing synchronicities everywhere I looked. They are numerous, occur regularly, and endlessly illuminate the path I'm traveling.

It's been a blessing.

— Elizabeth K. Goodine —

The Angel in Aisle Three

How beautiful a day can be
When kindness touches it!
~George Elliston

Years ago, I found myself in the local grocery store with my barely one-year-old son. I wore an owl sweater that covered my bony shoulders from weeks of eating as little as possible. My eyes were hollow with deep shadows of darkness underneath from countless sleepless nights. My hair was crimped from braids the night before. It was the most I could do to attempt to look ready for public interaction and to face a new day.

My husband had told me several weeks before that he wanted a divorce. My kids were ages three and one. I was heartbroken, which quickly carried over to the anger-and-rage stage I had stayed stuck in far too long. I was physically starved for food. Emotionally starved for love. And spiritually starved for understanding and peace after my world was turned upside down in one single, horrible conversation.

As I did my usual grocery shopping early that morning, I tried to put on my bravest face — if only for the small child smiling back at me from his car seat carrier perched in the front of the grocery cart. I needed to be strong for him and his older brother. They were my saving grace during that time of traumatic emotional upheaval.

I recall walking to the dairy aisle. I hated that aisle. It was cold, unwelcoming, and made me want to shiver my way far from the butter, cheese and eggs, which seemed to mock my now typical awkward, troubled appearance. As I reached for a box of butter, I looked up to find an elderly gentleman directly beside me. He looked kind.

I smiled. He smiled. He looked deep into my tired, sad, lifeless eyes and said three simple words: "You are beautiful." With tears streaming down my face, I turned to thank him, but he was gone. He vanished as quickly as he had appeared, changing my perspective, mood and life with three simple words.

At the depth of my despair, I entertained this angel unaware. He touched my broken heart with words I will never forget. He reached into my spirit and gave it a breath of re-birth, forcing me to rise above and re-evaluate my spiritual worth.

I will never know if he was really there or a figment of my fractured imagination. I only know he brought a smile to my face and a song to my heart for the first time in weeks.

I still had a long road to recovery and accepting my new normal. Yet, my interaction with the stranger on that particular day was the beginning of a healing path toward forgiveness, acceptance, peace and a greater love than I had ever known. That experience changed the way I saw myself, from a rejected, empty shell of a woman to a beloved, worthy, precious, and beautiful child of God.

— Amannda G. Maphies —

The Still, Small Voice

God turned the adversity into a blessing.
~Lailah Gifty Akita

W e were three strangers — Marcus, Jim, and me — meeting for the first time on the first day of a new job. We were all in our fifties — not always a good place to be. However, we found that we worked well together. And, after a year, we decided we could do better working for ourselves.

We set up our business in a one-room office furnished with used equipment in a rundown building. We had no customers and were dependent solely on our own efforts to make a go of it. With great resolve and more than a smidgen of panic, we went to work.

By the end of our first two weeks, we had enough money in the company account to ensure that we'd each receive a paycheck at the first of the month and that the rent, electricity and lease on the equipment would be paid. We breathed a little easier.

We worked hard, and the business grew. At the end of the first year, there were six of us filling our new, expanded office. Things were looking good indeed.

Along the way, differences in management philosophy resulted in Jim's interest being purchased, leaving Marcus and me to run the business. At the end of our second year, we'd grown to twelve employees and had again expanded our space. The world was looking rosy.

Marcus and I met each morning for an hour before the business opened to discuss the events of the previous day, both successes and potential problems, needs of the business, and our personal lives. Marcus kept me informed of the financial side of the business, which was his responsibility. I, in turn, charged with generating revenue, told him about sales, pending sales, and large deals that were in progress.

We formed a deep friendship, going well beyond being business partners. We had a similar sense of humor and shared the same political philosophy and moral values. In those casual meetings, we discussed personal problems and our families. We laughed, cried and shared our victories.

In our fifth year of business, Marcus came to me requesting that I fill out a financial report for the state. "Just fill in the blanks, sign it and send it in," he advised. As finances were his department, I found the request to be out of the ordinary. Still, I willingly complied.

While filling out the forms, I discovered severe financial problems in the business that Marcus had never told me about. When confronted with my discovery, he shrugged off my concerns, saying the problems were "inconsequential."

The state agreed with my assessment. Within days, our business was closed and all the employees were terminated. My world collapsed almost overnight. Everything we'd worked for was lost and gone. I also lost a friend — Marcus.

During the next period of my life, my emotions ranged from rage at the betrayal by my partner to sorrow for the employees who were suddenly out of a job, to despair as I struggled with the total loss. I felt guilty; I should have known of the problems. I quickly found it difficult to trust anyone. All this gelled into one emotion — anger. Anger at Marcus. Anger at myself.

My blood pressure skyrocketed, requiring larger doses of medication. Even the thought of Marcus sent my blood pressure off the chart, my temples pounding, and my head throbbing. My stomach burned.

I put all my efforts into starting another company in an entirely different field. I trusted no one. It was my company; no one else was welcome to share. Two years passed in which I wrested a living from a slowly growing list of clients. There was little joy. Headaches were always with me, and I knew why: Marcus! Anger always boiled below the surface. Blood pressure hovered in that area that warned: danger!

One day while driving to an appointment, a voice spoke in my ear as though another person was in the car with me. I recognized it immediately. It was that still, small voice that I'd heard on a few other occasions. The voice quietly whispered, "David, you can't live with this anger in your soul. You have to speak with Marcus. Clear the air of the problem between the two of you."

On two other occasions, that voice has spoken to me, once as a direct answer to prayer about a problem in my life. It gave me detailed instructions on how to solve the problem that I had prayed about.

The other occasion was on a trip to Nogales, Mexico. A man was racing down the street, chased by a squad of military men with rifles at port arms. I stared with open mouth at the spectacle passing by. As the military people rounded a corner, the still, small voice spoke, "David, Get out of here." I immediately crossed the border back to the United States. I've never been back to Mexico.

The admonition to clear the air of the problem with Marcus was still echoing when I turned the car around and drove directly to Marcus's home. He answered the door, saying, "I was hoping for a chance to talk with you. I'm so sorry for what happened." He ushered me into his living room, where we discussed the loss of our business, trust and friendship for the next two hours. At the end of that time, we agreed to meet for lunch within the next two weeks.

Early one morning, a week later, the phone rang. A friend was on the other end of the call. His words gave me chills. "Marcus had a heart attack last night and died."

I sometimes still struggle with thoughts of "what might have been," but the debilitating hatred that earlier infected me is gone. I find contentment with memories of holiday meals that my wife and I shared with Marcus and his family, of the high-fives we exchanged when things had gone well, and of the laughter over silly jokes. Such is the power of forgiveness. Thank God for that still, small voice that sent me to Marcus before it was too late.

— D. Lincoln Jones —

The Accidental Messenger

Angels represent God's personal care
for each one of us.
~Andrew Greeley

With my hands on my hips, I glared at Joe as he lounged in his recliner, nodding off as yet another football game blared on the TV. I muttered under my breath loud enough to stir him, and he blinked up at me, confusion spreading across his face.

"What?" he said, his brow furrowing as he took in my scowl and angry stance.

"What?" I mocked. "I'll tell you what. I asked you two weeks ago to change the burned-out bulb in the chandelier in the dining room, and just now as I was dusting, I counted three burned-out bulbs."

Joe blinked, looking confused. "I said I'd do it," he said. "I just haven't gotten around to it yet."

I could feel my scowl twisting my face into an even uglier contortion. The look on Joe's face let me know that he couldn't understand my anger, which made me even madder.

"You promised me if I would agree to buy this old house that you would fix it up and keep it nice. You seemed to feel like you had all the time you needed when you persuaded me to move out here." My head jerked toward the TV. "You could have changed the bulbs during half-time if you could drag yourself out of that darn recliner long enough to keep your word."

Joe sighed deeply and shook his head. "Are you all that angry about a few light bulbs that need to be changed?"

"No, I am not," I said, slathering each word heavily with sarcasm. "I am this angry about everything around here that needs to be fixed, which you somehow haven't gotten around to taking care of. Like the dripping faucet in the guest bathroom. Like the garage door that won't rise up all the way sometimes, and I have to get out of the car and manually push it up. Like the loose board on the back porch." I heaved a heavy sigh. "I could go on and on."

"I'll just bet you could," Joe retorted. He grabbed the TV remote and turned up the volume to drown out any further complaints that I might have.

That made me angrier than if he had simply argued with me or withdrawn into silence as he often did when I vented.

"Tell you what!" I shouted as I stomped out of the room. "I'm going to visit my sister for a while. I'll get out of your hair, and you can sit and watch TV all day. Call me when you get some things taken care of around here, and I might come back."

I could hear nothing but the excitement of the sports announcer and the roar of the football fans in the stands as another touchdown was made. If Joe had turned off the TV and come after me, I don't think I would have carried out my threat.

But he didn't... and I did.

I didn't call my sister until I had driven slowly down the driveway and was about to pull into the street. I kept looking in the rearview mirror to see if Joe would come after me. With a sigh, I realized that he was being just as stubborn as I was. Even as I experienced a little twinge of regret, I drove away.

It was a three-hour drive to my sister's house. I kept expecting Joe to call and ask me to turn around. After I had driven more than halfway, I had to accept that he wasn't going to call. I glanced down at my gasoline gauge and realized that I needed to get gas, so I pulled into the next gas station that I saw.

I was regretting my decision to drive off in anger, yet I was still too stubborn to make the first move. It was a Saturday evening, and people were pulling in and out of the gas station in a steady flow. I pulled up beside the only pump that was available. A middle-aged woman was at the pump in front of me, and she glanced up at me as I got out of my car, giving me a polite nod and brief smile.

"Hi," I muttered as I thrust my credit card into the slot and selected my gas. Realizing how unfriendly I sounded, I turned to her. "This place sure is busy," I said in a friendlier tone. "They must pull in a ton of money."

She looked at me, and as her eyes swept over my face, I realized that she saw more than I intended to reveal. Evidently, my fake smile and false friendliness didn't hide my anxiety. Her kind blue eyes looked into mine as she nodded in agreement and turned back to fueling her car.

When she was done, she suddenly spun toward me.

"Go back!" she blurted. "Turn around. Now. He needs you."

Then her hands flew over her mouth and she looked alarmed. "I'm so sorry," she cried out. "I don't know where that came from." She looked frightened. "That didn't even sound like me."

I realized that she was right. The frightened voice that spoke to me now didn't sound like the voice that issued a command to me just seconds ago.

We both jumped into our cars. Both shaken. Both not understanding what had just happened. As she drove away, I hurriedly turned around. I was confused, but I knew that I must get home as fast as I could.

I found Joe in the dining room. Great pangs of guilt swept through me as I took in the scene. Joe lay beneath the toppled ladder, his body twisted at an odd angle. Blood seeped from his head where it had struck the edge of the dining-room table as he fell. I grabbed my phone and called for an ambulance before rushing to him and cradling his head in my lap. When I called his name, he opened his eyes halfway.

"I couldn't get to my phone," he whispered weakly, "so I kept praying that God would turn you around."

My tears fell on his face. "He did, darling," I said. "He did."

Joe had a broken arm, two broken ribs, and a concussion. He was in shock. He required ten stitches in his head. But he survived — because God used an unknowing stranger to turn me around.

— Elizabeth A. Atwater —

Get Out of the Car!

The most incredible thing about
miracles is that they happen.
~G.K. Chesterton

"See you Sunday," I told my fellow volunteers. It was a late autumn night, and we'd just finished our Wednesday evening kids' club at church. As always, it was fun but exhausting, and I was eager to go home.

Two hours earlier, when I'd arrived, it was still light outside. But by the time I returned to my car a couple of hours later, the area where I parked my car was pitch-black. Almost everyone else had parked farther down under the lights. I walked from the church sidewalk to the front of my car, unlocked it, tossed my things inside and started to get in. That's when I heard it. Or… thought I heard it.

What was that noise? I asked myself. It was barely audible but sounded like a tiny child laughing. I scanned the full parking lot and saw no one near me. But farther away, in the well-lit area, parents and kids were getting in their cars, talking and laughing.

That must be what I heard, I decided, dismissing it. But then a bigger voice — inside my head — told me, *Walk around the car.*

I didn't. Instead, I argued with the big voice. *I'm tired. I need to get home. My dogs are hungry by now.*

I opened the car door again and sat down in the driver's seat. But before I could turn the ignition key, I heard the tiny laugh again. I sat still and listened, but I didn't hear the laughter. What I did hear was that big voice in my head again, a bit louder and more urgent.

Get out and walk around the car.

I still didn't. I was tired. But I sat there, listening, wondering if I should just start the engine and go home.

That's when the big voice became a bellow.

Get — out — of the car — NOW!

Okay, okay, I'll get out of the car. I got out and walked from the driver's door to the back of the car and peeked around. *Nothing there,* I thought.

But then I saw him.

A little boy, less than two years old, was joyfully smacking the back of my car near the rear passenger side. I couldn't believe my eyes, seeing this tiny boy, all alone on a dark night in a parking lot. I'd come so close to starting the car and backing right over him. Would my back-up camera have seen him? I didn't know.

"What's your name?" I asked him, gently. "Who are you with?"

He didn't answer, but someone else did.

"He's with me," said a boy of about ten years old. "He's my brother."

Until then, I hadn't even noticed that a dark SUV was parked beside my car on the passenger side. The older boy swung the SUV door open wider so that the interior light came on, and I realized it was Mark, a boy I knew from the kids' club.

"This is your little brother?" I asked, grateful that the little guy was not lost.

"He wanted out, and he kind of got away from me."

Mark was a great kid, always polite and helpful. But that night, he wasn't such a great brother-keeper.

"Where are your parents?" I asked Mark.

"My mom is over there," he said, pointing to the far side of their SUV.

I walked around to see what was going on and found the mom — a woman I'd never met — deep in conversation with another woman. They were completely unaware of what had happened, and, in fact, the mom seemed quite annoyed that I'd interrupted her conversation.

"Your little boy was playing behind my car," I said calmly but urgently to make her understand the danger he had been in.

She reluctantly followed me to my car and looked at it.

"Did he do any damage?" she asked.

"Damage?" I asked, confused. "No, he was just playing, but I almost..."

"Well, I'm sorry if he got fingerprints on your car. Anyway, we have to go," she said, taking her toddler by the hand and strapping him into his car seat. And then they were gone

All the way home, my mind was like a ping-pong game, bouncing between disbelief and thanking God that nothing horrible had happened. I'd wanted to call the mother's attention to the fact that her little guy could've been seriously injured or killed.

Thank God He didn't turn me loose until I stopped and listened to His voice. I hope that next time He speaks to me, He won't have to bellow.

— Teresa Ambord —

Chair Repair

We are each of us angels with only one wing,
and we can only fly by embracing one another.
~Luciano de Crescenzo

I had just poured my second cup of tea that morning and sat down to read the paper. From somewhere, an inner voice said, "Go see Jeff and bring him the chair to repair. Go right now."

It was such a strong impulse that I hurriedly dressed and lugged a dining-room chair to his door. Jeff was a neighbor who had lost his wife a while back, and he occasionally did minor repairs for me on furniture because he enjoyed working with his hands.

I knocked on his door and waited a while. I was about to walk away when he answered. He looked like he was far away in his thoughts. I felt awkward about disturbing him so early. I greeted him and then asked if he could repair my chair. He invited me inside. We sat in his living room. He looked depressed and not his usual self. He said he had had a stroke recently, and while he was home now, he still needed to attend outpatient physical therapy. He had to build his strength back up. I apologized for the chair and told him, under the circumstances, I would just bring it back home. He said to leave it.

We talked for a while. It had scared him to be in the hospital. He hadn't been there since his wife had died. He said that, before I arrived, he was seriously contemplating suicide. So, my visit interrupted his darkness. Having worked as a mental-health therapist, I listened to how hard it had been since his wife passed and how much worse it was now since the stroke. The longer we talked, the more I saw his mood lighten.

We even started talking about his diet and how he had not been eating. He said the dietician had told him to eat more fruits and vegetables, but he didn't care for them. Mostly, I was concerned because he was not eating much at all. I stayed talking with him until I saw his mood lift and the tension leave his face.

After I left his home, I went to the grocery store and gathered ingredients. I made him a hot meal I suspected he would like. Carefully, I cut up vegetables and prepared stew for him. It smelled heavenly as it simmered on the stove. I believe it was the best stew I ever made. I made homemade biscuits and prepared fresh fruit for dessert. I realize there might have been healthier fare, but I thought a hot meal would lift his spirits. I dropped it off for him. He was delighted that someone cared. Emotionally, he seemed in a better place.

The next time I saw him, he said the stew was wonderful. Though I usually am skeptical of compliments, I knew it had been because I made it with love. He talked of his next physical-therapy appointment. I made sure he had transportation; I would gladly have driven him, but he had figured it out.

I did not see him for a while. Then, one day, he knocked on my door with my chair. He had repaired it. He said it gave him a reason to get his strength back. He had returned to his usual self, and his confidence had returned. I was so thankful for the inner voice that directed me to see him that morning.

— Faye Shannon —

Chapter 2

Angels in Disguise

Mechanic Angel

I am convinced that these heavenly beings exist
and that they provide unseen aid on our behalf.
~Billy Graham

He was the biggest man I'd ever seen — tall, wide and solid. As he approached my stalled van in the Lower Ninth Ward of New Orleans, every horror story I'd heard about the neighborhood rushed into my mind.

His tap on the window was surprisingly gentle for such a big man. A compassionate smile filled his face with warmth. I rolled down the window an inch.

"Looks like you have a problem, ma'am. Maybe I can help, if you want." His basso profundo seemed to resonate within me, and my fears eased.

"The engine coughed a couple of times as I came down the bridge," I said. "And then it just quit on me. It won't start, but the gauge says I have plenty of gas. I don't know what to do. I'm just glad I was able to coast out of traffic." I thanked God for the steep slope of the Judge William Seeber Bridge, which gave me enough momentum to get clear of the flow of cars on busy Claiborne Avenue.

In those days, before cell phones, I was cut off from all the resources I might have utilized.

"Let's just take a look under the hood," he said. "You just stay there in the shade. I'll be back in a minute."

He popped the hood, and I heard his cheerful humming as he

examined the engine. True to his word, he was back in a few moments. I rolled down the window a little more to hear his findings.

"All your connections and hoses seem tight. Let's try starting it again, if you would, please."

I nodded and turned the key. He cocked his head toward the engine compartment and listened to the grinding of the starter.

"Sounds like it's not getting any gas. But you said you have plenty?"

"Half a tank, according to the gauge, Mr. James," I answered, using the name embroidered in red over the pocket of his faded navy-blue shirt.

"Well, maybe it's a filter problem if you got gas and it ain't getting through. Let me just check that out." He disappeared around the front of the vehicle again.

By now, my pulse had returned to normal, and I wasn't afraid of him anymore. When he came back to my window, I was able to return his smile.

"I'm going to need one of my tools to get that loose." He pointed diagonally across the street to a tiny service station. "I'll go get it and be right back."

I watched him cross the traffic lanes, the grassy neutral ground (the local name for a median), and then the traffic lanes on the other side. For all his size, he moved as lightly as a dancer. He disappeared into the shadows of the repair bay. A few minutes later, he emerged with a tool I didn't recognize in his hand.

When he returned to the van, he gave me another of those billion-kilowatt smiles. "We'll get this now," he assured me. He dove back under the hood, and I heard clinking noises as he worked. In a few minutes, he straightened.

"I think this is the problem," he said, holding up a cylindrical part. "Got some grit in it, like you got some dirty gas." Before I could respond, he put the part to his mouth and gave a mighty blow. He might have been a bugler sounding the charge for all the energy he put into it. One, two, three strong puffs. I saw a little cloud emerge from the opposite side of the part. Was it the particles he mentioned, a cloud of gas, or the vapors of his mighty breath?

"Let's try it now," he said, and vanished under the hood again. I heard another round of noises. In another moment, he called, "Crank her now."

I whispered a prayer, turned the key, and heard the sweet purr of the engine.

James slammed down the hood, ensured it was closed, and then walked to my window.

"You should be fine for now, ma'am, but I'd get that checked at a garage first chance you get."

"Thank you so much. You're a lifesaver. What do I owe you?"

"You don't owe me nothing. It was my pleasure to be able to help," he said, smile beaming.

"But your time and your tools. And your diagnostic expertise." I was flabbergasted at his generosity.

"No charge, ma'am. Just using the talents God gave me."

"Well, you're my hero," I told him. "A real angel. Thank you."

He gave a little salute with his tool and headed back across the street. I continued on my way home, another forty-five minutes away, but I couldn't get him out of my mind. How could he stay in business if he didn't charge people for his services?

My husband took care of the mechanical details, leaving me to ponder a way to say thanks to my angel. I made up my mind to go back and pay him something for his efforts. A week later, I had the chance to make the trip.

I pulled into the little service station, and a thin man came out to greet me. He was much shorter than James and probably 150 pounds lighter. His skin was much lighter, too, more a café au lait than James's rich ebony.

"Hi, I'm looking for James," I said. "He helped me out last week, and I wanted to thank him."

"Nobody here by that name," the man said. "Just me and my cousin, Billy. I'm Walter." He pointed to the name on his stained khaki shirt.

"But he came over here to get tools," I told him. "A big man with very dark skin."

"No, ma'am, he wasn't here. I don't loan my tools to nobody. Are you sure you're in the right block?"

I looked across the highway to the place I had coasted in my stalled van and confirmed to myself I was in the right place.

"This is the place. I'm sure of it."

"Can't help you, lady." He shrugged. "I don't know him."

"Well, I made a coffeecake for him to say thanks. Maybe you'd like it?" I picked up the foil-wrapped package from the passenger seat and offered it to him.

"Why would you do that?" he asked.

I thought back to my giant angel. "It's my pleasure," I answered. "Just using the talents God gave me."

— Mary Beth Magee —

11

What No One Else Can Do

Your Angels stay with you through each precious day,
loving, protecting, and lighting your way.
~Mary Jac

I awoke in a hospital bed. How much time had elapsed since my husband of forty years hurriedly drove me through the deserted nighttime streets to the ER? Where was Don?

When I saw the intravenous drip line connected to my arm, I breathed a silent prayer. *Thank you, God, for relief.* The pain, now deadened by medication, had awakened me at home. Like sharp rocks grinding inside my abdomen, the pain had scraped against my ribs and ripped through my right side to my back, squeezing my torso in a viselike grip.

The ER doctor had been kind and efficient. "The symptoms suggest a diseased pancreas or gallbladder, or maybe a blocked bowel," he had said. "We'll know as soon as we do some tests and get the results. For now, we're fighting the pain and the infection. Get some rest."

How long ago was that? And how had I gotten to this room? I heard a female voice outside the door. "Things don't look good for her; her veins are collapsing," said the voice.

I'm dying, I thought as a woman walked into the room. "Your vein has collapsed here," said the nurse, gently tapping the inner elbow of my left arm. "Your IV has worked its way out of your vein, and I can't get it back in. I'm going to find someone who can do what I can't."

She left and I dozed, waking to the sound of a male voice speaking my name. "Robin," he said, walking around the foot of my bed to stand by my side. "I'm here to do what no one else can do. Give me your hand."

I gave him my right hand, and he began to massage it gently. Relaxing, I looked at him closely. I saw neatly cut brown hair, clear eyes, and skin as smooth and flawless as a baby's. And what an unusual white shirt! Much like shirts I had seen in vintage photos, the tips of the collar reached down to the middle of his chest, and a center fold in the fabric ran down the front, covering what I assumed were buttons.

"But before I do my work," said the man, "I have a question. Do you believe in God?"

"Yes," I said.

"No, you don't understand. I mean, do *you* believe in God?"

His emphasis of the word "you"—what did that mean? "*Yes*," I said, matching his emphasis. "Yes, I do!"

"Okay," he replied, continuing to massage my hand. "While I do my work, I want you to close your eyes and tell me everything you're grateful for."

I closed my eyes. Beginning with my early years, I listed my blessings. Good parents. A happy childhood. A wonderful world. A beautiful home. A loving husband. A reliable job. A dependable employer. Two children. Five grandchildren.

"Okay, Robin," said the man. "My job is done. You won't die today." I opened my eyes to thank him, but he was gone.

Later, a different nurse came into the room. "Oh, I see someone has already been here and reset your IV. And it's in the back of your hand this time. Wonder why they didn't hook it up?" she asked, checking its correct placement before connecting it to the drip line. "Who did this, Mrs. Weber?"

"I didn't get his name."

The nurse raised her eyebrows. "It was a man? What did he look like?"

"He was very well-groomed, with a neat haircut and perfectly styled brown hair. I'm a hairdresser, you know, so I notice such things."

"So, did he have on a white coat, or was he wearing scrubs?"

"Neither, and no nametag," I answered. I described his clothing.

The nurse looked puzzled. "Well, he wasn't a doctor because a doctor would have called for a nurse to reset the IV. And he wasn't a technician because a technician would never insert an IV without hooking it up to the drip. Anyway, no doctor or technician in this hospital meets your description — and, in this hospital, only nurses administer IVs. But it couldn't have been one of us because we don't have any male nurses."

The nurse left, shaking her head. A few days later, with the infection cleared by antibiotics, a surgeon removed my stone-filled gallbladder. I recovered, and the hospital staff never solved the mystery of who reset my IV, or why he didn't hook it up to the drip line.

To me, there was no mystery. He didn't connect the IV to the drip line because angels don't do what someone else can do. Angels do what no one else can do.

— Robin Weber —

12

Heavenly Messenger

When we are touched by something, it's as if we're
being brushed by an angel's wings.
~Rita Dove

L aura and I had driven down U.S. Highway 26 in Oregon hundreds of times and never encountered anything out of the ordinary until that day. Our favorite section of the highway runs between the cities of Sandy and Gresham. The distance is about twelve miles. Once past the city limits, the area turns into a rural corridor with open areas of pasture, dozens of nurseries with decorative shrubs and saplings, several Christmas tree farms, and a few business exits. Various species of broadleaf and conifer trees thrive on the hillsides. Houses dot the landscape. The roadway continues eastward through other little towns until reaching the Mount Hood recreation area.

Over the years, our travels up and down the highway became routine, with numerous trips to visit my mother in Sandy or excursions to the mountain for camping, hiking, and fishing. We knew the route by heart: every curve, and every uphill and downhill section. It was a pleasant drive, scenic and peaceful. On a clear day, visibility went on for miles.

One eventful day, we were riding in my old Chevy Suburban, returning from a day trip at McNeil Campground. We had enjoyed a nice picnic and walked the nature trail at the abandoned beaver dam. On the way home, we stopped in Sandy at the Dairy Queen for single-scoop ice-cream cones, filled our tank with diesel at the Shell gas station, and then headed down the highway toward Portland. Laura took in the picture-perfect scenery from the passenger side. The sun had begun to dip toward the west, casting shadows on the trees, some of which were showing their autumn colors early. We were cruising along at fifty-five miles per hour, almost halfway between Sandy and Gresham. A nursery was on the right, with an overgrown hillside of wild blackberries on the left.

In the distance, I noticed a lone figure on the right side of the road. The individual was either standing still or walking. I couldn't tell from that distance. As we drew closer, I could see the person's forward motion. "Hmm, I wonder if someone's vehicle has broken down or run out of gas." I asked my wife if she had seen any cars pulled off to the side of the road, but she answered no. Neither had I. "If not a stranded driver, then why would he be walking the roadway so far from town?"

A hundred yards away, I could make out more details. The person wore a golden jacket with matching slacks. Maybe it was the angle of the sunlight, but there seemed to be a glow reflecting off the clothes. Wearing a suit like that on a hot afternoon seemed a bit out of place and not too wise. After we came alongside, we could see that our highway walker was a man. A gold-colored vest covered his glistening white shirt. His long, golden-blond hair fluttered in the wind. He swung his right arm, holding the left one outstretched, fist closed, with his thumb extended. The man stood at least six feet tall with a slender build, his age between twenty and twenty-five years old. He took huge strides, almost at a jogging pace.

Most hitchhikers keep looking over their shoulders to see if a car might be slowing down behind them. But this person didn't seem to have a care in the world. His eyes stared straight ahead, seemingly unconcerned with the traffic speeding by him.

One might find someone similarly dressed if he were a master of ceremonies or a student attending a prom. However, that was not the case here. We were in the middle of nowhere, four to five miles to the nearest town, and no vehicles had pulled off the side of the road. In all the years I've driven that highway, I have never seen anyone walking it, let alone trying to hitch a ride.

Then a strange thought crossed my mind, so I blurted it out. "I wonder if this guy is an angel. He sure looks the part."

My wife nodded in agreement. "I was thinking the same thing."

"Let's stop and see if he needs a ride the rest of the way into town. Angel or not, it's still a long walk to Gresham. On a ninety-degree day, he might appreciate a lift." I hit the brakes and started pulling my truck over to the shoulder. That's when I heard the voice. "Thank you, Charles, but I am waiting for someone else to come along."

Momentarily stunned, I glanced over at Laura and asked, "Did you hear anything just now?"

"No, I didn't," she replied. "Why, did you hear something?"

"Yes, and I think it came from that hitchhiker." Laura listened expectantly as I relayed the message. A wide grin formed upon her face. I smiled, too. Then I repeated myself, wanting to mark the exact words in my memory. The message I had heard was specific and tangible, an inward voice, not my imagination, not something I made up. And, amazingly, it included my name.

Apparently, a heavenly messenger had been sent to that roadside spot for an encounter with someone else, and he would not be distracted from his intended appointment. If so, somebody would come along soon and offer this angelic hitchhiker a ride, a person who needed his encouragement or perhaps a miracle. My wife and I could only wonder in awe. If we had owned a cell phone, she would have taken a picture.

As I merged back onto the highway, I saw the hitchhiker in my rearview mirror. He gave me a final nod with his head and moved his hand forward, as if to say, "Move along." I kept checking my mirror as we traveled down the highway until he was just a golden blur on the roadside. I may not have been the one he was waiting for, yet I felt encouraged nonetheless. From what I've heard or read, most angels are invisible, so we may not be aware of their presence. Still, sometimes they choose to unveil themselves and their mission, just as our mysterious hitchhiker did for us.

Whether aware or unaware, occasionally or once in a lifetime, it is nice to see a little bit of heaven revealed, even if it's for someone else. Each time I drive Highway 26, I keep a lookout for something divine or unexpected. One never knows what heavenly encounter is waiting around the bend.

—Charles Earl Harrel—

13

The Ladybug's Angel

All God's angels come to us disguised.
~James Russell Lowell

I was five minutes out and relaxed, knowing that I would easily make it to daycare to pick up my daughter before the 6:00 P.M. deadline. Sometimes, I got out of work late, but that day I would make it with time to spare. Thank goodness it was Friday! I was tired and ready for the weekend to start. I pulled into the parking lot at daycare and went to retrieve my little girl.

As usual, she came running when she saw me and had a big hug and "Hi, Momma" to greet me. With honey-colored curls bouncing everywhere, the sight of her brought a big smile to my face. That day, she wore her ladybug costume for the daycare's Halloween party. The bonnet with two antennae had long since been discarded, but she still wore the rest of the outfit, wings and all.

"Did you have a good day, sweetie?" I asked.

"Uh-huh," she said. "Look at the picture I made." It was clear my three-year-old was quite pleased with her artistic ability, and she couldn't wait to share her drawing of our house and the dog in the front yard.

"Very cute! Good job!" I said. "Alright, let's get your things and get home." I gathered her day bag and her drawing in one arm, with Lindsey in the other, and headed for the door.

"Don't forget your treat bag," said Miss Ashley. She handed Lindsey a small paper bag with her name on it in crayon, and we went to the parking lot.

I let Lindsey down beside the car, unlocked the door, and pushed the seat forward to access her car seat in the back. A two-door car wasn't ideal for a toddler, but I loved my Mustang and wasn't ready to part with it yet. I took off her wings so she could sit in the car seat. Once she was fastened in, I set her things on the seat beside her, clicked the front seat back into place, and got in myself. We headed toward home.

"So tell me about the Halloween party today. Did you have fun?" I asked. She said she did and told me about the costumes her friends wore and how Billy tried to eat all the Halloween cookies before anyone else could get some. I smiled as she explained, and I continued driving toward home. I was watching traffic and listening to her until she was finished telling me about her day. We were quiet for a couple of minutes as the radio played, and I started to think about what to make for dinner. I did not feel like cooking that day.

"How about when we get home we'll call for some pizza for dinner?" I asked her. When she didn't answer, I wondered what she was thinking. I knew she liked pizza, but maybe she wanted something else this time. "You like pizza, don't you?" Still, she didn't answer.

I looked over my shoulder and saw her face turning beet red. She could not speak at all. "Oh, my God! What happened?" I asked. I had just passed a four-way stop, and there was a wide, grassy shoulder on the road where I pulled off and jumped out. I ran to the other side of the car and freed her from the car seat. She was still bright red and could not speak. Clearly, she was choking! I was hysterical and pounding my hand against her back, trying to save my daughter. Nothing was changing.

Suddenly, a tall man in jeans, a western shirt, and a cowboy hat appeared next to me and took Lindsey from my arms. He didn't ask if he could help or say a word. He just did what needed to be done. His pick-up truck was parked behind us as he held her against him with her back against his stomach. She sat just above the huge silver belt buckle he wore, and he thrust his clasped hands into her abdomen, trying to dislodge whatever was choking her. Nothing happened.

Another family in a minivan pulled over ahead of us. A woman hopped out and ran toward us, saying she was a nurse and could help. Suddenly, a butterscotch disc flew from my daughter's mouth and rolled across the grass in front of us, its sticky surface collecting dirt. *The treat bag,* I thought, horrified at what had just happened.

I thanked the man profusely and took my daughter into my arms. I held her to my shoulder while she cried — that beautiful sound — and her face returned to normal color. The nurse was there and rubbed her back to help calm the child as she recovered.

"Thank you so much," I said as I looked toward the man who had saved my girl. But I didn't see him. "Where did he go?" I asked aloud.

"Where did *who* go?" asked the nurse.

"The man — the cowboy who saved her!" I said.

"There's been no one here but us, miss," she said in her British accent.

"But… he was right here, and his truck was over there," I said, pointing behind my car. "He saved her from choking." I sank to my knees, holding my daughter. The nurse knelt beside me and held Lindsey and me.

The nurse prayed, "Lord, thank you for sending your angel to watch over this small soul and her mum today." I will forever remember her words. In the growing darkness, until the nurse was satisfied that Lindsey was okay, we sat beside the road in quiet reverence. She stayed with us for several minutes while we recovered, and she checked Lindsey's vital signs to ensure we were good to go home.

I put my daughter back in her car seat for the rest of the drive home and moved the treat bag to the front seat beside me. As I closed the passenger door, the nurse hugged me and said, "You did great, Mum! Take care of your beautiful daughter!"

"Thank you so much!" I said.

Exhausted, I slogged back to the driver's seat and drove the few blocks to my home. I pulled into the garage, leaned my forehead against the steering wheel, and thanked God for saving my girl. It was quite a while before I felt okay again, although Lindsey was ready to play. Even as I told my husband what had happened, I was still in awe and trembling that my daughter was saved by an angel that day. I never knew his name, how he knew to stop and help, or where he went. All I knew was that God was not ready for my little girl that day.

— Kim Cook —

14

The Massage

Don't give up before the miracle happens.
~Fannie Flagg

I was expecting our second child, whom I felt was going to be a boy. We already had a sweet, little girl who was going to be four, so we wanted a boy to complete our family.

When I had given birth to my daughter, it was not an easy experience. Labor was not only long and painful, but the epidural had to be redone. The memory of it caused a lot of anxiety for this upcoming delivery. I prayed faithfully every day that this would be a pleasant experience.

The baby was due on my birthday but came four days later. The pain started around dinnertime, but we held off on going to the hospital until the contractions were coming at an intense rate. We left at midnight to take the thirty-minute ride to the Catholic hospital.

I realized I was having back labor, which was very different from the labor pains I had experienced with my daughter.

On arriving at the hospital, I was wheeled into a room and looked at by two nurses. They announced that I was not even dilated, and it would be morning before I delivered. They decided to go ahead and prep me for delivery anyway.

After they had prepped me, I felt the baby's head in the birth canal. I yelled for the nurses to alert them the baby was coming. They told me that I was not even dilated, so that could not be. I told them I knew what it felt like, so they'd better check.

Check they did, and panic ensued. They told me not to push because they had to call and get the doctor to the hospital. I told them not to worry; I wouldn't push.

The back labor became so intense that I asked for an epidural. As I was starting to panic, a little white-haired, blue-eyed nun in her habit came over to me. Without saying a word, she began to massage my back. Suddenly, a warm sensation washed over me. I told her that I did not know what she had done, but the pain was gone. The relief I felt was unbelievable, and I thanked her profusely. She still never said a word, just stood there smiling. A wonderful energy of peace and calm emitted from her presence.

And then the doctor was there and told me to push, so I completely forgot about the nun. Out came my son in two pushes. I had a short labor and an easy delivery with the help of the nun.

I was then taken to the recovery room where I rested for a bit. A while later, one of the nurses came to get me. As she was wheeling me to my room, I asked her where the blue-eyed nun was who had been in the delivery room. I wanted to thank her.

"Honey, nuns are not allowed in the delivery room," she said. "You must mean the other nurse."

"No, the other nurse had red hair. This was a white-haired, blue-eyed nun in her habit. She came over and massaged my back, and all my pain vanished," I exclaimed.

"Look," she said as she wheeled me over to a book on a table outside the delivery room. "This is where everyone in the delivery room must sign in. There is only the doctor, the other nurse and me."

I was dumbfounded, and I think she was, too!

Later, when my husband came back, I asked if he had seen the nun. He said that he had, and that she had come over to massage my back. She had white hair and was wearing a habit. I felt relief to know that I was not seeing things.

Her angelic presence, and the peace, calm and comfort I had felt emanating from her, made me think that she was indeed an angel.

— Rosemary Collins Horning —

15

The Cashier

We all have a Guardian Angel who is loving,
kind and caring, who'll be there when we
need someone to share the load we're bearing.
~Author Unknown

It was another late night at Capital Health Medical Center in Hopewell, New Jersey. I managed to order a hot meal of Salisbury steak, potatoes, and green beans before the cafeteria closed for the night.

"Twelve dollars even," said the cashier, a twenty-something woman whose curly hair peeked out from a purple turban. Was she new? It was the first time I saw her, and I had been eating dinner at the hospital for more than a month.

"Thanks," I said, as I took the change.

"Are you okay?" she asked.

"Yes," I said softly. "A bit tired."

"Do you have family here?"

"Yes, my mom. She's on the fourth floor."

"Oh, my goodness. What for?"

"She has a broken femur. They operated on her for that, but then she got pneumonia. She was put on a ventilator in the ICU for a while and recovered, but after so many respiratory infections, they decided to give her a tracheostomy. She can't talk now, so we have to communicate with pen and paper. My dad is upstairs with her. He ate earlier."

"Man with a cowboy hat and cowboy boots? I think I saw him a few hours ago."

"Really?"

"Yup. He got the Salisbury steak special, too, but he didn't finish it."

"Typical Dad. He doesn't eat much. Even less so these days."

"He must be worried about your mom." She smiled and then carried my tray to a table.

"Thanks. So kind of you."

"No worries. Now, you sit down and eat. You need to take care of yourself."

"Thank you. I'm Rita, by the way."

"Nice to meet you, Rita. My name is Kayla."

Kayla wiped the table, as well as the other tables, and began stacking chairs and taking out trash. She laughed, sang and conversed with the other workers, who sipped soda and mopped the floors.

I savored the Salisbury steak, mashed potatoes and beans. It was exactly the comfort food I needed on that cold January night. Dad and I would be staying the night with Mom, sleeping on the recliner sofas that were on either side of her bed. This was our ritual. Right after work, we ate dinner in the cafeteria and then stayed the night with Mom. On my days off, I stayed the whole day with her, bringing my notebooks, sketchbooks, and lots of reading material while I held her hand as she slept.

Despite the seriousness of Mom's ailments, I enjoyed staying with her. I treated the hospital nights like a slumber party, bringing my favorite pajamas, teddy bear, slippers, and microwave popcorn (which I cooked in the common-room microwave). I enjoyed dressing up for the next day and putting on my make-up as the nurses attended to her.

As I finished my food, Kayla signaled that some coffee was available.

"Would you like a cup?"

I nodded and was about to pay when she shook her head and said, "No, our treat. We're just closing it all up." She brought some sugar and creamer and sat down with me.

"Are you Catholic?" She gestured toward the Miraculous Medal I wore on a safety pin on my dress.

"Yes."

"I'll pray the rosary for your mom. For you and your dad, too."

"Thank you. I really appreciate that."

As she sipped her coffee, she smiled, and I could not help but notice her energy and fits of laughter as her co-workers high-fived her and danced around with the mop.

"I'll pray for you, too, Kayla. Do you have any particular intentions?"

"For now, no, I'm good."

"Wow, this is really good coffee. Did you make it?"

"Yes."

"It's phenomenal."

"Cool. Please tell me your mother's name so that I can ask Mama Mary to help."

"Josephine."

"Josephine. And your father?"

"Reynaldo."

"Okay. Josephine, Reynaldo, Rita. May God heal you all. You know, if you come here tomorrow, I'll have some prayer cards for you — St. Michael the Archangel, as well as St. Jude and St. Rita. Come here tomorrow for dinner. Same time. Maybe no Salisbury steak — we'll have another special — but just show up for dinner, and you'll find the prayer cards. I think you really like the food here, no?"

"Yes, it's the best cafeteria food."

"Food here is cooked with love, for sure."

We finished our coffees. She wiped down my table, and as I went toward the elevator, the lights dimmed, and the workers exited toward the back.

The next night, I went to the cafeteria and looked for Kayla. She wasn't there. I ordered the special, which was chicken cacciatore with egg noodles and Caesar salad.

I approached the cashier and asked about Kayla.

"Who?"

"Kayla. A little taller than me. African-American, curvy. Curly hair, purple turban."

"There's no one here with that name and description. Are you sure she was here?"

"Absolutely. She was here last night around this time. She said she would give me something."

The cashier shrugged and looked at me strangely. As I counted my change and picked up my tray, I noticed a clear plastic bag by the register.

"Oh, this is it!" I picked up the bag and looked at the cashier, who just shrugged and said, "Take it. People often leave lost items here, right at the register. If it's yours, it's yours."

My hands shaking, I sat at the nearest table. Although I was hungry, I ignored the plate of steaming hot chicken and opened the bag. Within were the prayer cards she had mentioned — St. Michael, St. Jude, and St. Rita — but also a tiny pink one-decade rosary.

I walked around, trying to spot the workers I had seen last night, but I could not find a familiar face.

A janitor walked by to collect the garbage, and I rushed up to him.

"Excuse me, sir, but is Kayla around?"

"Kayla?"

I described her, and he shrugged. "I don't know anyone of that name or description who works here. Are you sure she was here?"

"She was. I talked to her. She even made me coffee."

"Sorry, miss, can't help you."

I ate slowly, savoring each bite while looking around every now and then to see if she was around. But, no, I didn't see her or the other workers.

I stayed until closing time, grateful for the quiet. Outside, the waterfall feature in the garden rippled, not yet frozen.

— Leonora Rita V. Obed —

Midnight Encounter

Faith is not only daring to believe;
it is also daring to act.
~Wilfred Peterson

It was late, and I was tired. I had suggested to Richard, my husband, that we spend the night in a motel in Lake County and drive the fifty miles home in the morning, but he assured me he was fine to drive, and he preferred sleeping in his own bed.

"That means I have to stay awake," I reminded him. We had agreed that when he drove, I co-piloted.

"We'll be fine," he assured me. "We'll stop for coffee."

He had forgotten there was nowhere to buy caffeine that time of night between the sleepy Northern California town of Clearlake and Santa Rosa.

My exasperation increased when he took the "shortcut"—a cut-off road that eventually met up with the main highway. Though grateful it would make the trip shorter, I was nervous, as the narrow, isolated road was fraught with turns, S-curves, and embankments that dropped down into ravines.

I locked my door and settled in for a torturous ride, coming up with any conversation I could think of to keep him awake.

"I'm disappointed in my new book. Francine raved about it, but the author used every cliché there is, and I am only on chapter three."

"Going to finish it?"

"I paid $16.95 for it. I'll finish it."

"Your choice."

Politics, sports, my cousin's ugly divorce... I ran out of topics. The silence felt welcome.

It was then that I saw it. An animal. A Shepherd-looking dog. *It must be a coyote,* I thought. Then Richard exclaimed, "Did you see that dog?"

"Yes, I saw it. Probably a coyote or maybe a wolf."

"No, there are no wolves here." He insisted it was a dog. "No coyote looks like that."

We rode about half a mile. A dog. Out here. No people. No houses. No farms. No campgrounds. My vision of the dog would not go away.

"Richard, why would there be a dog out here alone? There's no one around...."

"We need to go back."

"Yes... He's lost and hungry and..."

Richard turned the car around, and we began to search for the Shepherd. He drove slowly.

"There!" I shouted. "By the side of the road. I see something." He slowed and shone our headlights toward my discovery.

"Oh, my God," I said. It was not the dog but a man lying in the brush, not moving.

"What should we do?" I asked as he stopped the car, panic sounding in my voice. "It might be a trap. If we get out of the car, we might get ambushed. They'll take our wallets and—"

"We'll call 911," he said, sounding confident that he knew what to do. As he reached for his phone, I chose to ignore his shaking hand. He punched in the numbers. "No service. We're in a dead zone. Wait here," he said, getting out of our warm car. "Keep the car running so you don't get cold."

He put on his coat and closed the car door quietly, as if to not disturb the body. He cautiously walked toward the man. "Hello? Sir? Are you okay?"

No movement. *He's dead,* I thought. *I know he's dead.* I tried to remember what one should do when one finds a dead body on a desolate road at midnight and 911 cannot be reached, but my memory failed me.

"Be careful, Richard," I repeated through my cracked-open window.

Then movement. The body rolled onto its back and groaned. Drawing closer, Richard said, "Are you okay?"

"Sleep," I heard him mumble. "I need sleep. A minute."

"How did you get here? Did you lose your dog?"

"Walked. No doggy. Don't 'member gettin' here. Cold... Wet my pants. Sleep. Just need sleep." His words were slurred. He closed his eyes and rolled back onto his side.

"We need to get him to a hospital," said Richard as he reached for the handle on the car's back door.

"No," I protested. "We can't put him in our car. We just need to wait."

"Wait? For what?"

"Someone to come. Drive to the nearest town and make a phone call. Find the fire station. Call an ambulance. We can't leave him, but he's not getting in this car. I'm sure someone will come along."

"Guess we don't have a choice," he said, sticking his hands in his pockets and shivering.

He got a blanket out of our trunk and covered the man. Then he knelt next to him, talking and keeping him awake. "He's wearing a medic-alert bracelet," he called back to me. "Epilepsy."

Richard paced and talked to the man. I found myself dozing off.

An hour had passed when we heard the sound of a car.

"See. Told you so," I announced, sounding like a bratty sibling.

Richard waved down the car. Thankfully, it pulled up beside him.

He explained the situation to the young driver. The car, full of friends, was returning from a party. The group lived in Guinda, the next town. It had a firehouse, and the kids said they knew exactly who to contact this time of night to get help.

They sped off on their mission, and again we waited.

Forty-five minutes later, we heard sirens. Suddenly, the area was filled with flashing red lights.

From our warm car, we gratefully watched the man being lifted into an ambulance.

A patrolman interviewed us above the sound of the parting siren, as if we were suspects of a major crime. "How did you see him? He was off the road. What made you stop? Where you from? Where you headed? Charlie," he yelled to his partner, "check their trunk."

"A dog. We saw a dog. We came back to—"

"There's no dogs out here. I patrol this area. Only deer."

"Coyotes?" I asked.

"No. No prairie wolves here. We have your info. We'll be in touch if needed," he said accusingly. "You can go—for now."

As Richard started to drive away, the patrolman waved for us to stop. *No,* I thought, *they're going to hold us overnight in jail for more questioning.*

"Wanted to thank you," he said, smiling. "Think you saved that man's life. It's starting to freeze."

We didn't speak for several miles. "Richard?" I said, breaking the silence just as we merged onto the main highway.

"Yeah?"

"The patrolman said there were no... Had we not seen that dog... It is as if he knew we would turn around, come looking for him. He brought us to that man who would have died. I don't think it was a dog at all. I believe he was an angel. A real angel."

"I know. Just what I was thinking."

Twenty-five years later, we still believe it to have been so.

—Cheryl Potts—

The Compliment

*Sometimes, reaching out and taking someone's hand
is the beginning of a journey. At other times,
it is allowing another to take yours.*
~Vera Nazarian,
The Perpetual Calendar of Inspiration

It had been almost a year since my husband Don died, and I was still grieving. He was a Missoula County police officer in Montana. Anyone who knows police officers knows they are a tight-knit group of people who have their own inner circle of friends. Don and I were part of this very close group, but following Don's death, everyone was trying to cope on their own terms. I suddenly found myself on the outside looking in, alone and searching for my own answers as to why God chose to take Don.

On this particular morning (like many previous ones), I awoke feeling extremely weepy, and that familiar painful cloud hung over my head. I had learned from counseling that I needed to make a new life for myself, so I'd joined the church choir. I made up my mind I would attend practice that evening. I went through the day on autopilot trying to occupy my mind with my work.

As the evening approached, I got dressed for choir practice. I looked in the mirror and wished again I could just hear Don say, "My, you look really nice tonight." Many people would say that, but it was only special if I heard it from him. I drove into church and found a seat next to a close friend of mine.

About halfway through choir practice, we took a break, and my good friend Billie looked at me and said, "You really look like you need a shoulder to cry on. How about we skip practice and grab some coffee and talk?" She couldn't have suggested anything I needed more. I hurried to the car, thanking God all the way for such wonderful friends who still understood how much I needed them.

At the restaurant, we got a booth in the corner and settled in to talk. We chatted for a while about things in general until Billie finally asked what was upsetting me. Then she said, "You know, you really look nice tonight." Immediately, I burst into tears.

"Oh, Billie," I said. "That is what's wrong. I miss Don so much and probably feel I shouldn't. When does the hurting stop? I just want so much to hear Don say one more time, 'You really look nice tonight.' It is so kind for others to tell me, but I need to hear it from him. It just seems it's the little things that hurt the most."

Billie put her arm around me, and we walked out into the empty parking lot. It was closing time at the restaurant, and all the customers had left some time ago. We didn't put on our coats even though it was a brisk October night in Montana. It was about 10:00, and the only lights were from the restaurant sign and streetlights that illuminated the parking lot.

Suddenly, about twenty feet away, a lady appeared to be walking straight toward us, as though on a mission. Even in the darkness of night, I clearly saw this woman. Her appearance made such an impression on me that, to this day, I can still recall every detail of her outfit. She held a book, which looked like a Bible, under one arm and her purse in the other. I noticed she wore a navy pillbox hat tilted to one side of her head and was wearing sensible "Grandma" laced shoes. I noticed her legs, and it amused me that they looked like Don's. I remember thinking the hat was very odd for Montana, especially that time of night.

She stopped a few feet from us and said, "My, you ladies look nice. Where have you been?" We were both taken by surprise but began to explain about skipping out of choir practice to which she nodded and said, "Oh, I see."

After a brief pause, she looked straight at me and continued, "Well, I just came to tell you that you look really nice tonight." I couldn't believe this stranger was saying the very thing that we had just been talking about!

As she passed us, we turned around to thank her. Suddenly, we realized the parking lot was empty, and she had disappeared.

By this time, Billie and I were in complete shock. I couldn't comprehend the hat, so unique and out of place. Then I realized from stories I had read that angels on assignments usually had something about them that caused you to wonder if it was truly an angel. Then I thought about the statement she had made while looking right at me about how she had just come to tell me I looked really nice. It felt as though she had been sent on a mission just to deliver that message, and the effect it had on me was profound. I knew in my heart that the message was from Don, and God had sent His angel to speak to His hurting child.

I called Billie the next day and asked her what she thought of our encounter. She replied, "It had to be an angel as the message was just for you."

—Ann Sharon Siweck—

18

My Guardian Angel Drives a Ford

Impossible situations can become possible miracles.
~Robert H. Schuller

bout twenty-five years ago, our family of four lived in Central Ohio. Being within driving distance of Cedar Point, and having a sunny day at our disposal, we decided to drive north and ride the roller coasters.

At the time, we had a sedan that was dependable, but it had more than a few miles on it. I kept the oil changed, the belts, hoses, and fluids replaced, and the tires rotated and balanced. It just kept on running like an old sewing machine. For weeks, however, it had been trying to warn me that it had a problem. Occasionally, when I turned a corner, I could hear something that is best described as the sound of a softball rolling around in the trunk. I would open the trunk and find nothing, look under the spare tire and find nothing, and check under the car and see nothing. The noise did not seem to get louder, and sometimes it would not be heard for days.

Having had such good service from this car, I decided that whatever was making that sound could wait a little longer, and we headed out for Cedar Point. The drive up was uneventful.

As expected, my wife and kids were having so much fun that they wanted to stay until the amusement park closed, so we did. We were among the last to leave, and then we started the long drive home.

After midnight, the kids were asleep, my wife was nearly asleep, and I wished that I could get some sleep. I took a drink of something with caffeine when suddenly, without warning, the car started swerving all over the road and filling up with smoke. It was pretty much out of control, and I was scared. An ear-piercing, screeching sound was coming from the rear, and the smoke smelled like burning rubber.

Fortunately, we were the only car for miles, and we did not hit anyone as I tried to regain control. I stayed off the brakes and eventually was able to work my way over to the berm. When the car came to a stop, I threw it into Park, and we all jumped out, thinking the car might be on fire. It was not, thank goodness.

When the smoke had cleared, I got out a flashlight and found that the left rear tire was leaning inward and rubbing the car body inside the wheel well. The upper ball joint had broken! The car was not drivable, and it was now approaching 1:00 in the morning. We were helpless at the side of the road, in the middle of nowhere, without a cell phone, and it was getting cold. The sights and sounds of the night were setting our nerves on edge. Sometimes, a car would slow down and then pass us by. This did not help our anxiety. We noticed that it was not only getting cold, but fog was rolling in as well.

Now our danger radars were on high alert. Would a patrolman come by? Would someone stop to help? Would someone stop to harm? Would a drunk driver drift over in the fog and hit us? This would have made a great opening scene to a horror movie! For the first time in a very long time, we felt completely helpless. We had no option but to sit, wait, put a white towel in the window… and silently pray.

After an hour or so, an old pickup truck pulled over and backed up to the front of our car. At those hours, it was easy to wonder if we were about to be helped, about to be robbed, or worse. Thankfully, it turned out the driver did not put on a mask or pull out a chainsaw like in the movies but instead offered to help.

The driver was a kind, old gentleman who looked a bit familiar. He asked what had happened and where we were going. He told us that he was going in that direction, and his destination was not far from our house! We asked if all four of us could fit in the cab with him, and he said, "Of course!"

He got behind the wheel, the kids sat on our laps, and we talked all the way home. Among other things, he told us he didn't have a family but enjoyed his work, that helping others made him happy, that he wished everyone lived by the golden rule, etc., etc. I asked him his name and where he worked, and after a pause that seemed like he was deciding whether he should, he told me his name, the name of his company and where it was located.

After a few hours, we arrived at our house. He refused any payment for his gas or assistance. He said only that I should help someone else someday, shook our hands, and said goodbye. We were amazed and grateful for his over-the-top helpfulness. After another prayer (of thanks this time), we took quick showers and got a few hours of sleep. We felt very fortunate. We went from being totally helpless to being home safe and sound.

The next day, I was able to locate a repair shop that would tow the car and replace the ball joint. I had worried the repair would be like the movie, *National Lampoon's Vacation*, but it all went very smoothly. My wife and I were amazed that this incident, which could have ended in an accident and injury, turned out only to be a minor inconvenience.

The following week, I decided to stop by the gentleman's workplace to tell his supervisor how grateful I was to have been rescued and see if I could leave a gift card. I wanted to tell his supervisor that his employee had really helped us out and was a credit to his company. But after I drove to the location he'd given me, there was nothing to be found but shrubs. When I looked up the business name, it did not exist.

It was then that the hair on the back of my neck started to tingle. I thought his face looked familiar, and I began mentally reliving other close calls when I might have remembered that face. I thought of those potential tragedies and near disasters, and concluded that perhaps, and most likely, I was being looked after. I have shared this story several times and have been told that we were probably "entertaining angels unaware." The longer I think about it, the more I think that we were.

If that is the case, I now know that my guardian angel is named Gary and he drives a Ford F-100.

— Thomas Brooks —

19

The Bus Station

The more that you trust and believe in angels,
the more they will pour their blessings upon you.
~Denise Linn

"I've been invited to New York for Christmas! May I go?" I appealed to my parents. "Please, say yes!" They stared at me as if I'd lost my mind.

All I wanted for Christmas was to visit my friend. For weeks, I waged a campaign to go. My parents were aghast and felt I'd give up sooner or later, preferably sooner. They were wrong. I was seventeen, a college freshman, albeit living at home, and felt quite old enough to make the trip. But I did need their permission as well as their help to pull it off.

Never mind that I was born and raised in Atlanta, and I had never traveled beyond the deep South — and then only with my family to visit relatives who lived in neighboring states. But how hard could it be? I'd take a plane to New York City, even though I'd never flown before, and then get to the bus station for the rest of the trip. Easy. People did it every day. So could I.

With encouragement from my grandparents, aunts and uncles, my parents finally gave in. They weren't happy about it and secretly hoped I'd change my mind before it was time to go. But I was a teenager, and I had the world at my fingertips.

The December evening finally came, and my parents and younger brother drove me across town to the airport and accompanied me to my seat on a Capital Airlines Viscount plane. Soon, I was looking down at my hometown city lights, mesmerized by their beauty. Most of my fellow flyers on board were already dozing, but I was too excited to sleep.

When we landed, I retrieved my suitcase and lugged it to the taxi queue in front of Idlewild Airport.

New York City was alive and bustling, just as I'd envisioned it. The Port Authority bus terminal was near Times Square and swarming with people of all ages and types. I dragged, shoved, and sometimes kicked my heavier-by-the-minute bag into the depot. A tall, young man came to my rescue.

"Hi," he said, flashing me a smile. "Let me help you with that."

Before I could say thanks, he grabbed the handle and began to move rapidly away from me.

"DROP IT!" came a commanding voice from behind me. "NOW!"

My "knight in jeans" glanced over his shoulder and then did as he was told, letting my suitcase fall as he began to run away.

Then I stared into the face of a short, stocky, well-dressed gentleman. He had a beard and blue eyes that crinkled as he smiled at me. Just for a second, he reminded me of Santa Claus, minus the red suit.

"Where are you from?" he asked.

The minute I uttered my first words, he knew and shook his head.

"You haven't traveled much, have you?" He smiled at me and then continued. "You have to be very careful here. People like that…," he paused and nodded at the growing crush of humanity surrounding us, "…will take everything you have."

I was surprised, not only at his words but at my own naivety.

"Do you have your ticket?"

When I answered, "Not yet," he nodded toward the side wall. "Let's go over there."

As we got nearer, I could see the row of booths. When my round-trip ticket was safely in my purse, he showed me where my bus would load and depart in a few hours. He asked if I was hungry as I drank deeply from the water fountain, and when I told him no, he smiled.

"Follow me."

We took turns carrying and pulling my suitcase across the ever-more-crowded floor and headed to a roped-off corner of the station.

"There. Find yourself a seat and don't move until you hear your bus number and destination called." He swept the area with his eyes and then added, "Don't leave. It's safe and police-patrolled, and you won't have any problems here."

He smiled at me, his eyes gentle and caring. "When you come back on your way home, don't stay here. Go directly to the airport. It's less crowded, cleaner, and a much safer place to wait."

"Thank you so much. You saved me from a ruined holiday."

"It was nothing. You just needed a wee bit of looking after. It was my pleasure. Take care of yourself, Jeanie Girl."

As I sat down, I was stunned that he knew my name. I didn't remember telling him. Turning to ask him, I looked around, but he was nowhere to be seen.

Gone. Completely.

I stood and searched for any sign of him, even standing on my tiptoes, but he had vanished as quickly as he had appeared when I'd first needed him.

Who was he? And how did he know my name?

Was he a kind gentleman who spent his time helping others, especially travelers out of their familiar surroundings?

Or my own special guardian angel?

I have no way to prove either, but I know how I feel about him, even now, some sixty years later. I am so very grateful and, yes, even blessed.

Because the only other person to ever call me "Jeanie Girl" was my own sweet father.

— Jean Haynie Stewart —

20

The Comforting Visitor

When angels visit us, we do not hear the rustle of wings,
nor feel the feathery touch of the breast of a dove;
but we know their presence by the
love they create in our hearts.
~Mary Baker Eddy

I got the call to take my friend Debra to the hospital to have her baby. Her parents were supposed to take her, but they were away and the baby came a bit early. I drove her there and got her settled in, and then the tears began to fall. Debra wasn't married, and her parents were already helping to care for her one-and-a-half-year-old baby boy. This new baby was being adopted.

I couldn't imagine Debra's anguish. My heart was hurting for her. She truly wanted to keep the baby, but with no husband or job, it was unfair to her parents. Still, she struggled with the final decision, even though the new parents had been chosen months before. I offered my best loving and compassionate words but somehow knew they were inadequate.

The precious little girl was born, beautiful and healthy, and the new parents would be there the next day to take her home. My friend was distraught over the decision. Was she making the right decision, or would she hate herself forever and pine for the little girl she never had the chance to know?

Finally, I had to leave her for the night with the promise that God loved her dearly and was there to help her through. My prayers would be the same as hers. I told her I would pick her up the following afternoon.

The next day, I picked up Debra as planned. She was calm, even smiling. She liked the couple very much and knew she had made the right decision. The future for all looked bright and happy. She told me she had cried endlessly the night before, asking God to help her figure out what to do. The night nurse had come in, aware of what was to take place the following morning, and found Debra immersed in her sorrows.

She sat down to comfort Debra... and she stayed for hours. She spoke words of love and comfort to her from a God who knew her better than she knew herself — and loved her even more. She assured her that God understood her pain and the difficulty of her choice. He was not angry or upset with her in any way. In fact, He was so incredibly pleased and proud of her for making the most important choice of all nine months ago — the choice to have the baby.

Through this wonderful nurse named Annie, God told Debra that He would watch over her little girl for all her life, and He would bless her with abundant love, talents, and beautiful things to enjoy. Nurse Annie also assured Debra that the new parents would love the baby with all their heart and soul. They would give her a blessed life because this little one would make their lives perfect and complete, full of love and joy.

As Annie talked to her, Debra felt a wonderful peace come into her heart. The next morning, Debra asked the day nurse how she could thank this great nurse named Annie who had stayed with her during her darkest of nights. The day nurse said they didn't have a nurse named Annie working there. She also said the night nurses have so many patients to see that they would not be able to stay more than a few moments — certainly not hours.

At once, Debra and I looked at each other and exclaimed at the same time, "She was an angel!"

Yes, we knew. God had sent His loving approval to Debra's

heart-wrenching prayer through the voice of an angel, not a nurse. And everything would be okay—better than okay—because God's special messenger told her so.

—Kathryn Kemp—

Chapter 3

Messages from Heaven

Listening to The Boss

I think miracles exist in part as gifts and
in part as clues that there is something
beyond the flat world we see.
~Peggy Noonan

My wife Betsy was always a Springsteen fan. When we were first going out in 1983, she stopped by my house unexpectedly one night to drop off a book, and my mom told her to go upstairs to my room. I had Springsteen's *Born to Run* album on the stereo, and the song "Thunder Road" was playing when she came through my door and scared me half to death. She smiled brightly, tossed the book on my desk, and sang the last line loudly. She said she didn't know I liked Springsteen, and it was the best of many signs from the Universe that we were "meant to be" and would be together always.

We saw Springsteen (aka The Boss) in concert four times, her favorite being the first in July 1984. A guy standing next to us yelled at the stage, "Bruce! You're the only Boss I listen to!" She'd often reference this line when we disagreed, and she'd remind me how she was the only boss I should listen to.

Betsy and I were married for thirty-one years when she died of liver cancer on August 4, 2018. We'd had many adventures together over the years — exotic journeys like traveling through Egypt, and many far more modest like getting rid of a large hornets' nest or hiking with the dogs through the woods — and I felt lost without her.

I woke up the morning after she died feeling as though I'd died myself. Our twenty-three-year-old daughter, Emily, had come home, but the house still felt enormously empty. That day dragged on slowly as I cleaned the house and tried to start planning the funeral service. Emily was a huge help and family members came by, but I still felt completely alone. I could not see how I would ever feel any differently.

Betsy always made me feel better when life knocked me down, and I celebrated every victory with her. We literally finished each other's sentences, and at least once a week one of us would say something when the other would respond, "I was just about to say that exact same thing." How was I supposed to go on living without her?

That evening, Emily's friends Krista and Heather came over. They were in the living room when I went into the kitchen to wash the dishes. As usual, I put on some music while I was cleaning up, and that night it was this "Music Through the Years" CD, a compilation of songs that Betsy had made for us years ago. This was an anthology of tunes we had loved from 1980 onwards on multiple CDs, and I put on one she always especially liked from June 1990. As I was listening to the songs, Monty the dog had to go out, so I hit Pause and went outside with him.

When I came back and hit Play, I should have heard the next song on that CD, which would have been Leslie Phillips's tune, "Answers Don't Come Easy." Instead, I heard Bruce Springsteen's "Backstreets." I was confused and reached out to hit the Forward button, thinking that the CD had gotten stuck, when I realized that this version of "Backstreets" wasn't on this CD, and it wasn't the song that had just played before Monty showed up. I stood still, just listening, and felt a tingle at the back of my neck and goosebumps running up my arms. When "Backstreets" ended, it was followed by "Born to Run." I stood in the middle of the kitchen just staring at the stereo on the far wall.

As the song played, I half-stumbled into the living room and said to Emily, Krista, and Heather, "You've got to hear what's happening in the kitchen."

Emily said, "That's okay. Springsteen's not our thing."

I said, "No, you don't understand. I'm not playing these songs.

She is." I quickly related what was happening, and they were suitably freaked out.

I went back into the kitchen, and "Born to Run" was followed by "Jungleland" and then "Thunder Road." Two of those songs are not on that CD at all. In fact, "Jungleland" isn't on any of the "Music Through the Years" CDs.

The four songs that played that night were Betsy's four favorite songs on the *Born to Run* album. Betsy used to sing "Thunder Road" to Emily when she was an infant and asked me to play the *Born to Run* CD in just that order so she could finish listening by singing "Thunder Road" to Emily, acting out the song in dance and pantomime.

When "Thunder Road" ended that night, the machine stopped playing anything. As I said, this is a multi-album-length CD with many songs on it, and something should have come on after that song ended. The machine was working perfectly. I put in another CD to test it. Then I put the "Music Through the Years" June 26, 1990 CD back in, and it played the songs it always had.

I can't explain how those Springsteen songs played that night out of nowhere, but I know how they made me feel: I wasn't alone anymore. I knew I wouldn't be waking up the next morning to make her breakfast and we wouldn't hold hands as we walked the dogs or finish each other's sentences as we watched TV anymore. But I felt her presence in the room that night, and I knew that, even if I couldn't see her the next morning, she hadn't left me. She'd told me, that long-ago night when she burst into my room, that we were meant to be together always. And, the night after she died, she came back to let me know that not even death could change that.

—Joshua J. Mark—

Nanny Knows

Angels are never too distant to hear you.
~Author Unknown

I closed my eyes to numb myself to the news I feared was coming as the thick, icy gel spread across my bare stomach. A heart-shaped gold locket with a fuzzy ultrasound picture hung from a delicate chain around my neck. I twisted it nervously, silently praying for the tiny image inside.

One week earlier, the ultrasound technician had smiled as she pointed to the flickering heartbeat on the screen. The white bean shape on the grainy black screen became real to us. "It is a weak heartbeat," the doctor warned.

Now, the same technician pursed her lips and said, "I'm so sorry. There is no longer a heartbeat." The future we had imagined suddenly vanished.

The next morning, I awoke with a high fever, vomiting and excruciating abdominal pain. I fell in and out of consciousness as Travis rushed me to the ER. Doctors and nurses raced my bed down the hall as septic shock caused my blood pressure to plummet. Their urgent shouts echoed behind my agonizing screams. The OB/GYN on call performed an emergency surgery to save me from a rare septic miscarriage. I woke up physically healed but emotionally scarred.

I left the hospital grateful for my life, but after nearly losing it, the thought of another pregnancy was terrifying. Still, we longed for a sibling for our three-year-old son, Kyle, to complete our family. But the frightening experience left us afraid we might never be ready to try again.

I placed the heart-shaped locket with the ultrasound picture in a small, velvet bag in the corner of my jewelry box. When I was grieving the loss, I would take it out and trace the beautifully engraved "I love you" written in delicate cursive lettering. The sentimental piece of jewelry had been a gift from my late great-grandmother, Nanny, and the perfect place for the picture to stay.

Nanny had raised three girls on her own and was the tough and strong matriarch of our large, extended family. Her daughters' families and their children's families all gathered at her beautiful, old, Victorian-style, three-story home in Philadelphia for each holiday, birthday, and occasion in-between.

Nanny took care of me when I was a baby after my parents returned to work. As a teenager, I was her travel companion to visit cousins across the country.

My favorite memories took place in her kitchen where she taught me how to bake an apple pie from scratch, carving an "A" with a butter knife into the delicate homemade crust before placing it in the oven. We shared a close bond that I treasured until she passed away while I was in college.

Eerily, I knew the moment she died and I cried to my room-mates. They were dumbfounded when the phone rang and my parents confirmed the news.

Years later, I learned how much our bond transcended heaven and Earth. Three months after my miscarriage, Nanny delivered a message about the baby I lost — and one that was to come.

A friend invited my cousin Linda to be a last-minute replacement at a group session with a popular medium. Skeptical, she agreed to fill the seat as a favor.

Almost immediately, the medium asked if anyone in the room had a close relationship with a "Margaret." Linda immediately thought of Nanny but was reluctant to participate.

At the end of the session, the medium pleaded with the group, telling them this Margaret woman was determined and was not going away until she delivered her message. Linda said to herself, "That sounds an awful lot like Nanny, the feisty Margaret I knew. But there's no way this is real."

The medium stressed, "This woman named Margaret has an important message for a Jennifer." He closed his eyes to concentrate. "She is showing me a pie with an 'A' on it. Does that mean anything to anyone?" Stunned, my cousin slowly raised her hand.

"She needs you to tell Jennifer that she is holding the baby that she lost. Tell her that she is going to have another baby. She will become pregnant again within a year with a baby boy. You must tell her that everything is going to be okay."

When Linda hesitantly relayed the powerful message to my parents that night, she was astonished to learn of my recent traumatic pregnancy loss.

Six months later, I was pregnant, but an early ultrasound revealed a serious fetal abnormality. A nurse solemnly ushered us into a genetic counselor's office and handed us brochures about grave medical problems. The stoic counselor wrote down a long list of potentially life-threatening disorders. Many of the conditions meant our baby might not make it to term. We felt helpless clutching this list of terrible things.

As I sobbed on the car ride home, I reminded myself of Nanny's message: *Everything is going to be okay.*

The next week, a doctor performed a test to extract DNA from the fetus. I repeated those words in my head as the long needle entered my stomach. When I closed my eyes, I saw the list of terrible things and whispered to myself, *Everything is going to be okay.*

I thought of those words during sleepless nights when tears stained my pillow. I repeated them through the long days until the doctor called and said, "The chromosome results are normal. And your baby is a boy."

The list of potential problems remained long, so I repeated my message from heaven through fifteen ultrasounds, countless genetic tests, and a fetal echocardiogram.

One by one, we crossed off the scary words with a thick black marker, eradicating the harrowing, handwritten warnings. Finally, only a kidney disorder remained, but tests showed growing concerns. My

C-section was moved up as a team of specialists awaited the birth in the OR.

As I lay on the operating table, I repeated Nanny's words until a delicate baby boy was lifted above the curtain and briefly nestled against my cheek before being whisked away by the neonatal team. I believed those words as I anxiously waited for news in recovery. I repeated them until a relieved Travis and a smiling doctor arrived holding a healthy baby boy with two well-functioning kidneys.

The day we returned home from the hospital with our healthy baby, Tyler, I placed his newborn picture on the other side of my special locket, thankful for the divine words of courage and comfort I received when I needed them most.

Twelve years later, the locket still holds the ultrasound picture of the baby we lost and the one she told us was to come.

Sometimes, I still trace the beautifully engraved "I love you" delicately written in cursive lettering, eternally grateful for what Nanny knew.

— Jennifer Kennedy —

23

A Message Delivered at the Museum

The love of a mother is the veil of a softer light
between the heart and the heavenly Father.
~Samuel Taylor Coleridge

"Come see this oil painting," I called out to my sister. "It so reminds me of the beach landscape, you know the one with the beautiful lighthouse Mom painted years ago."

My sister was busy studying a sculpture across the room. She turned her head, and as she approached the painting, her eyes grew wide. "My goodness, it certainly does," she exclaimed.

It was early on a Saturday morning, and the two of us were wandering through a museum waiting for an art-appreciation workshop to begin. Weeks prior, my sister had seen an advertisement in the local paper for the workshop. We decided to register and attend together in loving memory of our mother, a talented artist who in her lifetime did more than dabble with paintbrush and palette. Her works of art were true masterpieces and prominently displayed on the walls of homes far and wide.

I struggled tremendously with the loss of our mother. My heart ached to hear her voice once more, to feel her caress, always gentle and reassuring. I found it challenging to remain focused on simple tasks. Recurring thoughts about heaven and the existence of an afterlife weighed on me. I wondered where my mother was and if she was okay. Daily, I prayed for a sign.

My sister and I meandered a bit more through the museum's exhibits and stumbled upon a fascinating artifact collection. Then we heard an announcement that all registered participants should report to Room 125. The workshop would begin in ten minutes.

Upon entering the room, we were greeted by a man who introduced himself as the workshop instructor. He invited us to take seats anywhere we chose. The seats were arranged in a horseshoe shape. My sister and I selected two seats next to each other, placed our purses on the chair backs, and comfortably settled in.

As other participants entered the room, I was curious as to their personal motivation to attend the workshop. Some arrived with notebooks tucked under their arms. Others held laptops, and a few carried tote bags with easels and sketch pads protruding. The instructor loudly cleared his throat, welcomed the class, shared his credentials and stated that he would begin the workshop with a lecture, and then take questions, followed by a twenty-minute break.

The instructor was undoubtedly passionate and knowledgeable about art history. He was interesting and engaging. However, I found myself suddenly no longer captivated by his PowerPoint presentation. Instead, I became completely mesmerized by an older woman who sat directly across from my sister and me. Her petite frame, delicate features, and flattering pageboy hairstyle with wisps of white bangs that softly framed her face immediately reminded me of my mother. I was completely astonished by the striking resemblance.

Our eyes eventually met. I initially felt more than a tinge of embarrassment at my staring, but I quickly found comfort in her response: a smile, a nod and a gentle wave. I nudged my sister and whispered, "Does the older woman in the pink cardigan…?" Before I could finish the sentence, my sister responded, "She most certainly does."

I continued to hear the instructor's voice, but to me his words were a string of garbled sentences as I was completely inattentive. I had drifted far from Room 125, overcome by waves of emotion, flooded with memories of my mother.

At one point, I heard the instructor ask if there were any questions. I quickly regained focus. Hands were raised. I looked at the older woman and desperately hoped she would raise her hand, ask a question, and share something about herself. I wanted to hear her voice. I wondered if it would sound just like my mother's or possess the same soothing and sweet cadence.

She never did raise her hand. The instructor answered the last question and announced it was time for the break. He encouraged the class to look around at some of the exhibits, visit the coffee shop or stroll the museum gardens.

My sister and I, both outdoor enthusiasts, decided to explore the well-manicured museum grounds. We discovered a bench directly under a dogwood tree in full bloom. Its pastel pink petals were breathtaking. I turned to my sister and was about to say, "Mom loved dogwoods, especially the pink ones."

Before I uttered my thought aloud, I heard a voice say, "Hello, girls." I turned my head, and my heart raced. It was the older woman in the pink cardigan! I was speechless.

My sister responded, "Good morning. Are you enjoying the workshop?"

A smile graced the older woman's face. "Oh, I most certainly am. It is wonderful." Her voice was as melodic as my mother's. She continued, "By the way, girls, my name is Eileen Patricia. What do you girls think of the class?"

My heart raced even faster. I could feel beads of sweat on my forehead. My sister, much more composed than me, eloquently expressed our complete shock. She said, "My goodness, my name is Eileen." She turned and looked at me and said to the older woman, "This is my sister, Patricia."

The older woman smiled, nodded and did not seem surprised by our shared names. It was as if she knew. But how? No nametags, no formal introductions. Since childhood, my sister and I had always called one another "Sis," so it was unlikely she had overheard our names. My sister proceeded to ask her why she had signed up for the workshop. Her eyes, just as blue as my mother's, sparkled.

"Well, girls, I used to paint landscapes, portraits, and still life, but I became ill, seriously debilitated. I was in horrific pain, but you see, girls, I no longer am. I am painting again and happily pursuing all my passions. I am free; the world is now mine to roam."

The older woman then looked down at an old Timex watch, tapped on it and said, "Oh, look at the time. The workshop will resume shortly." My sister asked if she would like to walk back with us. She responded, "No, thank you. I'd like to sit here a bit longer under my favorite tree. Isn't it lovely? No worries, girls, I am not far."

As my sister and I walked back to the museum, a steady stream of tears rolled down my cheeks. I managed to say aloud, "My prayers have been answered, Sis."

We returned to Room 125. The instructor began to lecture, and once more I was distracted, anxiously waiting for the knob to turn and Eileen Patricia to enter. She never did return. But her message was indelibly painted on my heart.

— Patricia Ann Rossi —

24

Butterflies in January

*Love is like a butterfly: It goes where it pleases
and it pleases wherever it goes.*
~Author Unknown

For nearly a decade, I have worked in a long-term nursing facility. As indicated by its name, most patients — or residents, as we are bound by law to refer to them — are not in good health, and most of them will never leave the community. Because the facility is Medicare-certified, most of the residents are quite old, have lived a long life, and seem prepared to begin the next chapter — wherever that may lead them.

That said, sometimes our facility admits what we refer to as an "outlier" — a younger person who qualifies for Medicare and is quite compromised physically. One such "outlier" was a handsome, middle-aged man named Geoff who was in the final stages of kidney failure. Along with his quiet sense of humor, quick intellect, and deep-set eyes, Geoff brought along his beautiful, ginger-haired wife. Lisa was as vivacious and outgoing as Geoff was reserved and private. They personified that age-old axiom that opposites attract.

While our nursing staff cannot play favorites among our residents, Geoff and Lisa were certainly at the top of everyone's list within a few days. This was due to their ages — both were so young to be dealing with a terminal diagnosis — and, secondly, to their positive attitudes. Not only did they accept their situation with dignity and grace, but they brightened the days of every staff member and resident by their daily presence.

As the weeks passed, I grew to know Lisa better. She was a gifted "crafter" and had such talent in creating exquisite flowers, butterflies, and gift baskets out of crepe paper, twine, and straw. When Geoff was asleep, I would often stop by his room, and she would be sitting there quietly watching him while she coaxed a beautiful calla lily or a monarch butterfly to appear from what seemed to be nothing at all. Her serenity astounded me.

During those quiet interludes, we shared many conversations. I learned that Lisa was adopted, and that she and Geoff had adopted two children. She shared the serious health-related challenges that both she and Geoff had faced early in their marriage — not only his, but also with their children. While she didn't practice any particular religion, she described herself as a spiritual person, and she believed that angels were one of the strongest forces in this life, professing openly that angels had transported her adopted children from across the world into her waiting arms.

Not long after Christmas, Geoff's condition deteriorated, and before the New Year, he was gone. Somehow, the post-holiday decorations, bleak winter sky, and barren landscape seemed to make his death even more depressing. Lisa, the ultimate trouper and supportive spouse, was with him when he passed on.

A few days later, I saw her in Geoff's former room, folding his clothing, packing up some family photos, and distributing some of the butterflies and flowers she had made to our staff. I just stood there and gave her a hug. What was there to say?

While words escaped me, she whispered something to me. "Don't worry," she said. "Geoff is at peace. He's on his own journey now. And when he arrives safely, he will send me a sign. Please, don't worry. I know that he is okay."

I pressed her for more information. Here she was — a new, young widow — and I was the one who needed reassurance. "What do you mean?" I asked. "What sign, and how will you know?"

She hugged me back, and then looked at me. "Geoff and I spoke of the time when he would have to leave me. He told me that he wasn't afraid, and when he finally arrived, he would send me a sign. I told him that I wanted something definite, something so out-of-the-ordinary that there would be no doubt that the message came from him." She leaned toward me and whispered, "I told him to send me butterflies in January." I just nodded and hugged her again. Butterflies in January? Here in the Northeast? Impossible.

The New Year arrived with a vengeance, and Old Man Winter raged on. Though our staff continued to mourn Geoff and miss Lisa, life did continue. Another resident moved into his room — a lovely lady in her late eighties. She had fractured a hip and was what we call "pleasantly confused." I think all of us were relieved that it was not a young person. Losing Geoff had affected all of us.

The following week, I received a text from Lisa. Her message was simple. "On your way home tonight, stop at Michaels." *That was odd*, I thought. The craft store was located only a block from our skilled-nursing facility. And while Lisa with her talent for such pursuits was a routine customer, I only ventured inside to purchase holiday wrapping paper, balloons, or the occasional birthday card.

After 5:00 that evening, I parked the car outside the store, which appeared to be nearly empty. It was mid-January, too late for Christmas, too early for Valentine's Day. Still, I expected to see red, white, and pink hearts strewn throughout the store.

However, when I opened the door, I could not believe what I was seeing. Hanging from every overhead lighting fixture mixed in with an assortment of flying, winged Cupids were hundreds of butterflies in every color of the rainbow. Standing under the canopy of color, I was mesmerized by the sea of wings, angels and butterflies. I continued to stare at the ceiling until one of the store clerks approached me.

"Are you okay?" she asked. "Is something wrong?" All I could do was shake my head. Finally, I found my voice and said, "I had expected to see valentines this time of year, not butterflies. Butterflies in January? I never heard of such a thing. Where did they come from?"

She smiled and said, "I know! Aren't they great? It's funny because we were expecting our routine shipment of valentines, but when we opened the packaging, this is what we discovered — a million different butterflies mixed in with our standard winged Cupids. Angels and butterflies — it's even better than valentines. It's like a colorful blanket from heaven."

A colorful blanket from heaven... Yes, that was exactly what I had been thinking.

At that moment, my phone buzzed, and a text appeared from Lisa. Four words lit up my screen: "Geoff made it home."

— Barbara Davey —

25

Silver Strings

Do you think the universe fights for souls to be together?
Some things are too strange and strong to be coincidences.
~Emery Allen

A few years ago, I visited an old friend who had recently moved to Canada. He was a notorious atheist with a great passion for argumentation. The subject wasn't important; it was the arguing he savored. I always joked with him that he could start an argument in an empty room.

I had driven to Vancouver from Los Angeles, so all I wanted to do was relax. But within an hour of my arrival, my friend engaged me in a heated discussion that lasted almost an hour. To make matters worse, I had no interest in the subject. But it seemed important to him, so I went along. When the argument was over, I was annoyed, as any sane person would be. He, on the other hand, sighed deeply and said, "Wow, that was great. I haven't had a good argument like that in a long time. These Canadians are so passive." The fact that he enjoyed it so much only annoyed me further. Fortunately, his good qualities outweighed the frustration of the occasional debate.

The one subject he always avoided was religion, which is usually a sign of good manners. However, his reason, as he put it, was, "I don't want to damage your faith."

When he first told me this, I replied, "How very kind of you."

He thanked me, completely missing the sarcasm.

"I'm kidding," I clarified. "You're either underestimating my faith or overestimating your power."

He continued to lay off spiritual matters. One day, however, after we had just watched a movie, he couldn't help himself. The main character had seen and spoken with the spirit of a recently deceased loved one. I heard my friend scoff while we watched that scene and knew why but didn't expect him to bring it up later.

"What a crock," he said as we walked out of the theater. "When someone dies, you never see them again. They're gone. I can't stand that sentimental hogwash."

I didn't bother answering because I knew his anger and lack of faith were rooted in the pain of his own losses, especially that of his mother who had passed away ten years earlier. Whenever he heard of some catastrophe, he would say, "There goes God, moving in mysterious ways again."

One day, I asked him, "Does life feel like nothing to you, or does it feel like a mystery?"

Without hesitation, he replied, "Nothing."

I added, "I have a lot of questions and doubts too, but I've also had a lot of mysterious experiences that were too coincidental to be accidental."

After a moment, he asked, "Like what?"

I told him I had dreamed that a friend came to visit me. I greeted him cheerfully, but he started to cry. I hugged him and asked what was wrong, but he was inconsolable and unable to speak. In the twenty years that I'd known this friend, I'd never seen him cry. He'd always been cheerful, which made this dream even more bizarre. It felt so real that I was compelled to check on him the next morning. When he answered, he sounded as if he had been crying. It was as if the dream and reality were melding. I asked if he was okay, and he answered, "My wife and I have been crying all night because her mother was just diagnosed with dementia."

My atheist friend wrote this off as coincidence, so I told him a few more stories. My father had died a few years earlier and had "visited" me several times since, each time within an hour of my praying and asking him to let me know he was okay. The first was when my toddler, who was just learning how to speak, said a word I could easily identify my father by. Another time, a perfect shamrock appeared in a puddle of water. (My father was fiercely Irish). Yet another "coincidence" was when my eldest daughter correctly guessed the birthday of a dog we adopted as May 11th, my father's birthday. (A 1-in-365 chance!)

I don't pretend to know how these events are orchestrated. Some say coincidence is God's sense of humor. Others say that our souls are joined to the souls of our loved ones by a silver string that seems as wispy and delicate as mist but is actually very strong, and that these strings, or soul connections, are how we find each other in the afterlife. I don't even try to explain it, but I have felt and experienced the connection.

When I finished telling my atheist friend about these bizarre events, he joked, "You watch *The Twilight Zone* too much." However, since then, he has often asked, "So, have you had any more crazy experiences lately?" I usually have. In fact, they happen so often that I started keeping a kind of "X-file" on myself to keep track of them.

One day, with tears in his eyes, he confided in me, "I wish I had your faith. I don't enjoy being an atheist. I wish I could believe I'll see my mother again when I die. I don't even dream about her."

I implored him to pay attention to his dreams, saying, "Life is full of signs and omens, but you have to be open to them."

He called me one morning a few weeks later, very excited, and said, "Mark, I was with my mom in a dream last night! She sang a song she used to sing to me when she was tucking me into bed. She said she couldn't find me before because it was too dark. When I woke up, the room smelled like her!" He interpreted "too dark" to mean the darkness inside himself.

It was all I could do not to cry too, hearing him talk about his beloved mother as if he had just seen her in person. He was absolutely certain she had visited him.

Some say dreams are only the products of an imagination fed by despair, stories we tell ourselves to alleviate unbearable grief. But I believe they are ethereal places, as real as any other, where spirits meet, though the language of the next world is sometimes hard to decipher.

Fortunately for my friend, his mother spoke to him clearly. She was not alive in his dream. She knew she was dead, and she was finally able to visit him because he had removed the walls of cynicism and anger within himself. He doesn't scoff about spiritual matters anymore.

His mother has visited him many times since then. He falls asleep every night hoping to see her again. He has accepted the beautiful mystery of life — and death.

— Mark Rickerby —

26

When Cardinals Appear

May you come to find comfort in and remember —
cardinals appear when angels are near.
~Victoria McGovern

I wholeheartedly believe the adage, "When cardinals appear, angels are near." Throughout some of the most emotionally difficult and uncertain times in my life, one of these scarlet messengers has serendipitously emerged, encouraging my resilience. "You will get through this," it declares with its distinctive song.

While the spiritual symbolism of these crimson creatures varies slightly from culture to culture and religion to religion, they are universally regarded as a positive force. The word "cardinal" has its roots in the Latin word *cardinalis*, meaning serving as a hinge. A hinge is used to open a door, and the cardinal was/is assumed to facilitate a similar purpose — opening a door between heaven and Earth. Any time I see one of these divine messengers, a feeling of peace washes over me due to both their visual splendor and the belief that an angel is nearby.

This symbol of resilience and hope is one I enjoy sharing with friends when they are faced with emotional challenges and uncertainties. I keep miniature cardinals on hand at all times to give to friends who are going through difficulties.

In the fall of 2019, I received a phone call from my friend and work colleague, Jen. She had lost her mother, Joanne, earlier in the year. I had a cardinal to give her, but, through a series of events, the opportunity had not yet presented itself. Jen was calling to inquire if I knew of someone who might be interested in several boxes of glass hurricanes that had been used to hold candles and other decorative fillers for various family events and celebrations throughout the years.

Jen explained that she and her sisters were assisting their father in sorting and repurposing some of Joanne's items and wanted to ensure that the hurricanes would go to a good home. I assured Jen that I would find the perfect place for them, and we subsequently made plans for me to pick them up from her house. Since we had not seen each other in person for quite some time, we also made plans to go to lunch.

On the scheduled day, I pulled up to Jen's front door. She and I loaded the boxes of hurricanes into the back of my Dodge Caravan. I left my vehicle parked in Jen's driveway and hopped into her car. We headed to a nearby bistro for lunch. During lunch, I gave her the cardinal. I explained the symbolism and provided an example of when a cardinal had appeared in my life, after my mother died.

I hadn't seen my mother for eight years when she died. She had struggled with alcoholism and drug addiction her entire life, and she had chosen to distance herself from my siblings and me. I did talk to her frequently, but I still felt a deep sense of guilt, confusion, and anger regarding how her final years played out—a waste of a life, or so I thought at the time. I sobbed uncontrollably for days.

Then, one day shortly after her passing, I decided to take a walk around a lake near our home. There was a light summer rain that helped to hide my tears. As I walked, I contemplated the meaning of my mom's life. I began thinking about all the contributions she had made to the greater good throughout her career as a nurse. She had obtained her nursing degree while caring for three small children and while being pregnant with her fourth. Throughout her career, she had worked in hospitals, provided home care to the terminally ill, worked in care centers, and served Native American populations through a traveling nurse organization. I also began recalling her talents as a published poet.

Suddenly, I had an epiphany. A familiar feeling of calm began to replace my anxiety. My mother did have addiction challenges, this was true, but those challenges did not define who she was, nor did they negate her many accomplishments. As I thought about this, the rain subsided and a glorious full rainbow appeared on the horizon beyond the lake. As I was identifying the brilliant colors of the rainbow using an acronym I had learned as a child — Roy G. Biv — red, orange, yellow, green, blue, indigo and violet, I heard the faint song of a northern cardinal. I walked a short distance and spotted the crimson bird standing along the edge of the wooded area that surrounded the walking trail. I could sense my mother's presence, reassuring me that she was okay, I would be okay, and there were definitely better days ahead.

With my tears welling, I relayed this story to Jen. We had a delicious lunch and a wonderful conversation about her own mother, including her mother's tendency to be what Jen referred to as "a saver." Joanne saved everything. On the very rare occasion that Jen and/or her sisters were able to convince Joanne to part with a particular item that she no longer needed or had not used for a long time, Joanne needed to know exactly where it would be going and what specific purpose it would be used for. If it met her specifications, then — and only then — would she allow the item to be removed from her home.

Following lunch, Jen and I continued our conversation on the ride back to her house. When we pulled into her driveway, I looked over toward the van where we had earlier placed Joanne's hurricane collection. I noticed a solitary cardinal by the back of the van, suspending itself at window level by feverishly flitting its wings.

"Jen, look!" I exclaimed, pointing to our brightly colored visitor. "It's looking right into the window!" We watched the bird for a few moments as it flitted from one window to the next, with its beak seemingly right up against the glass as if it were surveying our handiwork in packing the boxes. The bird turned his head and looked toward Jen and me as if it were looking for an explanation for why Joanne's precious keepsakes were now packed in my van.

Jen spoke in the direction of the inquisitive bird. "Don't worry, Mom. Shelly will make sure your hurricanes go to a good home." With that, the bird turned back for one last look into the van window and flew away.

The hurricanes have indeed gone to a good home and are now being used at weddings by couples beginning their new life together. Jen has assured me that this is something that Joanne would most definitely have approved of.

— Shelene Codner —

27

Let It Go

*Sometimes our grandmas and grandpas
are like grand-angels.*
~Lexie Saige

All the grandchildren loved the unique player piano that sat in my grandmother's living room. This piano was manufactured in the 1960s, and we could purchase paper rolls of our favorite songs. The music roll was relatively easy for a young Mozart like myself to hook up, but the very best part was *how* we got the roll to move to make the piano play. At the bottom center of the instrument were two pedals, and if we pumped the pedals at the speed at which we pedaled our bikes when racing with friends, we could make just about any song sound like a honkytonk melody. By the end of the song, we kids started to lose steam, and our honkytonk tune switched to the pace of a church hymn. The beauty of the piano was that it could also be played manually by those fortunate enough to have the skill.

Grandma loved to watch the grandkids enjoy her music maker. We had an old upright at home, but it wasn't nearly as awesome as Grandma's modern piano. Our ancient relic had belonged to my dad's aunt, who was a piano teacher in my small hometown. The top layer of the keys had been broken off over the years, which created the illusion of asphalt under our fingertips rather than the "tickle" of ivory. Nonetheless, I loved it and sat for hours at that old piano until I taught myself how to play a few songs. I couldn't read a note of music, but I had the ability to listen to a song and echo what I heard through my fingers.

Upon arrival at my grandma's house, I'd run to the piano to serenade her with my latest accomplishment. Mom would join us in the living room, and the two would engage in adult conversation. Sooner or later, I'd tire of playing or stop because I feared missing some important bit of information they were sharing. Grandma would always cease talking and ask me to keep playing. She may have truly enjoyed my juvenile concerts, but now that I'm a grandmother myself, I can't help wondering if that was her way of keeping me occupied while they discussed topics too mature for my little ears.

When I was twenty-five, Grandma passed away, ten days after my grandfather. All their belongings would be dispersed amongst family members or sold at an estate sale. Needless to say, I wanted the piano. I guess the better statement would be that I felt I was *entitled* to the piano. Wasn't I the one Grandma always asked to continue playing for her? I was her private pianist, and that was my fondest memory with her.

I immediately let my mom know how I felt about the piano and that I intended to claim ownership of it. She presented the idea to the family, but there was an issue. One of her six siblings wanted it, too, and they had seniority over a mere grandchild.

Daily, I harassed my mother about the piano. She needed to understand that I was counting on her to be my voice, my legal representation, whatever it took! An appraiser had placed a monetary value on some of the more expensive belongings of the estate, and a value of $350 had been placed on the piano. My husband and I didn't have an abundance of money at the time, but I'd been saving for a trip and was more than willing to sacrifice my vacation fund if it meant securing this treasure.

As the weeks went on and decisions were being made, I got more aggressive in reminding my mom that Grandma would want the piano to be mine. She would want my future children to enjoy it as much as I had, and Mom had to stand up for what should rightfully be mine. I knew she was growing weary of my demands, but I was relentless. At some point, my aggressiveness crossed the proverbial line from determination to obsession.

One night after again reminding my mom that her parental obligation was to diligently represent me, I went to bed and fell into a deep sleep. Sometime during my slumber, Grandma appeared to me in a dream. She had the same smile that made me gleam with pride when I'd play for her, but her message shocked me. It was simple and straight to the point: "Let go of the piano." I couldn't believe what she was saying! There had been no doubt in my mind that she wanted me to have it, and now she was telling me to let go of it. My first instinct was to argue with her, but as quickly as she appeared, she was gone, leaving no time for discussion.

I woke up still wanting to plead my case, but to whom? A dream? My mother, who had already grown weary from my badgering? What I had to do was crystal-clear. I had to let go of the piano. I called Mom that morning and told her I no longer wanted her to fight for the piano and to please let the other family member know I was surrendering. No doubt she was curious how I had arrived at this decision, but I never told her about the dream.

Several more weeks passed as the family continued to divide up the belongings. I attended the estate sale and picked up a few mementos to remember my grandparents by, but I never asked about the piano.

The final days of settling the estate were drawing near when I got a phone call from my mom. After a bit of small talk, she asked me if I was still interested in the piano. I couldn't believe what she was asking! Of course, I was still interested! The siblings had decided to allow each grandchild to pick one item from what hadn't already been taken, and, much to my surprise, the piano remained. The greatest news was, if I wanted it, I could have it for 10 percent of the appraised value. So, for a mere $35, Grandma's beloved piano became mine.

The piano sat proudly in my home for more than twenty years. My daughters played with it but never really expressed an interest in learning to play it. A few years ago, just as Grandma had delivered the message for me to let go, I knew it was time for me to physically let go of the piano I had emotionally fought for so long ago. We desperately needed more living space in our small home, and the renovations required utilizing the space where the piano sat. I joyfully passed Grandma's piano on to my cousin.

The lesson I learned through that last visit from my grandmother is one that will never be forgotten. I had been selfish, and my grandmother had given me so much in her lifetime that I didn't need an object to remind me of the things I loved about her. After she convinced me to let go, I was rewarded in a way I never "dreamed" possible.

— Tamara Bell —

28

Message from Mom

Where flowers bloom so does hope.
~Lady Bird Johnson

Mom always said, "Angels watch over our gardens and our souls." Those words were on a wooden garden stake in her garden.

Mom had a green thumb. From azaleas to zinnias, she could make anything grow.

Growing up, I helped Mom tend to her flowers in the garden. Her favorite plant was a red geranium that grew in a terracotta pot with a BELIEVE metal angel stake nestled amongst the leaves. It was a hardy mother plant she took cuttings from to propagate other geraniums. It thrived on the front porch during the spring and summer and through early fall. During the winter months, it resided inside the house on a two-tiered metal rolling cart.

After I was launched into adulthood, I married, and our son was born a year later. Our apartment was small but cozy and perfect for the three of us, and I had to be content viewing and admiring flowers being cared for by the gardeners in the apartment complex.

Upon Mom's first visit to our apartment, she was elated to see an empty space in our kitchen alcove. "A home's not a home without a plant or two," she said. "I know exactly what you need in that bare corner."

During Mom's second visit, she filled the vacant spot with a small two-tiered metal rolling cart. Pink and white potted ivy geraniums adorned the shelves.

Oh, how those colorful geraniums brightened my days, especially when I had sleepless nights caused by a colicky baby.

Two years later, when my husband's tour of duty in the military ended, he accepted a job on the West Coast. To relocate across the country from the Midwest to Silicon Valley, we had to pare down our belongings to the barest of essentials.

"Don't feel sad because your geraniums can't make the move," Mom said when I returned the cart and potted plants to her. "I've heard that geraniums grow wild in sunny California."

Adapting to the new climate was easy. Springtime was glorious. It was sunny and warm during the day, and cooler temperatures prevailed at nightfall.

Our relocation budget was meager, but yard sales and thrift shops were treasure troves for us. Not only were we able to furnish our new abode, but we had enough left over for a lawn mower, gardening tools and a gardening handbook for our planting region.

As I watched my husband cut the lush green front lawn, I was pleased at how beautifully landscaped the front yard was. It needed little care.

Fortunately, the neglected back yard wasn't visible from the front of the house. The lawn had sparse areas that needed reseeding, and the only plant in the yard was a scraggly pink geranium bush growing along the back fence. I had to be frugal in landscaping the back yard, but I was up to the challenge. I knew the solution to adding color was propagating the pink geranium plant.

It took only two weeks for the plant to respond to my coaxing and tender, loving care. As that geranium thrived, I began to take cuttings from the new growth and planted them directly into the soil of the flowerbed alongside the mother plant. By the beginning of summer, the flower bed had blossomed in pink splendor.

Mom was right: Geraniums flourished in the Golden State.

I shared my gardening skills with Mom and deluged her with photos of my beautiful geraniums. I anxiously awaited her first visit.

After Mom arrived and unpacked, she emerged from the guest room waving a blue plastic bag. "Lead the way to your garden!" she shouted, and I gave her the tour. "I'm so proud of you," she said and handed me the blue bag. "Here's something that would love to grow in your magnificent garden."

I was elated the gift in the blue bag was a cutting from Mom's red geranium mother plant, rooted and ready for planting in my garden.

There was a tug at my heartstrings when I bid Mom farewell at the airport, but we vowed that living across the miles wouldn't hinder our family. Over the years, our lives and plants continued to flourish as we made frequent visits from coast to coast.

In later years, Mom's health began to deteriorate, and she was unable to travel. It was worrisome being so far away, but we flew back to visit as often as possible.

One summer morning, to my dismay, I discovered that my prize red geranium, which began with a cutting from Mom's garden, had gone from a vigorous plant to a wilted, sickly one overnight. With gentle coaxing and doses of fertilizer, I managed to stabilize the plant, but it didn't fully recover.

As Mom's illness progressed, the red geranium went into a dormant state, while the other geraniums were in full bloom.

After Mom's funeral, I returned home and hoped that tending the garden would help me cope with my loss. It was heartbreaking to find my red geranium still droopy and losing its leaves.

For a moment, I was engulfed with sadness, and my eyes welled with tears. Suddenly, I remembered the keepsake still in the side pocket of my suitcase and quickly retrieved the small BELIEVE metal angel stake that once belonged to Mom. Then I headed back to the garden and placed that garden stake in the soil in front of the ailing red geranium.

The next morning, a sense of calm, peace and serenity washed over me as I stood in front of my grandest red geranium. Miraculously, it was no longer limp. I knew it'd soon be healthy again. I was also aware there was more than an angel stake involved in this phenomenon. It was a message from Mom.

I, too, believe a gardening angel watches over my garden and my soul.

— Georgia A. Hubley —

29

A Very Busy Bee

The busy bee has no time for sorrow.
~William Blake

I lost my friend Rachel to cancer in the early summer of 2021. Her two great loves in life were teaching, which she did with great skill and flair at an elementary school in Portland, Oregon, and photography, which she used to capture all the natural beauty of the Pacific Northwest. When she got too sick to teach, she still took beautiful shots from her garden of all the tiny bugs and flowers most people are too busy to really see. And when she got too sick to do that, she stayed indoors and made cards from the photos she'd already taken, painstakingly handcrafting the perfect greetings for everyone she loved.

The last card I received from Rachel was a congratulations for earning my bachelor's degree. It featured an awe-inspiring close-up of a bumblebee. The photo was so clear and detailed that I could count the hairs on the bee's fuzzy back and easily see that its legs were laden with golden pollen. "Here's a little something to celebrate all your hard work, my busy academic bee," read the inside. "May your future be just as bright and full of golden treasure as this little lady's!"

Rachel passed away a few days after I received that card. Oddly, I started noticing bumblebees everywhere after that: in the flowers outside my bedroom window, pollinating the tomato plants outside my grocery store, and flying around my face every time I went outside. Occasionally, one would alight on my shoulder and sit there lazily for a while, which freaked out everyone except for my friend Margot, who had also known Rachel well.

Margot had gotten her own "last card" from Rachel the week before she died. Hers featured a ladybug, and she had experienced a rash of ladybug sightings. One afternoon when we sat outdoors at a coffee shop, a ladybug landed on the lid of Margot's cup a few seconds before a bumblebee landed on mine. We both stared in silence until the insects flew off, at which point Margot said, her eyes teary, "I think that was Rachel's way of saying hi." All I could do was nod through my own tears.

That fall, when I moved to attend graduate school at the University of New Mexico, the very first thing I did in my new apartment was put my bumblebee card up on my refrigerator. I used my strongest magnet because the card was somewhat fragile. Rachel had made it by gluing her professionally printed photo to cardstock, and the top of the photo wasn't glued down as carefully as it might have been had Rachel been well.

I thought of the card as my lucky charm, and at first it really seemed that it was working. I was able to get all the classes I needed despite registering late and I received a small extra scholarship I hadn't expected. Alas, when the bursar's bill arrived, I received an unpleasant shock. My program, unlike every other graduate program at the university, was subject to an extra three-thousand-dollar tuition charge I hadn't known about. Even with the unexpected scholarship, I had no idea how I was going to cover it.

My friends and family really came through for me when they heard the story. Some gave me ten dollars, some far more. But when all was said and done, the day before my bursar's bill was due, I was still two hundred dollars short. I was sitting in my kitchen trying to figure out what I was going to do when a bee flew through my apartment window — the biggest, fattest, fuzziest bumblebee I'd ever seen, with a deep buzzing drone that seemed to fill the entire room. It flew straight toward me.

Now, I'm the kind of person who normally stays quite still when a bee comes my way. I figure it's best to simply stay calm and wait for my insect visitors to leave of their own accord, rather than risk getting stung by trying to swat them or run away. This time, though, the bee was so big and noisy that my usual serenity deserted me. I jumped out of my chair and stumbled backward — straight into my refrigerator, where my shoulder hit the magnet that was holding Rachel's card in place. I knocked off the magnet, and it went clattering to the floor. Rachel's bumblebee card went fluttering down after it, the photo loosening as it went. And what I saw when it landed made my heart stop.

There were two hundred-dollar bills tucked behind the picture.

It took me several moments, but I finally understood. Rachel hadn't mis-glued the photo to the cardstock. Instead, she'd intentionally left the top open to create a pocket for my graduation gift, the "little something" she'd alluded to in her message. I have no idea how Rachel could have known that I'd need that exact amount so desperately. Perhaps she hadn't known at all. But I do know that I never would have found it if the extra-large honeybee hadn't made me knock the card off my refrigerator.

I never saw that extra-large bee again. But when I went to the bursar's office to pay my bill in full, the roses outside the door were alive with its smaller cousins, happily pollinating the last few flowers of the summer. When I left the office and one flew perilously by my nose, I smiled.

It was just Rachel's way of saying hi.

— Kerrie R. Barney —

Walter's Last Wave

Flowers grow out of dark moments.
~Corita Kent

I'm late again, I thought as I raced through my apartment getting ready for work. No matter how I tried, I never seemed to get ahead of a school bus that stopped at every corner. I resigned myself to another morning of stop and go. However, that morning, at one of the stops, a new little face raced to the back of the bus, and his eyes met mine through the rear window. He was a good-looking little guy, about ten years old, with dark hair, dark eyes, and a beautiful smile. He gave me a big wave, which I returned. From then on, I found myself purposely trying to end up behind that bus so I could see that angelic little boy.

As a storyteller for children, I was blessed to work for a corporation that embraced not only my corporate skills but also my artistic talents. I was often invited to entertain the employees' children at our on-site daycare center. One morning, I decided to share one of my puppets with that darling little boy on the school bus. I was stopped behind the vehicle, waiting for all the kids to board. He was always last but always made his way to the back window in time to wave to me. The look of surprise on his face when I propped my puppet up on the steering wheel was unforgettable. He shared two waves that day — one for me and one for my puppet. From that day forward, that puppet and I were partners in receiving waves and smiles from that little boy.

One late night, while organizing my props for a company story time, I was thinking of how my little school-bus friend would love to see my show. I wished I could perform at his school. My thoughts were interrupted by a hideous, bone-chilling scream in the woods behind my apartment. I called the police, who said it was probably an animal being attacked. However, they promised to investigate.

I assumed I had panicked for no reason but spent the night tossing and turning while trying to sleep. That scream echoed in my head all night long.

The next morning, as I raced with my puppet to catch those special waves and smiles from my favorite little fan, there was no sweet little boy boarding the bus. I was worried. Was he late? Maybe he was ill or perhaps his parents gave him a day off. A few more days passed and there was no sign of that child. *Maybe he moved,* I thought, and sent a little prayer his way.

That weekend, when my newspaper arrived, there on the front page was a picture of that darling boy's face. Now he had a name: Walter. He had been brutally murdered in the woods behind my apartment. Something died in me that day, too.

A few days later, the entire community mourned his death at a church memorial service. Everyone contributed something to help his family. I attended his celebration of life and was in awe of the hundreds of bouquets of flowers that covered and overflowed the altar. I was one of the last to say goodbye. I had brought something special just for Walter from me. Next to his coffin, I left a little wrapped flowerpot with a package of forget-me-not seeds and a note for him to "Plant his dreams!" It's something I share with all the little children I entertain.

A week passed, and I decided to visit my family gravesite. Nearby, I couldn't help but notice the mountain of bouquets on top of another grave. I was surprised to discover it was Walter's, who was now laid to rest close to my family. Remembering his smiling face and little waves, I found myself making several trips to visit his grave, heartbroken that he never got to plant his dreams. With each visit, I noticed fewer bouquets until one last bouquet of weathered, dried roses remained. That seemed to make me sadder. Beautiful blooms, giving their all, were now tossed and gone just like this little boy's life.

As I walked closer to his grave, I decided I would take that last bouquet and scatter its petals in memory of him. As I removed the dried flowers, I was shocked to find my little wrapped flowerpot nestled under the dead roses. And then, a miracle! The seeds of forget-me-nots I had placed in the pot had pushed their way through the package, and little flowers were blooming! I knew those little blossoms were a last wave from Walter, letting me know he would remember me. With the angels in heaven, he was planting his dreams!

— Lainie Belcastro —

Chapter
4

Guardians and Protectors

My Imaginary Friend

*Children often have imaginary playmates. I suspect
that half of them are really their guardian angels.*
~Eileen Elias Freeman,
The Angels' Little Instruction Book

I was in the park with my brother, patiently waiting for my turn on a swing, when we heard the explosion. For almost a minute, a deathly silence settled over the park that only seconds before had been filled with the shouts and laughter of energetic children enjoying their summer vacation.

The sky began to blacken with smoke, and everyone started to run past me, almost knocking me over as they headed toward the sound of the blast. My oldest brother, Eddy, rushed by to join them across the street where a field faced a building engulfed in flames.

"Stay there!" he ordered over his shoulder. "I'll be right back."

I looked around at the now empty park. All the kids were watching the fire with morbid curiosity. The swings I'd waited so long for were finally free, except for one. A little girl about my age of six grinned at me, and I ran to join her. As I approached, I noticed her fingers and the back of her hand were covered in large, unsightly bumps.

"Hi!" she greeted me. "I'm Theresa. Do you want to play with me?"

"I'm Marya," I replied, staring at her hands. "What are those?" I asked, realizing quickly that I was being rude.

"They're warts," she told me. "But don't worry. You won't get them unless you touch them."

"Well, then, I won't touch you." I shrugged. "Let's swing!"

While people continued gathering to watch the horror that we were too little to understand, Theresa and I became fast friends, laughing, playing, and enjoying having the whole playground to ourselves. She told me no one was ever allowed to play with her because of her warts and was glad it didn't matter to me.

"This is fun!" she giggled gleefully as she swung higher and higher, her sneakered feet trying to reach the sun.

When we tired of the swings, we tried the monkey bars, and then the slides. All too soon, my brother came back.

"Oh, good! You listened," he told me. "It's time to go!"

"Five more minutes!" I begged. "We're having so much fun!"

"We?" he mimicked. "Who's 'we'?"

I turned to point to Theresa, but she was gone.

"Her name is Theresa. She was here a minute ago."

"I didn't see anybody," Eddy insisted. "You're a little old for imaginary friends, don't you think?"

"She's not imaginary. She's real. She has bumps on her hands called warts, and she said no one ever plays with her because of that!"

"Well, you shouldn't either!" he admonished with all the sternness and pompous authority of someone a whole five years older than me.

The next day, my other older brother, Joe, grudgingly brought me back to the park. Forgetting I was no longer a baby, he dropped me off at the sandbox and went off to hang out with his friends nearby.

I looked toward the monkey bars and was delighted to see Theresa again. We dangled by our hands and our legs, laughing uproariously when she slipped and almost fell. Other kids stared at us strangely, and I felt bad. They must have seen Theresa's hands, so I suggested we go and sit on the grass for a little while.

Theresa sat facing me with her back to the outer fence as we chatted. I told her we were leaving the next day to go to our country house like we did every year during my father's vacation.

"I won't be here when you get back," Theresa told me.

"Where are you going?" I asked. "When will you be back?"

"When you need me," she told me, standing up to brush the grass from her shorts. "Thank you for being my friend when no one else would be, Marya. I have to go now."

At that moment, I heard my brother call me. When I turned around, Theresa was gone again.

"You know you look stupid sitting there talking to yourself," Joe told me. "You're embarrassing me."

"I was talking to my friend," I insisted. I hated that my brothers always teased me and pretended not to see things that I did.

"Yeah, right!" he muttered, yanking my arm. "It's lunchtime. Let's go home."

Our country house was located close to a river, beach, woods, fields, and waterfalls. It had no electricity, running water, or toilet, just a well and an outhouse. About a week into Papa's vacation, Mama announced she was going to the river to wash some laundry by hand. Since everyone else was out somewhere, she made me go with her.

Bored, I sat on a large nearby rock watching as she scrubbed bedsheets, attempting to get them pristine white again. Suddenly, from the corner of my eye, I saw a movement. It was a rabbit!

Without thinking, I began to follow it as it hopped away. Each time I got close, it scrambled into bushes to hide. I don't know how long I continued to chase it, but when I finally looked around me, everything was unfamiliar. I couldn't even hear the roar of the river anymore. I found myself deep in thick woods, having completely lost my sense of direction. I was beginning to get frightened when I heard a familiar voice behind me.

"Hi, Marya!"

I whirled around to see my friend from the park.

"Theresa! What are you doing here?" I exclaimed.

Before she could answer, I looked down at her hands, stunned to find them smooth and unblemished. She also had an odd glow surrounding her — as if the sun was bouncing off her back and ricocheting into rays all around her, which was odd because the forest was dark and damp.

"Your warts are gone!"

"Are you lost, Marya?" she asked, ignoring my words.

"I think so," I replied. "Mama will be mad. I was supposed to stay nearby, but…"

"That's okay. I'll take you back before she notices that you're gone. She's still washing stuff. Follow me."

I did, and she led me to my mother. Her back was still to us as she rinsed and wrung out laundry, carefully placing it into a bucket.

"Thank you, Theresa!" I said. "Can you stay and play?"

"No, I have to go, Marya. I came to say goodbye."

"Are you moving?" I asked, puzzled.

"Sort of." She smiled. "I have to go be with my mom and dad. I'll miss you."

"I'll miss you, too," I said sadly and watched her walk away. I turned to see Mama was finally finished. I never told her about Theresa or the rabbit, afraid she'd be angry I'd wandered off.

I never thought about that day again until another old childhood friend and I were reminiscing about the past, and he happened to mention that gas explosion of long ago. Only then did I learn that three people who'd recently moved into the area died in the fire — a mother, father and six-year-old girl.

"Do you recall her name?" I inquired, feeling strangely chilled.

"No," he replied. "But I remember no one would play with her because her hands were covered in warts."

— Marya Morin —

32

God Protects Children

I think that someone is watching out for me, God,
my guardian angel, I'm not sure who that is,
but they really work hard.
~Mattie Stepanek

t was 1970. My friends and I were eighteen, away from home for the first time. We were attending the University of Miami and, in the way of college students, felt immortal. Our entire lives were ahead of us. What could happen?

In those halcyon years, freshmen weren't allowed to have cars on campus. Miami had no mass transit to beaches or Coconut Grove — all the places we wanted to go. Mother Nature had solved the problem by giving us thumbs. We thought, foolishly, that if we hitchhiked in groups, we were safe. Oh, sure, there were stories — the ghost of Tahiti Beach Road, the unsolved disappearance of coeds at Crandon Park. Everyone heard about them. Everyone had a friend who had a friend who knew someone who'd seen the ghost or went to school with a missing woman. It was thin evidence as far as we were concerned.

On this particular day, my roommate Cyn and I set out with our suitemate Carrie for Peacock Park in Coconut Grove. We stuck out our thumbs, and two cars — one a big blue Chevy and the other one of those early Hondas that looked like a high-top sneaker — pulled up to the curb. We opted for the bigger car. A lone male sat behind the wheel of the Chevy. He looked to be in his early twenties with long, light brown hair that curled over his shoulders. His eyes were the bluest blue I'd ever seen. He instructed Cyn and Carrie to get in the back seat and pushed open the passenger door for me. It seemed odd that he wanted one of us in the front. Most drivers wanted the entire crew in the back.

The three of us climbed in. The man assured us he was headed for Peacock Park and he'd be happy to take us the entire way. That was huge. Most drivers only went as far as one of the U.S. 1 cross streets into the Grove, and hitchhikers were left to try for another ride or walk. Traffic was heavy, and the man turned down an unfamiliar side street. We exchanged glances, but it was daylight. We were headed in the right direction, and we were on surface roads with lots of stop signs. No cause for concern. After a few minutes, he circled back toward U.S. 1, pulled off in the parking lot of an abandoned gas station, and instructed me to open the glove box.

The glove box door fell open and revealed a revolver. I'd grown up with weapons and saw immediately that it was loaded. My friends scrambled to leave the vehicle only to discover that the doors were locked and the interior releases missing. I'd like to say my entire life flashed before my eyes, but I hadn't lived long enough to have much life to review. The man reached over and flipped the glove box closed. Then he said, "Don't be afraid. The person who pulled over behind me had different intentions. Remember what could have been if you decide to hitchhike again." There was a click, and the car doors unlocked.

The three of us exited, and when we turned back to the vehicle, it was gone. Traffic was stopped in front of the driveway. If the car had managed to squeeze into traffic, it would still have been on the road in front of the building. It was nowhere to be seen. We never spoke of the event among ourselves, and we never hitchhiked again.

— Kait Carson —

33

Snow Angel

*Our perfect companions never
have fewer than four feet.*
~Colette

One stormy night, on my way home from work, my car slid off into the ditch just outside of town. I had been driving in a blinding blizzard, and there was no one around. I trudged for miles through the snowstorm and finally reached the edge of town. At the first exit, I made my way up the ramp, shivering from the cold. But at least I was now only a couple of miles from home, I told myself.

Suddenly, a carload of drunks pulled up beside me and began harassing me. They offered me a ride, but I was sure they had other things in mind. Scared out of my wits, I uttered a quick prayer. "Jesus, help me!" In an instant, a beautiful Collie appeared at my side. The dog began snapping and snarling at my tormentors, and they quickly left. *Thank goodness, the dog showed up to protect me*, I thought.

As I trudged on through the snowstorm, my new companion stayed by my side, guiding me through the blizzard. It was if the dog knew exactly where I lived and how to get there. Finally, after struggling through the blizzard for two more miles, I came to my house. The dog followed me onto the porch. I was so thankful to be home that I quickly unlocked the door and turned to bring my new companion into the house and out of the nasty weather.

But when I turned around, the dog had disappeared. And, to my astonishment, the only tracks in the snow were mine.

— Christine Trollinger —

The Watchers

The unlikeliest people harbor halos beneath their hats.
~Author Unknown

The call came late at night, as such calls often do. Apparently, my teenage cousin had not returned home after hunting in the woods near his house. What followed was a heartbreaking phone tree and plans to travel out-of-town for his funeral.

When someone dies, especially when that person is young, we often find ourselves philosophizing on the meaning of life. My older sister and I did just that as we lay on her bed the night before the funeral. Our aunt had told us that her son's body had lain in the woods where wild dogs were known to roam, yet not one dog had come near him the entire evening. "God assured me that several angels had been assigned to stay with him throughout the night and to remain with him until the end," she had told us.

We weren't really sure how to take her explanation of several angels watching over our cousin's lifeless body as he lay in the still of the woods. Yet, we knew about the wild dogs that roamed those woods, and it did seem very peculiar that they had not gone near our cousin's body the entire night.

At the funeral the next day, my sister and I sat with my aunt in the designated area for family. After the eulogy and special music, the funeral director asked family members to come view the body. That is when I noticed about ten or twelve men of various shapes and sizes walk to the front of the room. The men, all dressed in dark suits, walked in single file toward the casket. Then, one after the other, they looked at my cousin's body and walked out the side door of the funeral parlor.

At the time, I assumed the mysterious guests were relatives of my uncle, especially since they were the first to view the body. My aunt and uncle had been divorced for several years, and I didn't know many of his family members. So, I patiently waited my turn and then fell into step behind other family members as we took our opportunity to pay our last respects.

Later, I asked my younger sister about the mysterious men in the dark suits.

"What men?" she asked.

"All those men in dark suits who walked up to view the body before we got to go," I answered.

"No one went before us," she contradicted. "We are family, so we went first. It's tradition."

I knew I hadn't been seeing things. Sure, I felt numb, and nothing seemed real, but only in the way that our minds protect us when someone we love dies. Feeling shock is completely different from hallucinating.

So, I asked my older sister if she had seen the men. She had, but she was just as clueless about their identity as I was. We decided to ask our aunt. Surely, she would know who they were.

"You *saw* them?" my aunt asked, her eyes widening.

"Yes," I said. "They each walked in a straight line, right up to the casket. They looked at the body and walked out the side door, one behind the other."

My aunt smiled. "Those were the angels that God promised would stay with my son until the end. I thought I was the only one who could see them."

Well, that was my cue to do some investigating. I needed to find out if anyone else at the funeral had seen the men in the dark suits. As it turned out, several people had seen them but dismissed them just as I had — as family members they did not know. Many others remained adamant that no one fitting the description of the men in dark suits had been there.

I am not sure why only some of us were able to see them, but after that day my view of guardian angels has never been the same.

— Cynthia Zayn —

He Spoke My Name

A God wise enough to create me and the world
I live in is wise enough to watch out for me.
~Philip Yancey

I was sixteen years old, and he was seventeen. He was not my first love and certainly not my last. He wasn't even someone that I was really interested in, but I knew he was crazy about me, so I gave in and dated him. As teenagers, it was mostly hanging out and doing things that we really had no business doing. Definitely not the makings of prom queen or king. No, we were just kids trying to grow up too fast.

From the start, it was a rocky relationship. I soon discovered that he had a jealous streak a mile long, and it seemed I could do nothing right. This was not something that I had experienced in the past, and I quickly realized it would be difficult to break free.

Early into this relationship, I started feeling trapped. I was missing the boy I had previously dated. He was always so sweet and kind. It hurt to know that I had hurt him, and I wanted to be able to talk to him. So, I called him one day. Huge mistake. It wasn't long before it got back to my jealous boyfriend that I had made that call. But, of course, as stories do, it had grown from a friendly "I'm sorry" call to an "I want to secretly meet you."

I knew this was going to be ugly, and it was. He didn't confront me until we were alone. Abusers are manipulative that way. From the moment we walked into his house, he started. It's tough to admit it, but I was smacked, shoved, shaken, thrown, and finally reduced to cowering in a corner begging him to stop. He was red-faced, angry, and extremely threatening. After what seemed like hours of terror, with him berating and threatening me, he pulled out a rifle and held it to my head.

"All I want you to do is breathe," he said. I could do nothing but sob and pray.

Suddenly, everything went silent and still. Out of nowhere, a loud voice filled the entire house. It was a man's voice, deep and strong, as crystal clear as if it was in the room with us. And it spoke only one word: my name.

Immediately, my boyfriend ran out of the house and into the yard, yelling, "Who's out there?" But there was no one there. He lived in a remote area, away from any other houses, and there were dogs in a pen outside. If someone had been outside, we would have known it. There was no one there. When he came back in, he had a look of fear on his face, and he was ready to take me home. We were both unnerved. I don't remember much of what happened after hearing the voice. After that night, I was finally able to break free from this abusive relationship.

Twenty years later, I ran into him. As adults, we had moved past our troubled youth and spoke as if we were good friends.

"Do you remember the night?" I said.

He answered, "Of course. How could I forget?" And I knew we were on the same page.

"So, what do you think it was?" I asked.

"God," he answered.

I told him that no one would ever believe us if we spoke of it, and he agreed. But it happened, and we will always know it.

Recently, I was on social media chatting with friends when up popped a familiar name on my friend list. Here we were, twenty years after our last conversation, and again I asked, "Do you remember the night?" Of course, we talked about it again.

I don't know who or what it was that night many years ago. What I do know is that it stopped the attack. I will never forget the voice. I can still hear it as clearly as when it echoed throughout the room that night. I can still recall every emotion I felt, and it still shakes me to this day. I've heard the old adage, "It was a miracle I survived," many times in my life, and for me there is nothing else that it could be.

— Lacy Gray —

Kept from Harm

One thing you can say for guardian angels: they guard.
They give warning when danger approaches.
~Emily Hahn

That early morning, with my ten-week-old baby girl in my arms and a warm bottle in the diaper bag, I walked to the house next door. As I let myself in, I smelled the fresh brewed coffee and heard Mom's voice from the kitchen.

"I'm pouring you a cup right now."

Mom took DeBritt from my arms, and then we both sat at our usual places at the table.

Dad always joined us a few minutes later to feed and play with DeBritt before he left for work. He kissed her goodbye on her forehead, as he always did, before handing her back to Mom.

That had become our routine since two weeks after the birth of my daughter. She usually fell asleep in Mom's arms as we sipped our coffee, talked about nothing or simply sat in comfortable silence while reading a book or magazine for the next hour or so.

That scenario played out exactly the same, almost word for word, every single morning. It would finally end with me saying, "Well, I guess I should go."

Mom would respond, "Oh, you may as well have another cup." I would agree and then stay for another fifteen to thirty minutes. It was just like *Groundhog Day*, the movie.

But, on that morning, as soon as Mom said that I should have another cup before I went, I had an extreme, desperate urge to leave immediately. So, I answered, "No, Mom, I have to go right now. Give her to me!" I quickly stood up and reached for DeBritt.

Mom, with a shocked look on her face, stood up and took a step toward me. As she placed DeBritt into my arms, the large, heavy glass light fixture fell from the ceiling and landed squarely on the seat of Mom's chair. It hit with such force that it exploded into hundreds of pieces that scattered across the floor.

We stood in stunned silence while DeBritt lay in my arms, undisturbed by the noise.

I put my free arm around Mom's shoulders, drew her close, and asked, "Are you okay?" She didn't answer my question, but, still in her confused state, she hesitantly asked, "How did you know?"

I shrugged my shoulders and said, "How? Honestly, Mom, I have no idea. It was an overpowering, urgent feeling… an instant knowing. I just knew I had to leave immediately — I didn't have a choice! I don't know how else to explain it."

I looked down at Mom's chair. It had several chunks ripped from the wooden seat, and a few shards were still embedded in it.

After several seconds, Mom asked, "Do you think it was an angel?"

Smiling, I answered, "Yes… keeping us safe."

— Zaquynn Phoenix Iamati —

See You Soon

The bond between friends cannot be broken by chance;
no interval of time or space can destroy it.
Not even death itself can part true friends.
~John Cassian

A very dear friend was dying from cancer. My last visit with her was at the hospital before her family took her home to Kentucky. It was what Connie wanted, and hospice arranged it all.

As I was ready to leave, Connie called me to her bedside, and we hugged. I held her hand, said goodbye to her, and told her how much I loved her. Connie pulled me down to her and said, "I will see you again real soon."

My husband and I walked down the hall, and I told him what Connie had said to me. We both thought it quite strange since she was dying.

Four days later, as I was waking, I had a strange feeling. Lo and behold, Connie was standing next to me. She took my hand and placed it on my right breast. I gasped as I felt a baseball-sized lump in my breast that I never knew existed despite checking regularly.

I sat upright in bed, in shock. Connie was no longer next to me. I gathered my courage and went out to the kitchen where my husband was having coffee. I poured a cup of coffee and said, "Connie is going to heaven today." He asked me how I knew, and I told him that she had one more task to complete. Now that it was done, she was on her way.

I then told him what had happened in the bedroom and how Connie had taken my hand and placed it on my right breast.

Connie did pass on that evening, and I have no doubt that she saved my life by coming to me. I was diagnosed with Stage 2 breast cancer.

Surgery and radiation followed, and I continue to be on chemo drugs, but I am alive and thriving due to Connie. I can't wait to thank her for what she did when I get to heaven one day.

I realized that when she said she was going to see me real soon that she knew in the hospital bed what she had to do. Not a day goes by when I don't count my blessings for this miracle.

— Sue Pasztor —

My Husband and the Firewall

No evil shall befall you, nor shall affliction come near
your tent, for His angels God has given command
about you, that they guard you in all your ways.
~Psalm 91:11 (AMP)

My husband Scotty and I had been talking for weeks about camping with friends from church, and we'd finally found a weekend when it would work for all four of us. Even more amazing, we'd checked the web and discovered there would be an available spot for both our trailers in the one campground we all considered the very best and one of the safest.

"This is going to be such a great getaway," I'd said more than once, grateful that we would be miles from anything that even resembled a town, surrounded by towering evergreens, camping under a truly big Montana sky. We would play board games, pop popcorn, and have as many s'mores as we wanted.

Meanwhile, each of the four of us had said we would be happy to take on any or even all the cooking. Scotty said he wanted to at least prepare the first night's entire meal himself. The rest of us were to sit back, enjoy a glass of wine, and relax.

The three of us chatted and watched while Scotty peeled potatoes, diced onions, and made mouth-watering hamburger patties. With the inch-thick burgers sizzling and the potatoes and onions keeping warm on a platter, the fragrance from our incredible-looking supper began to fill our camping space.

"He's really an excellent cook," I bragged. "In fact, he often cooks at home."

Scotty preferred, however, to do his cooking outdoors over a campfire or on a propane stove. Because he'd done quite a bit of our outdoor cooking, he owned a fine collection of excellent tools. For this camping adventure, he'd even packed his newest, three-burner stove, which he was preparing to shut down after announcing, "Dinner is served!" The rest of us were preparing to move to the table and my husband was unscrewing the black hose that supplies the propane to each of the burners, but he'd forgotten to turn off the valve that would fully extinguish the flame. The propane burst into a towering flame not even a foot from his face.

We all froze, although I wanted to leap from where I was seated, grab my husband's arm, and yank him completely away from the stove. I was just about to make that move when, just as suddenly as that flame erupted, what appeared to be a solid Plexiglas shield shot straight up from the top of the camping table and settled in place between Scotty and the blue flames that continued to burn. And then, while our friends and I continued to stare, that same shield remained in place until Scotty was able to close the valve. He hadn't been touched by even one lick of flame!

So, do I believe something divine took place in that Montana campground at the exact moment when something divine was needed? No one and nothing on the face of this Earth will ever persuade me to utter one single word of disbelief.

— Nancy Hoag —

39

Not Quite an Airbag

Miracles are instantaneous. They cannot be summoned,
but come of themselves, usually at unlikely moments
and to those who least expect them.
~Katherine Porter

It was 2:00 in the morning. My brother, Chase, was driving us home from our weekly chore of cleaning the church. It was a tiny church, so they entrusted the cleaning of it to just my brother and me. We were both getting sleepy, so we picked up a couple of energy drinks at a gas station, and then jumped onto the freeway and headed home.

The ride was fine. My brother was focused, so I snuggled into my seatbelt and closed my eyes. I woke up when we were close to our exit, but something was wrong. The car was veering off to the right. I laughed it off at first because Chase is a goofball who messes around sometimes. But it didn't occur to my foggy, sleep-riddled brain that it wasn't a joke at all.

Not until it was too late.

I shouted my brother's name at the top of my voice. He woke up from his slumber in time to slam on the brakes, though the brakes did little to slow us down. We crashed into a streetlight, sending us bumping down the dirt hill of the off-ramp.

Then I saw something white and bright shoot toward my chest. I thought nothing of it, assuming that it was the airbag. It hit me and left me breathless but saved me from the dashboard.

The streetlight swung around, hitting two other cars, and then crashed back onto the hood of our car. One inch closer to us, and Chase and I wouldn't be here today. A kind man helped us out of our car, and the police came to assist. Chase and I sat in the back of the police car and a policeman came to talk to us. Somewhere in the conversation I mentioned the airbag that had saved my life. The policeman looked at me and then at Chase.

"There are no airbags in that car," he said.

Our dad arrived on the scene in his car and drove us home. As soon as I walked through the door, I headed to the bathroom. I lifted up my shirt to see an enormous black bruise from my abdomen to my collarbone. The paramedics said there were no broken ribs, no internal bleeding. Whatever that white thing was that came at me and protected me had saved me from injuries much worse than a bruise. My brother was much better off, with only a cut and a bruise on his arm from where the seatbelt had tightened against him.

I believe that an angel was sent to protect us that morning.

And I believe that angel has watched over us ever since.

— E.S. Arnold —

Chapter 5

Answered Prayers

Feeding a Family on a Prayer

Through the eyes of gratitude, everything is a miracle.
~Mary Davis

At nine years old, I had been through more than the usual amount of excitement and change for a girl my age. In the past few months, my stable and predictable life had been turned upside down when my father, who was a nurse, was laid off from his job at a local hospital. This set into motion a series of events, including my parents losing our beautiful Victorian home and forcing our family into a fifteen-foot pull trailer we had previously only used for weekend camping trips. My parents also withdrew me from my private school and began homeschooling my brother and me.

Life in the trailer was tough. I contracted scarlet fever and remember being sicker than I ever thought possible. We were incredibly crowded. I'll never forget the first time we sat on the tiny couch together, the one that served as my parents' bed at night. When Mom, Dad, my brother, and I all sat on the couch at the end of the trailer, the entire front end began to tip in our direction, forcing one of us to jump up and scramble to the front. This settled the trailer back on the ground. Furthermore, we were running out of options for places to park our mobile house. It finally got so bad that we had to park the trailer in our church parking lot.

Things were getting bleak. I remember my mom's shrieks as a gray mouse ran across the floor and under the stove. One day, she sat at the cramped table and made out a shopping list while the last of our food, fried chicken, sizzled on the stovetop. "We need to pray," she said aloud. "We don't have enough food to last the week." And so, we joined hands and asked God to provide not only food but all our pressing needs.

Then Mom got up and started putting the chicken on a plate for dinner. I opened the tiny door and let the smell of dinner follow me as I wandered outside to find my dad. He was working on our broken-down truck. As Dad leaned over the engine, I noticed a disheveled man walking up to our humble abode.

"Can I help you, sir?" my dad asked in his friendly way.

"I'm hoping you can," he said. "I'm hungry and was wondering if you had any food to spare."

I looked up at Dad, knowing we didn't have much.

"Sure!" Dad chirped without hesitation. He brushed off his hands and went inside, returning with a fresh piece of fried chicken wrapped in a paper towel. The man's grimy face lit up. He devoured the home-cooked food, and I happily listened to a friendly conversation between the two men. The stranger mentioned that he had some canned food that he couldn't use because he didn't have a can opener. Dad offered him our can opener, but the man refused, saying he'd bring the cans by later. Dad said that wasn't necessary, but the man insisted.

After dinner, our little family locked our dog and cat in the trailer and walked across the parking lot for Wednesday night service. Doing something we used to do, before losing our home, was a comfort to our family. The small congregation was warm and familiar. The evening activities consisted of all the things a midweek service should have: homespun music, heartfelt prayer, and encouragement.

When we returned to the trailer, we were surprised to see three brown paper bags near the drop-down step leading up to the door.

"Well, that man said he was going to leave us some canned food…" Dad's voice trailed off. Dad had left the conversation with the impression it was a few cans, not a few bags. Mom and Dad brought in the bags and began to unpack them on the table. About two bags in, Mom's eyes filled with tears. She grabbed her list from under a magnet on the empty, pint-sized refrigerator. Dad took it from her and began to cry himself, something I rarely saw throughout my lifetime. I glanced over his shoulder and saw it in black and white. It was a simple grocery list, written in Mom's fancy cursive.

"This is unbelievable!" Mom gasped. "Every item I listed, even down to the 'tuna in water,' is on our table! Milk, eggs, noodles, bread…" The list went on.

It was enough to get us through another week. Dad sat us down and thanked God for providing for us in such an immediate, specific way. Then he got out his big brown Bible and began thumbing through the thin pages until he found the book of Hebrews. "Chapter thirteen, verse two," he said in a shaky voice. "Do not forget to show hospitality to strangers, for by so doing some people have shown hospitality to angels without knowing it" (NIV).

From that day to this, our family has always referred to that man as an angel. Life got better for my family after that. Dad began working as a traveling nurse, and we upgraded to a thirty-four-foot Class A motorhome. This fit our new homeschooling lifestyle like a glove. We all recall the years spent on the road with great fondness, seeing just about every state west of the Mississippi. It was a time of bonding and memory-making that could never have happened in the Victorian house.

"Remember the angel?" my younger brother often said, which conjured up the memories. We would retell the tale of the day an angel visited a trailer and fed a family on a prayer.

— Hosanna Barton —

41

Miracle in the Blue

Believe in guardian angels. They believe in you
and are forever by your side.
~Author Unknown

It was a perfect day for the beach. I was thirteen and my brother was fourteen. We were meeting our friends on the northeast side of the island, a beach we seldom visited due to the strong currents and undertow.

Dad dropped us off an hour before everyone was to arrive. I watched my brother take off into the crystal-blue ocean. He was a diehard body surfer.

I decided not to wait for our friends either. Instead, I ran down to the shoreline as the water began to rise, forming a perfect wave. I held my breath and dove through the swell. I was under the surf, with my eyes wide open, the water like silk flowing over my body. It was cold, like liquid ice waking up my senses.

I pulled my body to the surface, allowing fresh air to fill my lungs, and then went back under. I pretended to be a mermaid, a dolphin, anything that lived under the sea.

After a while, I thought it might be a good idea to head back in and see if our friends had arrived. I looked toward the beach and realized I had gone farther out than I should have. I was the only one this far out.

I wasn't too worried though. I was a pretty good swimmer. But, as I tried to swim in, I realized I was making no progress. After what felt like a long while, my body began to feel heavy, and my arms grew tired. I took a deep breath and went under the water in search of the ocean floor, thinking I could kick off the floor and give myself some momentum.

I couldn't find the bottom. I began to think I might drown out there, apparently caught in a rip current that was carrying me farther away from the shore. It didn't matter how hard I tried to swim; I was not moving any closer to the beach.

Exhausted and terrified, I began to pray and ask God to help me. I cried, "I don't want to die this way!"

My arms could barely pull through the water. I tried yelling for help, but could only whisper, "Please, please, God. Help me. Don't let me drown!"

Before I could take another breath, a stranger appeared in front of me. "Give me your hand," he said firmly.

I reached out and felt a firm grip wrap around my fingers. The stranger told me to kick, but my legs were numb and lifeless. I could feel his strong arm pulling me out from the deep.

I don't know how long it took us to get to shore, but he picked me up out of the water and carried my limp body onto the sand, away from the crashing waves.

I held my face in my hands and began to sob uncontrollably. A few seconds passed. I looked up to thank the stranger, but he was gone. My eyes scanned the uncrowded beach, but there was no sign of the hero who had rescued me.

I am a grandmother now, and I have told this story a hundred times throughout my life. People often ask me, "Do you think he was an angel?" My reply: "Without a doubt."

Forty-three years ago, God sent an angel to save me. It changed my life forever.

— Jamie Williams —

42

Angel On My Shoulder

Angels are all around us, all the time,
in the very air we breathe.
~Eileen Elias Freeman,
The Angels' Little Instruction Book

I hated driving in the New England snow and ice. But on this day, with my husband's encouragement, I decided to try to let go of my fear. After all, I convinced myself, we were only going to the local library a couple of miles away on the back roads—no major highways! Surely, I could do this.

I always considered myself a spiritual person who believed in the possibility of the universe offering help and direction, but I had never asked for guidance—until then. For some reason, I felt compelled to do so on that wintry February day. Not knowing exactly what to do, I chose Archangel Michael and asked him to protect us, visualizing a benevolent face and beautiful expansive wings surrounding the car. Then I took a deep breath and slid behind the wheel.

The start of our "adventure" was without incident. Tightly clutching the wheel while pasting on a smile, I told my husband that this was going to be "a piece of cake." (I was really trying to convince myself.) But the minute we approached the four-way intersection, everything changed. I nervously looked in both directions. Not seeing a car in sight, I exhaled a brief sigh of relief and proceeded forward on the slippery road with caution, determination, and sweaty palms. So far, so good.

Then it happened. A blue van came barreling from our left, aiming directly at us as a green pick-up truck skidded toward us from the right. It was terrifying to see these two vehicles careening toward us on the icy road.

It felt like a presence completely took control of the steering wheel. My hands loosened their grip, barely touching the wheel, as we witnessed the steering wheel moving on its own. Our car swerved sharply to the left, just missing the van by a hair. Then it turned right and dodged the truck. That presence controlled the wheel and steered us to safety.

We stopped on the other side of the road unscathed, just a bit numb and in awe of what had happened. Back in control of the wheel, I continued driving down the road in silence. But a few minutes later, I pulled into a parking lot and stopped the car. My husband and I, both of us now shaking, looked at each other and whispered, "What just happened?" We both knew that I did not steer us through that potential accident. I couldn't possibly have maneuvered the wheel that nimbly.

It had to be divine intervention that saved us. My husband, a pragmatist at heart, concurred. He confirmed that I barely touched the steering wheel that adeptly navigated us to avoid danger. I realized then that my request for protection had been answered. I thanked Archangel Michael.

Now, fifteen years later, we live in Florida. And although we have escaped hazardous, wintry road conditions, we still have to contend with some unpredictable drivers. Driving can be dangerous and risky, but I have become more confident, knowing I have an "Angel on My Shoulder" that I can call on when needed.

—Judy Stengel—

The Shadow

*The guardian angels of life fly so high as to be beyond
our sight, but they are always looking down upon us.*
~Jean Paul Richter

The California sun shone brightly upon my face. I had a basketball in one hand and a Slurpee in the other. My best friend Kim was challenging me to a shootout, like we did every week.

As we played on the court, sweat dripped down my cheeks. We continued playing the game, not realizing how late it was. As the sun began to sink, Kim got a call and had to go. I watched her parents pick her up, and I decided to head home, too.

I only lived a few blocks away, so I figured I would walk home instead of running so I could enjoy the fragrant night breeze. But there were no streetlights, and I could only see the headlights of the cars passing by in the darkness. I hated how dark it was, and it was getting colder, too. I felt more and more insecure about walking and decided that running was a better option.

Suddenly, I heard a loud noise. A big gray van with two men inside came up behind me. I thought nothing of it at first, but when they followed me around the corner, I became worried.

I ran faster. Whenever I stopped, they stopped. Whenever I turned, they turned. I was nearing my house, but I knew that if I went inside, they would know where I lived and might come looking for me another time, plus no one was home. What if they followed me inside?

I ran back and forth, up and down the street, trying to confuse them, but nothing worked. My legs became stiff. I was out of breath. Because they kept following me, I knew they wanted something.

As I thought of my future and my present, I began praying to God.

"Help me, God. Give me a second chance. I have no idea what to do. Please, hear me. Please, help me!"

I needed a sign. The men were coming closer and closer. I couldn't run anymore. Breathless and exhausted, I was giving up hope.

Then I heard a voice say, "Step into the shadow."

I looked around and saw no one. I thought I had just lost my mind from fatigue and fear. But again I heard the same voice. "Step into the shadow."

Who was saying that? I kept turning around and, as I did, I saw a skinny shadow from a palm tree. I knew I had to take a chance, so I stepped into the narrow shadow.

At that exact moment, the van pulled right up next to me. The men got out and came toward the palm tree. This was it.

As I tried to quiet my labored breathing, I could hear them breathing down my neck. I froze, waiting for them to pull out a weapon and push me inside the van.

One of the men growled, "Where did she go? We had her." He spit the words out with such anger. "How'd we miss her? Where is she?" Then I realized they could not see me!

Terrified, I stood as still as a statue right in front of them in the puny shadow. I watched them stomp back to the van and then speed around the corner. Once I lost sight of them, I sprinted to my house and ran inside crying, wondering what was going on. Then I went to the yard and watched through a hole in the fence as the van sped back and forth. The men kept stopping and jumping in and out of the van, looking for me, getting meaner and angrier each time. Finally, the screeching tires raced away.

When my mother came home, I ran to her. Trembling, I told her what had happened. She told me to fall upon my knees and praise God for sending an angel to save my life. I went to my room and did just that. I thanked God for saving my life. I realized my faith in Him had saved me.

I went to the window and looked out into the pitch-black night. It was then I realized there had been more than one miracle that night — not only the voice that had directed me, but there was no moon… no moonbeams to create a shadow from the palm tree.

Later, on the news, I heard that a girl had been abducted and murdered around the same time by two men in a gray van. They were captured, found guilty, and sent to prison.

I still fall on my knees and thank God for saving me that night. I tell all who will listen, including the students in my religious-education classes, that anything is possible with Him… even a shadow on a moonless night.

— Nancy Curtis —

Lifted

Are not all angels ministering spirits sent to serve
those who will inherit salvation?
~Hebrews 1: 14 (NIV)

The bright headlights came straight at me. With my hands on the steering wheel, I stared at them but could not move. I had become like a passenger in the driver's seat, unable to turn, swerve, or get out of the way as my car sped down the highway.

The headlights came closer and closer, glaring into my tired eyes. Still, I could not move.

It had been a long day. Between working and client appointments, all I wanted to do was go to sleep. But as the mom of two teenage daughters who played on their school's volleyball team, I could not miss their away game that night. I was proud of my daughters and attended virtually all their games.

So it was that I found myself driving home late that night after a glorious victory. Riding in the church van in the lane to my right, the team was in a celebratory mood, and I wished I could have shared in the fun of their exuberant ride home. But the girls were required to ride in the church van with their coach, so I had taken my own car.

Entranced, I stared helplessly at the headlights that fast approached, wondering what they were doing straight in front of me. This was a four-lane highway, after all, with each pair of lanes going in a single direction. At a certain point, the highway would turn into a two-lane road, with traffic going in opposite directions, but we had not reached that point yet. Having traveled the road hundreds of times, I knew it well.

I kept staring ahead at the brilliant headlights that now blurred my vision. Closer and closer they came. Soon, they would be upon me, yet still I couldn't move.

Just as the headlights were about to overtake me, invisible beings lifted my car off the ground, carried it slowly through the air, and gently placed it on the grassy median at the side of the road.

Suddenly, I awakened.

All was still. I turned off the ignition and just sat there, stunned by what had just happened.

He gives His angels charge over you, to keep you in all your ways. Years before, I had memorized those precious words from Psalm 91 and had recited them regularly over my children, spouse, and myself. Now I had literally experienced their truth. God's angels had rescued me from a horrific, head-on collision.

From almost certain death.

With tears welling up in my eyes, I drew in a deep breath and thanked the Lord for His great mercy in sparing my life.

Soon, I heard the shouts of teenage girls running toward my car. "Mom, are you all right?" My daughters were the first in line.

"Dr. Diorio, are you all right?" the girls on the team asked. "We were so scared. We were praying at the top of our lungs that God would protect you."

Dazed, I looked at the girls. "What happened?"

Coach Debbie approached the driver's side window that I had rolled down. She laid her hand on mine. "Are you okay?"

"Yes, I'm fine." Deep peace had settled over me. "What happened?"

"You almost had a head-on collision. You were driving in the wrong lane on a two-lane highway."

A two-lane highway. How did I miss the changeover from four lanes to two lanes?

Coach Debbie's voice caught. "I kept blowing my horn to get your attention, but you didn't respond."

The seriousness of the situation dawned on me.

Coach Debbie's eyes glistened with tears. "The team and I watched God's angels lift your car off the highway and place it on the median."

I swallowed hard. "I must have fallen asleep at the wheel. Thank you so much for praying."

Coach Debbie smiled. "I don't think I've ever prayed so hard for anything in all my life."

She opened the car door, and I got out. Then, she and the team surrounded me and gave me a huge group hug.

"Girls," Coach Debbie said, "let's thank the Lord for this great miracle tonight."

With my two precious daughters close beside me, we all joined hands. Right there on the grassy median at the side of the highway, Coach Debbie led the team in a powerful prayer of thanksgiving for God's mercy in saving my life. His angels had protected me. And I would never be the same.

— MaryAnn Diorio —

Angels by Her Side

*A good man's prayers will from the deepest dungeon
climb heavens' height, and bring a blessing down.*
~Joanna Baillie

My mother had a twenty-six-year battle with cancer, having been diagnosed three times with the disease. She underwent many treatments over those years. In June 2018, we were told by her doctors that nothing else could be done. She was admitted to hospice at home. My brother Mark, sister Anne and I were sharing caregiver duties.

Mom began experiencing extreme agitation and delirium in her last days. We often heard my mother cry, "Mark, where am I? How do I get home?" "Anne, where is my mother? I can't find my house!" "Barbara, where are you? I can't find you!" In her delirium, she would be in a long-ago time, in a faraway place, with people we couldn't see. She was so frightened and lost. These symptoms were not relieved by medication.

We tried holding her, praying with her, talking about familiar things, and crying with her, all to no avail. Anne, Mark and I could not find a way to soothe her anxiety and fears. Each time she cried out "Help me, *please*," our hearts would break a little more. It seemed that we could not go with her to this unknown and terrifying place.

The hospice nurses were amazing and offered help constantly, but her symptoms continued without any relief. As difficult as this was for us to see, I can only imagine how hard it must have been for her. As our frustration grew, it was becoming extremely stressful for the three of us taking care of her because we were unable to provide what she needed. Mom's condition was getting worse every day, and it was hard to leave her side even for a few moments.

After a particularly difficult morning, Anne and I were sitting in the kitchen having a cup of coffee, feeling devastated and helpless. I said to Anne, "I don't know what else we can do for Mom. I think only God can comfort her." So, we held hands and prayed, "Lord, please send your holy angels to my mother to protect her, comfort her and show her the way to heaven. She wants our help so badly, but we aren't able to be with her on this part of her journey."

After praying, Anne, Mark and I thought it was time to put a security camera in Mom's bedroom so we could monitor her constantly. If we had to leave her room for any reason, we could still see her, which would help us keep her safe. As soon as Mark had the camera in place and working, he came to us and said, "Did you see the angels?" Mark was unaware of our prayer asking God to send his angels to Mom, but somehow he knew what he was seeing through the camera.

Anne and I looked at each other and said, "What are you talking about?" We quickly looked at the camera and saw these incredibly beautiful flashes of light moving around the room, surrounding Mom. We were surprised to see that she was sitting up in bed, looking around her. Perhaps she saw the angels, too. These flashes of light seemed to float around the room, hovering over and around her. Some were brilliant colors; others were pure white. We never saw anything like this when the camera was working previously in another room. It was unbelievably intense and beautiful.

There was no doubt in our minds that we were experiencing divine intervention. This was the help we had asked for in our prayer. These angels were sent from heaven to protect and comfort our mother in a place where we couldn't go.

The end came quickly after that. The angel lights remained with us until she was gone. The beautiful flashes of light then disappeared and did not return. When we so desperately needed help, for that brief moment in time, we received a gift we will treasure forever. We were able to see the angels that were by her side. At the end of her long journey, they came to show her the way home.

— Barbara L. Ciccone —

46

In the Mood

Music is well said to be the speech of angels.
~Thomas Carlyle

I was so blessed to have my father in my life for fifty-five years. He was a soft-spoken man with a heart of gold. One of his mottos was to always give people the benefit of the doubt. It amazed me how, in the midst of chaos, Dad was steadfast. His solutions were well thought out with common sense, intelligence and, most importantly, integrity.

Dad rarely became angry. I can honestly say that I have no memories of him "losing it," or even using curse words, for that matter. Maybe he went in another room to punch a pillow, but it impressed me how much he was able to keep his cool. But his "look," the one that I dreaded receiving when I crossed the line, could stop me dead in my tracks. I learned so much from that look. Boy, I sure do miss it!

I talk to Dad every day, even though he passed in 2008. A cherished photo of him is one of the first things that I see every morning. It instantly reminds me of the many reasons why our daddy-daughter relationship means the world to me.

Music was a definite connection. He introduced me to Dean Martin, Frank Sinatra and the Big Band Era. He was also my very first dance partner at a wedding when I was five years old. My shyness always caused me to hide behind his legs, peeking out at new surroundings and people. But when the music started and he picked me up, placing my feet on his shoes, I was on top of the world. Time marched on, and our dances together became our tradition at special occasions. I can still feel his strong hand on my back, guiding me through each dance, helping me become a strong, confident young lady.

I was passionate about art from an early age. Nobody, especially me, could figure out where my artistic talent originated. The mystery was solved when my father's father stopped by for a visit. He was carrying a large box filled to the brim with envelopes, books, and other relics. "I need to clean out my place," I remember him saying. "Too much stuff!" Well, I loved looking through old "stuff," so I started digging, and Mom helped. Dad sat in the living room watching television with minimal interest in our activities.

Vintage family pictures, treasured trophies from Dad's childhood and one of his old report cards were all fascinating to Mom and me. I was getting the absolute best "blast from the past" of my father's life. It was awesome!

"What's this?" I recall my mother asking my grandfather. She was holding some striking drawings that looked as though they'd been done by a professional artist. Cartoons, portraits, geometric sketches, and landscapes were just a few of the many images that were in a rather bulky folder.

"Oh, Johnny did those," my grandfather casually replied, referring to my father. My mom and I stood paralyzed for a moment. We gathered these newfound treasures and rushed to show them to Dad.

"Now we know where Gail's talent came from!" exclaimed Mom. "Why didn't you tell us?" she asked as she placed the pictures in my father's lap.

"You never asked," he replied.

I relied on memories like these after Dad's death to pull me through the grief. As time went on, I recognized many signs that were signals from him. It created an awareness that he was always there, no matter what. Somehow, they seemed to appear at just the right moment. A pair of deer walking across the back yard of the house that I grew up in; a bevy of butterflies fluttering in a bush on one of my "down days"; a gorgeous red cardinal sitting in a tree, looking at me. These were all personal remembrances that Dad and I had shared. I depended on them.

Rough patches are a part of life. During one such time, I found that each day was a struggle. Plopping into bed at night, pulling the covers over my head, and listening to some favorite tunes were good antidotes. But one evening during this tumultuous time, I realized that I had not "heard" from Dad lately. There had not been any indications of his presence whatsoever. I found myself saying out loud, "Where are you, Dad? I really need you now!"

Life seemed relentless as it continued to throw curveballs at me. I started going to the gym to try and decompress. Tuning in my music as I worked out was a helpful and essential part of my routine. But on this particular day, it was just not meant to be.

As I climbed on the treadmill, my thoughts turned toward my problems. Focusing on the music in an attempt to flush them out of my head, I stepped up my pace. Suddenly, the music stopped. Struggling with the logistics of my iPhone and earbuds produced no results. Aggravated with this chain of events, I yanked out the earbuds, swore silently to myself, and stomped off to the locker room to fight with technology. Nothing worked. Feeling slightly sorry for myself, I walked back out to the gym and continued my workout without music.

I found myself growling at Dad. "Where are you, Pop? I really need you!"

Making one last valiant effort, I pulled my iPhone out of the pocket on my leggings. It fell to the floor. Quickly snatching it up, I jammed the buds into my ears, trying to keep my composure. As I got my rhythm started, I heard a melody. It was soft at first but then increased in volume. I had not touched anything, but my iPhone was directing music into my ears. Out of the 136 songs in my iTunes library, Glenn Miller's "In the Mood" was playing. It was Dad's favorite — and mine, too!

Goosebumps appeared on my arms. I could almost feel Dad's strong hand on my back again, this time guiding me through life. Sheepishly, I raised my eyes to Heaven. "Thanks, Pop," I whispered.

— Gail Gabrielle —

47

The Power of Prayer

There is power in prayer. When men work,
they work, but when men pray, God works.
~Angus Buchan

I t was April. The warmer weather had crept in, and I was tired. But something kept pushing me to work on my parents' house. I reluctantly grabbed the kids and hopped into the car to head over.

When we pulled into the driveway, my dad was out working on something in the yard. When he saw us, he tried to get up from what he was doing but began to stumble. After catching his balance, he walked to the car and stood at my window. His conversation was silly and strange. It was funny enough that the kids started laughing, thinking that Grandpa was being silly. But I wasn't laughing. I sent them to play and got out of the car. I followed my dad into the garage. I spoke to him cautiously, thinking maybe I was misunderstanding what was happening.

"Your mom's not feeding me," he laughed. And then he talked again... not making any sense. I stepped out to call my husband and sister, who both work in the medical field.

"Dad's not making any sense. I think there is a problem."

I returned to the garage where he laughed again. "Your mom's not feeding me," he repeated, still with the same grin. I went into the house and explained to my mother that I was concerned. She gave me some food to take out to him, thinking he was just being silly (as he was sometimes known to be).

He took a small piece of steak as I explained to him that my husband and sister were coming to look at him because I thought something might be wrong. He crossed his arms and angrily told me that he wasn't going to the hospital, and I was being ridiculous. Yet I noticed that he kept chewing on the piece of steak, but he wasn't swallowing.

My sister showed up first and quickly realized that something was wrong. She tried to reason with him, as did my husband. Despite his objections, we packed him into the car and drove to meet the ambulance we had called. When I opened the door for him, he was still chewing the meat, and now his eyes had a faraway look. I looked in his eyes. "Look at me. What's my name?" I asked, holding my breath. He just looked at me and shook his head like he didn't understand what I was saying.

The policeman on the scene tried to comfort me, patting me on the shoulder. "He's going to be okay. Your dad is one of the strongest men I know."

Then the battle began.... I got into the car to head to the hospital as I rallied the troops all the way there. I called my friend and told her to send out a message to pray. I knew she would. I knew the people she would call would do so, too. I was counting on it.

My father was a pastor, and I had grown up in church. I believed in God. I had seen the miraculous. But this was huge. Was this a miracle I could believe for? I had to. I fought with myself and God all the way to the hospital — reasoning, bargaining, pleading.

By the time we reached the hospital, the prognosis was grim at best. My father now couldn't speak. One side of his body was drawn up. He writhed around in his bed, mumbling over and over. The doctor came into the room to deliver the news. All signs pointed to a stroke. This was going to be our new normal, he cautioned. My mother looked at him fiercely, her jaw set. "He will be healed. And you will be here to watch it." It wasn't a question. It was a fact.

The next two days, we took turns staying in the hospital room, waiting for his fever to break and hoping that he would come back to us. He didn't make eye contact. He would toss and turn restlessly until they gave him medication.

Our people began to pray. It was not some passing "heal him" prayer. When we suffered from exhaustion after crying out to God, our friends, colleagues, and congregation took over. As a pastor, my dad had taught us the importance of prayer. The importance of believing, even when we couldn't see. The importance of believing that "where two or three are gathered," anything could be done.

The teachers and kids in our school stopped every time the bell rang to storm the gates of heaven for a pastor who had taught them to do so. We were surrounded and held up by adults and children in our church, our community, and across the country who had heard of the story through social media and people who were on their knees praying for my father's healing.

The doctors were baffled by the fever. Fevers don't come with stroke, so tests were run. Soon, the doctor returned with a strange look on his face. "He has not had a stroke," he explained. My dad had a brain infection, so they were going to throw every medication they could at him until they could figure out what it was or what had caused it.

On the third day, my mother leaned over him like she had many times before to talk to him quietly and explain what was happening. Suddenly, he looked at her, confused, and said, "What are you talking about?" For the first time in three days, he had formed a logical sentence. He didn't understand what had happened and how three days had slipped away without his knowing it.

The next two days were a whirlwind of doctors, nurses, and physical therapists coming in to talk to him and help him understand the importance of what he had just been through. All of them were shocked at the shift that had taken place in this man for whom they had held very little hope just two days before. It was meant to be a slow process, but if you know anything about my father, nothing is ever slow where he is concerned.

By the fourth day, he was ready to go. By the fifth day, they were ready (much to our amazement) to let him. The sweet doctor who had seen us through the whole process came to tell him goodbye.

"Thank you so much," my dad said to him.

"Don't thank me," the doctor replied. "I didn't have anything to do with it. You healed yourself."

My dad smiled. "I didn't, but I know Who did."

We all knew. The power of prayer is real.

—Corrie Lopez—

48

The Magic of the Moment

Miracles do not, in fact, break the laws of nature.
~C.S. Lewis

My mother, sister and I always enjoyed various craft-making projects together. But it wasn't until people started offering to pay us for certain items that we considered doing crafts professionally.

We got a business license, set up a booth at the Country Sampler store in Knoxville, Tennessee, and set about entering contests in the major craft shows that year and reserving spots for the next year. Starting so late in the season, we missed several deadlines but were able to get on waiting lists and were surprised when an opening came for a large, outdoor street festival. We were ecstatic, but we only had a few weeks to prepare.

At some point during all of this (before the age of keyless entry and remote start), Mom had managed to break off her key in the car door. With all the craziness in the weeks leading up to the craft show, she'd put off getting it repaired. She didn't think it was that important. Besides, she could still open the door by inserting the remaining part of the broken key into the lock. She had to use her spare key in the ignition, but that was just an inconvenience.

The two days before the festival were a frenzy of activity. The night before the craft show, we only got a couple of hours of sleep. We filled Mom's Corolla from the floor to the ceiling with ninety percent of the show merchandise. All the tables, chairs and displays were in my Ford Explorer.

We got there at 6:00 in the morning to set up our booth. Things seemed to be going well. Even though there was a problem with our tent, the organizers had a spare one to loan us. The space was ready, so we went to retrieve our crafts — only to discover that Mom had locked her keys in the car. Our little booth was empty.

We panicked because there wouldn't be a locksmith open whom we could call until after the street fair opened. We unsuccessfully tried a coat hanger but couldn't get the car open. We resorted to laughter mingled with tears and prayer, hoping for either a police officer or a would-be thief to miraculously show up.

As I recall, part of the reason we were so upset was because we had never set up for a show. We didn't have any idea how we were going to arrange our space, which is one reason why we got there so early. We knew some events were very strict and stated in their contracts that vendors would not be allowed to set up late. (We've been to enough shows now to know that probably wouldn't have been enforced, especially not in our circumstances, but we didn't know it then.)

We just resigned ourselves to the fact that we might have to wait until Sunday to set up, missing Saturday, the biggest day of the festival. We stood there looking into the car windows at our precious stash: glistening Christmas ornaments, fall floral arrangements, and tinsel festival crowns for children. We felt defeated.

Suddenly, a thought blasted through my mind, and I blurted it out without thinking how ridiculous it sounded.

"Hey! I own a Toyota, too. Try my key," I said. Luckily, I had the keys with me.

My mom and sister looked at me like I was insane and proceeded to explain why the key to my Toyota Tercel would not work, but we tried it anyway. What did we have to lose? Crazily, it worked! We were amazed. We hurriedly unloaded and had a fantastic show.

Between customers, we discussed the unlikelihood of my key working and what an answer to a panicked prayer that had been.

Being the kind of people who "have to know," we locked Mom's car and tried my key again. This time it didn't work.

How was it possible that my key had worked the first time when her keys were locked inside the car? It seemed too weird to be possible, as if the only time my key worked was in the magic of the moment, when the thought had popped into my head.

It didn't make any sense, but the only time my key worked to open the car door was when we desperately needed it to work. None of us could explain it. We just know that we prayed for the car to be opened somehow, and it was.

— Lorraine Furtner —

A Prayer in Time of Need

*The prayer that begins with trustfulness and
passes on into waiting will always end
in thankfulness, triumph, and praise.*
~Alexander Maclaren

The sound of the Harley motorcycle revving up my driveway causes me to smile. Not because I like loud noises or am a motorcycle fanatic but because my son is arriving for a visit, and he is alive.

It was tough when my son Tyler was struggling with drug addiction and depression. I begged him to stop using drugs. I tried getting him into therapy. I explored various recovery programs and joined support groups for families dealing with substance-abuse issues. I prayed for him and asked people in the church I attended to please pray for him, too.

One night, he overdosed in his bedroom. In a panic, I called 911, and his friend administered Narcan to him. He recovered just as the EMTs arrived. I was told that this wasn't the first time he had overdosed. I knew we were running out of second chances for him.

Finally, he hit bottom, losing his job, his girlfriend and a place to live. Tyler showed up at home hungover, shattered, and trembling. He agreed to sign himself into a residential treatment center called Teen Challenge New England. I was so relieved.

That morning, we called Teen Challenge and were told that Tyler had to complete an over-the-phone interview with the admissions director. So, we set up the phone appointment for 4:00 that afternoon. The day seemed to drag on as we waited for the phone call. If all went well, Tyler would be signed into the program the following morning.

Then, at around 2:30, two of his friends showed up in a station wagon with fishing poles hanging off the roof. I feared the worst, and sure enough they invited him to go fishing.

"Tyler, you have that phone appointment at 4:00!" I screeched. "You can't go fishing!" Besides missing his appointment, I knew that when these guys "went fishing," booze and possibly drugs went with them. I shuddered with a dreadful premonition. Call it mother's intuition, but I knew, just knew, that if Tyler got in that boat, he would not make it home alive.

But, assuring me that he would call the director from the car and reschedule, he left with his friends.

I collapsed on my bed, weeping. I was so frustrated. I felt powerless. But most horrifying was this strong sense that Tyler would not make it through another night of using drugs.

I cried to God for help. Then I thought to call my pastor. I told Pastor Matt everything through my hysterical sobbing. He calmly quieted me down and said, "Let's pray."

He prayed that Tyler would feel an overwhelming need, even if Tyler himself did not understand why, to turn around and go home. "Lord, even if You have to make Tyler all of a sudden feel an illness coming on," Pastor Matt said. He asked God to protect Tyler and get him home in time for the phone interview.

About ten minutes after I thanked the pastor and disconnected the call, the station wagon came rocketing up my driveway. The car door opened, and Tyler emerged and stumbled back into the house without saying a word.

His friend Robert jumped out of the car and started gesticulating wildly. "I don't get it!" He threw up his hands in exasperation as he complained. "He said he had to go back home. He said he felt really sick. We were supposed to go fishing!"

"Oh, well," I said.

Tyler was accepted during the phone interview that day. After spending the night in the house, Tyler did enter the Teen Challenge program the next morning. He stayed for ten months, attending Bible studies and group therapy, and enjoying fellowship with the other men in the program.

Tyler, as of this writing, has been clean and sober for almost three years. He may still struggle with the ups and downs of life, like we all do, but he is basically happy and pursuing various goals and careers. Last summer, he bought a new motorcycle and is now attending college to learn motorcycle maintenance.

I am so grateful for my son's life, my pastor, and a loving God who answered our prayers. Of course, seeing how powerful prayer is, I do still pray. Now, I pray for extra angels to please surround Tyler as he roars down the road on his motorcycle!

— Donna Paulson —

Chapter 6

Touched by an Angel

50

The Fall

*The most glorious moment you will ever experience in
your life is when you look back and see how
God was protecting you all this time.*
~Shannon L. Alder

It was 1959, and our Air Force family was stationed in Adana,
Turkey. Along with other military families, we lived in an apartment building off-base. Next to our building was another apartment building under construction. I was a four-year-old girl, and
to my friend and me, this was an irresistible play area.

Inside the building, the railings on the stairs leading up from
the foyer had not yet been installed. My friend and I climbed the
stairs higher and higher, taking turns lying on each step and peering
down to the foyer floor. Young children at play, we became a little too
rambunctious. A playful shove, and I went tumbling over the side.

I fell two stories, landing on my head on a concrete floor. I don't
remember the fall or the landing, but I do have a very clear memory
of toppling over the side, and then getting up with an angel standing
behind me. He had very large hands, which were resting tenderly on
my upper back and shoulders. I felt no pain or fear. I was wrapped in
the safety and comfort of an angel.

With his hands on my shoulders, he gently guided me out the
door where I could be seen. I remember walking with my head tilted
back because the bleeding from my forehead was flowing into my eyes.
Our neighbor jumped off his first-floor balcony upon seeing me and

ran to scoop me up. In Turkey, there were no ambulances to call, so my parents drove me as fast as possible to the base hospital.

I spent a short time in the hospital with a fractured skull, a scraped nose, two black eyes that any street fighter would have been proud of, and a scratch on the back of my hand. My mother told me that I talked about the angel who saved me.

I healed well with no permanent injuries. Not surprisingly, I have been afraid of high places ever since. And I have a vertical scar bisecting my forehead, a lifelong reminder of an amazing moment in my life. I do not remember seeing the angel, but I will never forget the feel of his hands on my shoulders.

—Julia Johnson—

51

A Miraculous Save

Make friends with the angels who,
though invisible, are always with you.
~St. Francis de Sales

My grandfather had been released from the nursing home (we call it "rehab" these days) after he broke his hip at the age of ninety-two. I adored my granddad and gladly volunteered to take care of him at his house while he recuperated. After all, I was in my twenties, capable and single. He was doing splendidly but still tottered a bit.

As he was taking his afternoon nap, I went to take a bath. He'd indulgingly let me paint the bathroom an astonishingly bright pink to cheer it up. There wasn't a shower in his house, but the tub was good and deep, and there was no one there to pound on the door if I took too long or used too much hot water.

I was about to ease myself into the tub when I realized the room was a little chilly. Across from the tub was an old-fashioned heat lamp that Granddad used. It was the kind of heater that was simply a metal, reflective heat disc — concave like those giant, swiveling receivers they use to detect radio waves in the heavens, only small. There was a convex metal cage over it, and in the center was a cone-shaped, ceramic-encased heat element that projected out like the stamen of an alien flower. Its outermost end was about an inch shy of the metal cage for a good reason: you wouldn't want its metal tip to touch the metal cage when it was on. And like the planetary radio receivers, it swiveled so that you could aim it for best effect.

My grandfather had been worrying about the heater because the central element had gotten a bit wobbly. Growing up on Texas ranches far from towns and stores, he was used to making do with what he had and inventing his own repairs. So, a while back, he'd taken a long, thin metal rod he had lying around the place and threaded it through the cage from one side of the reflective disc to the other, which neatly kept the cone-shaped heat element in the center firmly in place. But he hadn't remembered to tell me and I didn't notice what he'd done.

Anyhow, still dry, I plugged it in and aimed the heater toward me, and then got in the tub.

Between the nearly scalding water and the heater, I quickly warmed up. In fact, I was sweating. I realized that I had tilted the heater up too high. My face felt like it was acquiring a third-degree sunburn. I needed to aim the face of the heater down a bit.

Still sitting in the deep tub, I reached over to the heater to just nudge it downward a little. To my utter disbelief, it fused onto my hand, sending electric shocks up my arm and through my whole body. With water surging around me, I was flopping violently like a fish out of water. I had absolutely no control over my limbs, and the heater now hovered in the air over the tub, still clutched in my hand.

I couldn't let go of the heater but must have tried to retract my hand because then I saw it hovering right over the water, still plugged in. With a rush of grief, I knew I was going to die.

And my grandfather would never get over it. A wave of sorrow at my foolishness came over me, but there was nothing I could do. I couldn't even cry out.

And then I felt, quite distinctly, the fingers of a large hand enclosing mine and then prying the heater away, flinging it to the carpet outside the tub. Bruised from head to foot, I sobbed with relief and shock.

It wasn't my grandfather's hand. I knew his as well as my own—the smooth, long fingers, the tender pad of his palm.

This had been some other man's hand—larger, wider, with thicker fingers and a rougher palm—a worker's hand. I still remember the feeling to this day: warm and strong, even slightly hairy, and very...

there, although I couldn't see it.

When I dried myself and yanked the blasted electrical cord from the wall, I went into my granddad's bedroom, wrapped in my towel and still shaking, and told him what had happened. Shaken himself, he held me in his arms, hard, rocking his remorse away.

"It's all right now, Granddad. Don't feel bad. I'm okay." My heart rate was finally settling down.

He beat his head in frustration with a fist, mussing his beautiful white hair and blaming himself for being too old to remember to warn me, declaring he was going to throw the darned thing away and should have done it long ago. "We'll get a brand-new one, sweetheart. I'll give you money right now."

Pulling my towel around me tighter, I laughed feebly. "Maybe not right now. Let me get my breath back."

Stroking my wet hair, he responded in a choked voice, "My God, I nearly lost you. Lost my 'little Palomino.'" It was his old nickname for me when I was little, blond and ponytailed. We were both crying then.

"Granddad, what do you suppose really happened? That hand... I thought maybe it was yours somehow. You know, like an out-of-body thing."

He shook his head. "I wish it had been. Thank the good Lord someone was watching over you when I wasn't." Sitting close and quiet in the shade-darkened room, I stroked his lovely, blue-veined hand with its cool, smooth fingers.

That's all we ever said about the angel in the bathroom. But I'm pretty sure we both believed.

— Laurie Hall —

52

The Taxi

Angels are not merely forms of extraterrestrial intelligence.
They are forms of extra-cosmic intelligence.
~Mortimer J. Adler

I was on a night out with friends at a bar in Central London. It was a fun evening, but I had been at work all day. Around 11:00 P.M., I started to feel tired, so I told my friends that I was heading home. I walked to the bus stop near Trafalgar Square to get the bus back to Muswell Hill, North London. I had my bus pass, showed it to the driver and went to find a seat upstairs.

I got out my book and started reading to kill the time. About thirty minutes later, I looked out the window. I thought it strange that I did not recognise my surroundings. I was in a very rundown area of London. To my horror, I realised that I had got on the wrong bus. I started to feel panicky, so I figured the best thing to do was to get off at the next bus stop. Surely, another bus would come along and take me back in the direction that I wanted to go.

I had only been living in London for a few months. I am from a quiet village in the Leicestershire countryside, so to be lost in London late at night was the stuff that nightmares were made of.

There I was all alone in an area of London where nobody wants to be all alone at night. It was a dark and very chilly April night. There were all sorts of unsavoury characters lurking around, and I couldn't see another bus stop anywhere. My mobile phone wasn't working, and I had no money on me, just my bus pass. I did not know what to do. I was afraid. I pictured myself being mugged, attacked or worse. Frankly, I was on the verge of crying my eyes out!

I stood on the pavement and looked up and down the road, hoping that a police car might pass by. Then, out of nowhere, a taxi appeared and stopped right in front of me. It was strange as I hadn't seen the taxi coming or even heard the taxi approaching me. The taxi window came down.

"Are you okay, love?" said the driver in a friendly voice.

At that moment, my fear and panic disappeared. I felt calm. I knew that I was safe. I explained my situation, and the man happily gave me a lift back to Muswell Hill. I know that it may sound dangerous to get into a taxi in an unknown area of London when the driver knew that I had no money, but I always listened to my gut feeling, which was telling me that it was okay. This man was genuine and would do me no harm. I felt it.

Throughout the journey, I had a pleasant conversation with the driver. His voice was very warm, soothing and kind. I felt like I knew him. I remember, though, that I could not see his face. It was like there was always a shadow over it, or oncoming vehicle lights would shine onto it. I could never catch a glimpse of it, not even through the rearview mirror. But I felt safe and, to my relief, I was heading home.

The driver safely got me home to Muswell Hill. I told him that I would just run inside and get some money for him. Surprisingly, he did not want my money. He said he was heading home anyway and just wanted to help me out. He said that it was his good deed for the day! I started to insist that I pay him for his kindness, but he would not change his mind. His kindness warmed my heart. Not only had he saved me in my time of need, but he didn't want to be paid for it.

I thanked him and got out of the taxi.

"May God bless you, Hayley," said the driver, as he drove away into the night.

Never at any point had I told him my name.

Inside my home, I made coffee and sat at the table. I thought about the events of the evening, the danger I could have faced stranded in a rough part of London, and the kindness of the unknown taxi driver.

I felt so lucky to have been rescued. I emptied my handbag onto the table, and what did I find? There was a white feather at the bottom of my bag.

— Hayley Dodwell —

53

A Guiding Force

*I guess I have never really doubted that we
are all born to our guardian angel.*
~Robert Brault

"Mommy feels dizzy," I said. Then I slumped down in the seat of the car, and my foot pressed harder against the gas pedal. The car began to speed down the road with my eight-year-old daughter in the back seat.

Earlier that morning, I had called off work because I wasn't feeling well. But I still had to get Mikaela ready and off to school. Halfway there, on the highway, I passed out.

A retired trooper had been going in the opposite direction when my car nearly sideswiped his. He turned his vehicle around to follow us. He reported that he was nearing 100 mph when he drew up behind me. Mikaela and I were using our seatbelts, but she had unbuckled hers to try to get to me. She was in the back center seat. When she tried to crawl up to me, she must have fallen into the front passenger seat or the floor space. Completely out of control, my car left the road and careened up a steep driveway to the right. It sped past a tree and straight into the glass door of an elderly couple's dining room. Although it was 7:30 in the morning, no one was having their coffee or breakfast, or reading the newspaper. Remarkably, they weren't even home.

As for my daughter and myself? There was not a scratch or bruise on either of us! I don't remember anything from "feeling dizzy" up until

I looked at my child in a bed across from me in the ER. Her eyes were wide, bright, and shiny as she exclaimed, "Mommy, I saw an angel!"

Later, I was told by witnesses about the events that happened. When my car crashed into the house at great speed, a wooden beam flew through the windshield past my head and exited out the middle of the back window. That was right where my daughter had been buckled in just moments before. The trooper worked quickly on getting us out of the car because there was a strong smell of propane in the air as he approached.

At that point, I was conscious and walking around once I was helped out of the car, but I don't have a shred of recollection up until I was on the ER cot.

Mikaela remembers everything vividly, even now, ten years later. I asked her the day after the accident if she recalled telling me about an angel. "Oh, yes!" she exclaimed.

I calmly asked, "Do you remember where she was or what she looked like?" I was awestruck and covered in goosebumps by her response.

She said, "She was in the car, in the back with me. But she wasn't sitting. It was like she was floating."

She told me she looked like an adult with long, curly blond hair, green eyes, and tanned, glowing skin. She had no wings but had fluffy, little feathers at the bottom of her white gown. Mikaela added with skepticism, "But she didn't have feet."

I wanted to hear more, especially because she was giving such great details without hesitation. I prompted further, "What happened then?"

She got choked up and there were tears forming in her eyes. I asked her why she was about to cry. She told me she was so scared and shaking. That's when the angel appeared. She placed her hand on Mikaela's shoulder and spoke only four words: "Go to your mother." Then, she was gone. That was how my child ended up in the front passenger side of the car moments before crashing.

I told her how special and extraordinary it was for her to see, hear, and feel this being that others never get the chance to experience. I explained how rare it was to witness an angel. Although I've never personally seen an angel, I've heard that children are much more receptive to this type of spiritual encounter. I believe my daughter received forceful guidance from her own guardian angel that day.

— Corinea Andrews Duzick —

54

A Day at the Park

Miracles happen every day. Not just in remote
country villages or at holy sites halfway across
the globe, but here, in our own lives.
~Deepak Chopra

Twenty-five years ago, I was living at home with my parents. I was in my twenties and, like most people my age, I didn't think much about danger. After all, I had my whole life ahead of me. What could possibly happen?

Because of my carefree nature, I made a habit of solo outings, usually involving hiking and woods. This was much to my mother's chagrin. She constantly worried about me — so much so that, after a while, I didn't even bother telling her where I was going. I know now that was a big mistake. It is always better for someone to know your whereabouts in case of an emergency. But, again, back then I thought I knew everything.

One early morning I packed my car with a picnic lunch, basketball, blanket and good book. When I got to the park, the first thing I did was shoot some hoops. It was a good stress reliever for me, so I looked forward to it. After tiring myself out, I grabbed the other items and hiked to the bottom of a hill near the lake. It was an isolated spot that I thought would be great for privacy and quiet.

It started off great. I enjoyed my lunch and was deep in thought as I turned the pages of my book. I didn't even hear the footsteps approaching me. I was startled to see five men plop themselves down by me on the blanket. The one closest to me placed his hand on my leg and told me what he wanted to do to me. I immediately panicked. No one knew where I was, and I had no phone. I silently prayed and struggled to hold back the tears so they couldn't see my fear.

Just when I thought I was a goner, I heard more footsteps. How could this possibly get worse?

The new man was quite tall and very muscular. The funny thing is that I don't remember any of his features. I just know that I suddenly felt safe, even though he was outnumbered by the five guys already surrounding me.

He approached me and smiled. "Hey, honey," he stated. "Are you ready to go?"

Even though I didn't know him, I jumped to my feet and said, "Yes."

The man who kept grabbing my leg stood as well. He got into the other man's face and said, "She is staying with us. We're getting to know each other."

The tall man stepped into him. No threats. No raised fists. He simply smiled and said, "She is coming with me."

At that point, for some reason, the five bad men turned and ran.

I was flabbergasted and shaking uncontrollably. My hero helped me gather my stuff and walked me back to my car. We climbed the hill in silence, and after he loaded my vehicle, I sat in stunned silence for a moment. Finally, after regaining my senses, I opened my car door to thank him. There was no one around. It was a huge parking lot, and he couldn't have crossed it without my seeing him in that short period of time. When we had walked to my vehicle, it was the only one there.

So, where was he? I wasn't waiting around to find out. Those other men could still be around somewhere. So, I started my car and began my journey home, a little shaken but a lot wiser. And did I tell my mom? Of course not. What she didn't know couldn't be used against me.

All I know is that, looking back, I believe I had my glimpse into the supernatural world. I believe that God sent an angel when I needed one most. Sometimes, their comfort isn't in flowery words and such. Sometimes, it is in a quiet walk up a hill in a bubble of peace and safety.

—Pastor Wanda Christy-Shaner—

55

A Gentle Guide

Is death the last sleep? No — it is the last
and final awakening.
~Sir Walter Scott

Our first hint that my brother Peter was ill was in February when he couldn't attend a pre-graduation event for my daughter. At the time, I thought it was strange since he was rarely sick. I asked him what was wrong, but he had no idea nor did the doctors. With the busyness of life, I soon put the event out of my mind.

As the spring progressed, however, my older brother began to feel worse and worse. His energy level kept dropping, and his pain began to build. Peter was having more and more medical appointments and lab tests. From MRIs to X-rays to blood tests, he took them all, but there was still no diagnosis.

Finally, the doctors came up with a diagnosis of non-Hodgkin's lymphoma. This type of cancer was very difficult to manage and painful. For many people, it is incurable. At first, my brother stayed at home and limited his activity. But as the cancer progressed, he spent more and more time in the hospital. Eventually, he was moved into the hospital full-time. At times, his pain was almost unbearable, but he faced it every day with extraordinary strength.

Late one July night, I was sitting beside his bed in the hospital. The fluorescent light in the ceiling cast an unsettling off-white glow over the whole room. The IV dripped slowly into the tube that ran into my brother's arm as he lay motionless in bed. I could hear a constant low hum that seemed to pervade the whole hospital wing.

As I sat on the vinyl recliner at the foot of his bed, I counted the minutes as they passed. I struggled to keep my eyes open because the day had been long. Suddenly, behind the head of the bed, I sensed a strange white form. But, in my fatigue, I didn't pay attention to it.

My brother knew his time on Earth was short, and he had talked about it with me several times. He talked about all the things he wished he had done, and he worried about his wife and the future she would have. Peter had no doubt about his Christian faith. However, facing the inevitable moment when his heart would stop beating weighed heavily on him.

Two days later, my wife and I talked to the respirologist who had been working with my brother.

"How is he doing?" I asked.

"As you'd expect. He's struggling to breathe."

"What is his prognosis?"

"I'm not really allowed to say."

"Off the record, what is your expert opinion? You work with cancer patients all the time."

The woman, who was in her fifties with close-cropped brown hair, lowered her voice to a whisper. "He likely doesn't have a day left."

"Oh!" I gasped. We had to be ready for the worst, hoping somehow it wouldn't come so soon.

That night, a small group of family members gathered in his room. At 1:14 A.M., I was startled awake and had a vision of a very large angel in the hospital room. He was all white, and a strange glow emanated from him. He had a compassionate expression on his face as he moved quickly and with precision. He stood beside Peter's bed and looked down on him. He reached out his hand, and Peter's spirit took it. He was lifted off the bed. Some family members were standing around his bed, but the angel moved past and through everything and everybody nearby.

Even though my brother's spirit was transparent, I easily recognized him. Somehow, I just knew it was him.

The angel moved quickly and seemingly without much effort as he escorted my brother through the wall of his room and into the hallway of the hospital. My brother's earthly body, however, lay motionless on his bed.

I knew I was seeing something extraordinary, but I wasn't afraid. In fact, a strange peace settled over me. The fact that an angel was taking my brother with him reassured me that things were going to be okay for him. I had complete confidence that Peter was in good hands — in God's hands.

The angel had a firm grip on my brother's arm, guiding him along. As the two of them left his room, they passed through some medical equipment that had been left in the hallway. Although the angel moved very quickly, he didn't appear to be in a hurry. Instead, he was very focused and deliberate in what he did. His job was to escort my brother out of this life into the next.

Once they had both left the hospital, a quiet settled over the room and everyone who had gathered nearby. I don't know where the two of them went other than up through the roof of the hospital. But that was enough for me to know my brother's life on Earth had come to an end.

After the angel disappeared, I sat for a while in a state of wonder. I had witnessed one of the great mysteries of life — the end of this existence on Earth and the beginning of the next. I wasn't nervous, anxious or upset. I just accepted what I had seen moments before and allowed its reality to imprint on my heart.

I realized that, in the span of a few moments, Peter had moved from a state of constant pain where he struggled for each breath to his new life of perfect peace. Everything had changed for him, and he was free and in the hands of God.

— Rob Harshman —

56

Guidance Through the Fog

Never drive faster than your guardian angel can fly.
~Author Unknown

was in the middle of cooking dinner when my cell phone rang. Looking at the caller ID, I saw it was my friend, Anna. I was prepared to tell her I'd call back after dinner, but the desperation in her voice changed my mind.

"I hope I'm not disturbing you," she said with tension in her voice.

"Not at all," I lied.

"My car broke down. My husband is out of town, and I have the kids with me." Her voice cracked. I could hear her two young kids in the background crying. She had called a tow truck, but they wouldn't be there for at least an hour. Her kids were hungry and tired.

"Can you please come and get the kids?" she asked.

"Of course," I said without hesitation. I could feed them and let them relax until Anna called a car service so she could pick them up at my house.

I called out to my husband to take over cooking dinner as it would take me about thirty-five minutes to get to Anna. It was late autumn and already dark outside. A light fog was forming when I got into my van.

As I was driving to my destination, the fog progressively thickened. I was relieved when I reached Anna's car. With my headlights shining on her face as I drove up, I could see she had been crying. After a long hug, we put the children's car seats in my van and buckled them up. As I closed the door, I heard my friend say, "Drive safe."

With all the commotion of getting the car seats in and the children settled, I forgot about the fog. I would have my friend's children in my van, driving in thick fog. They were my responsibility. I couldn't help but be nervous, especially since the fog was thickening by the minute. I tried to put on a brave front for the children's sake as I navigated in almost zero visibility.

"Let's sing a song," I said in a pretend cheerful voice. After a few rounds of songs, the kids started to chatter between themselves. What seemed like hours of driving was a mere ten minutes. The children's chatter was getting a bit loud, and the fog was thick to the point where I could hardly see. My anxiety began to peak. I knew I had to pull over. But where? I couldn't even see the lines on the road.

I drove as slowly as possible, veering to the right where I thought the shoulder might be. I was disoriented and not sure where I was on the road. I stopped and put on the four-way flashers. I didn't want to scare the kids, so I told them we were stopping for a few minutes so I could make a call. I reached for my phone to call my husband to tell him what was going on, but, to my horror, I couldn't find it. I realized that I must have left it at home while rushing out of the house. An intense fear washed over me. I couldn't make a call or use my phone's GPS to at least let me know where I was and help me navigate home. For all I knew, I could have been in the middle of the road. The only thing I could do was wait until the fog dissipated.

My husband was probably looking out at the fog and worrying. He no doubt tried to call me, only to hear the phone ring on the kitchen counter where I left it. I stepped out of the van and took deep breaths of the dark foggy air.

"Please, help me get these precious children home safely," I said, looking toward the sky.

I stepped back into the van and sat silently for a few minutes contemplating what to do. My mind was on overdrive.

What if we're in the middle of the road, and a vehicle comes barreling and hits us? I thought fearfully. I silently asked for help once again.

"Are we leaving now?" a little voice broke the silence from the back seat.

"Yes, just one more minute," I assured the kids.

A few seconds later, flashing lights in my rearview mirror caught my attention. Red, white and blue lights. It had to be a police car. It was a huge relief seeing the police car as it got closer. I got out of my van to flag down the car.

The police car pulled up in front of my van. I started to walk toward the car. With the fog, I couldn't make out the police officer's face when he rolled down his window. He told me to get back into my vehicle and not walk out onto the road. It was too dangerous. The officer got out of his car, stood between our two vehicles, and called out to me to ask for my address. He instructed me to follow him. He would guide us home.

The officer took his time navigating slowly down the dark, winding roads as I followed. Finally, we arrived at my house. He pulled into my driveway as I eased my way behind his car. The kids were getting fussy, so I unbuckled them from their car seats and lifted them out of the van. I turned around to thank the officer, but the police car was gone. How could that be? He had been in front of the van. There was no way he could have pulled out and driven off.

I stood frozen in disbelief. Had I been hallucinating? The porch light switched on, and my husband stepped out the front door.

"I was so worried about you driving in this fog!" he said as he walked toward us.

I was just about to say a police officer had escorted me home when my friend's five-year-old piped in, "An angel brought us home!" Out of the mouth of babes, wise beyond her years.

I often wonder how I managed without a cell phone and GPS. That night as I lay in bed, it occurred to me that I managed just fine. I said a prayer and thanked my mysterious angel, the police officer who appeared and vanished in the not-so-thin air on that very foggy evening.

— Dorann Weber —

It's Not Your Time Yet

The golden moments in the stream of life rush past us,
and we see nothing but sand; the angels come to visit
us, and we only know them when they are gone.
~George Eliot

In my twenty-two years of life, I had always been a skeptic about the existence of guardian angels and a higher power. I always believed that we were in charge of our lives and that, whatever happened, we faced it alone. Until the day when my guardian angel decided to say hello.

By the fall of 2019, I had been in therapy for depression, borderline personality disorder, and anxiety for almost four months. I had been struggling, and things didn't seem to improve. Each day, I fell asleep on a pillow wet with my tears. The slashes on my wrists had gone deeper. I was spiraling downward, and fast.

One night, when the depression became too severe to handle, I was sitting on my bed crying. My face was all puffy, and my eyes were red. My hands were shaking, and I could not see any hope. In that moment of immense weakness and despair, I gave up.

I overdosed on my anti-depression pills along with a few others I could find. As I recall, I popped close to sixty pills that night. I thought that my pain would finally be over, and with that thought in my head, I went to sleep hoping to never wake up.

Oddly enough, I woke up six hours later in a hospital bed. I had a tube in my nose and an IV in my hand. My father was talking to

Touched by an Angel | 177

the doctor, and my mother and my boyfriend were next to my bed. I felt strange and out of place. *I shouldn't be here*, I thought. And yet, somehow, I was.

When I was discharged from the hospital two days later, I was sitting in my room when my father walked in to check on me. I asked him, "Dad, how did I end up in the hospital?"

My father's expression changed to something I couldn't understand. He sat down on my bed and said in a heavy voice, "I was asleep when you… when *it* happened. Suddenly, I heard a voice that told me I needed to see you. At first, I couldn't understand. I thought it was your mother talking in her sleep again. But then, the voice became more urgent. Even though the room was dark and my eyes were closed, I could see a strong, bright light. I somehow knew that you needed me. When I came to your room, you…" My father was a huge man who had never even been sad, as far as I could remember, but he had tears in his eyes.

I remembered seeing a bright, shiny light before I woke up from my overdose. I felt warm and calm, and I kept hearing the voice of a woman. It was rich and low-pitched, almost a whisper. She said, "It's not your time yet. You need to go back."

She kept saying this, and I told her I didn't want to. I don't know how I was able to, but I could hear my voice in my head saying, "I don't want to go back. I don't feel happy there. I feel alone and lost."

And she said, "You are never alone. You will always have me watching over you, Yashna. Now you need to go wake up."

These were the last words she said to me before everything went dark again. The next thing I knew, I was awake, and the voice I heard was gone.

Fast forward to the winter of 2020. COVID has already stopped the world, and we were all locked in our homes, unable to go out. I got the news of my cousin's passing due to COVID. Everyone in my house was really depressed, more so since we couldn't be with her family because they lived in another state. It was late at night. I was sitting on the floor with my knees close to my chest. I was hyperventilating. All the thoughts that had tormented me the year before were once again taking over.

I don't remember how long I stayed like that, but at some point I felt a warm embrace around me. I felt like someone had hugged me from behind and held me as I cried and rocked me back and forth. I felt safe and comforted. Even though the door to my room was locked from the inside, and I know that no one had opened it, I knew I wasn't alone.

It's been almost two years since I first encountered my guardian angel. I am in a much better place emotionally. I feel grounded and calm. I no longer indulge in self-harm, and I am off the pills. I only go to counseling once a month. Whenever I feel lost, scared or alone, I just look up to the sky and know that someone up there is looking out for me.

Many non-believers will have a lot of theories, but only I know the gravity and reality of what I experienced. Never before have I shared these incidents with anyone. But I know for a fact now that I never was — and never will be — unprotected and alone.

— Yashna Malik —

An Uninvited Guest

If you can heed only one piece of advice from the
universe, make it this... Pay attention. Do this
and everything else will fall into place.
~Bryan E. Wright

We had almost reached the climax of our bedtime story when the children and I heard a noise. I couldn't tell if the thud had come from outside or indoors, but a quick glance out the window showed nothing. I motioned to the children to stay put on the couch while I tiptoed across the floor to the open railing overlooking the basement. I hung my head and listened but heard nothing except my pulse pounding in my ears. The oldest had ignored my request and stood next to me, peering into the darkness. Relieved to hear nothing, I was about to give the all-clear when we saw the basement light turn on.

All color drained from the girl's face as she fell against me, grabbing my shirt and whimpering that she was going to faint. She hung on to me while I quietly struggled into the bedroom, grabbed the baby, and wrapped him in a blanket on our way out of the nursery.

Although I'd recently started seventh grade, I'd been babysitting for many years. I'd had plenty of childcare training in church and school and had gotten it drilled into me that, during an emergency, I should phone for help, starting with my parents who lived a few blocks away. Frightened beyond my wildest dreams, I figured I'd call first and then get the children out of the house.

Back then, we had no 911 number. Thankfully, the phone was right there, but as my hand brushed the receiver, a warning thundered through my head. "Get the children out of the house now!"

Remarkably, I didn't doubt the command at all.

As the bangs and thuds crescendoed downstairs, the four children held tighter, pinching my flesh as we struggled to get to the front door only feet away from us. I feared for our lives.

When we finally reached the front door, the terrified children refused to let go of me to pass through the door one at a time. How our mass of arms and legs made it through the doorway, I'll never know, but we did. None too soon, we heard footsteps starting up the stairs.

Outside in the darkness, the children clung tight as we cut through bushes, saving time and staying hidden. Afraid the intruder might follow us, we felt a wave of relief when we finally made it up the road to the neighbor's house.

By the time the neighbors headed down the road to check out the house, our uninvited guest had vanished.

Back at the house, we found the outside door to the basement open wide, and debris littered the floor.

A shiver raced down my spine as I stared at the recreation-room floor where the telephone lay upside down. Its receiver was off its hook, rendering the upstairs phone dead and useless. Had I tried phoning for help, we would have lost precious time. It was then I knew that the warning I'd heard had probably saved our lives.

The neighbor's oldest son offered to stay with us until the parents arrived home, an offer I couldn't refuse.

Before calling it a night, the children and I cuddled together on the couch and finished our bedtime story, reveling in its happy ending. And as I tucked the children into bed, I felt ever so grateful for the prompting I'd received, which allowed our chilling story to have a safe and happy ending.

—Jill Burns—

Strong Arms

Prayer is the best weapon we possess,
the key that opens the heart of God.
~Padre Pio

I woke up early, like I do almost every day. I had a bunch of orders to get through, and I needed to pass through some fabric shops in the overcrowded part of town. I prayed as I got ready, which is something that I try to do every day. I asked God to bless my day and to send His angels to protect me as I travelled and did my work. I asked for my life to reflect God's goodness and glory.

I made my way to the Central Business District using the time that it took to get there to catch up on work messages and make sure I had a comprehensive list of what I needed to buy. I had to go to at least three shops, and I hoped and prayed that they were stocking the materials that I needed. I knew that, being a weekday, there was likely to be a lot of foot traffic in the parts of town where I needed to go. I was dreading the crowds, the stench of sweat mixed with cheap perfume, and the noise of people shouting to be heard over each other and over the speakers blaring at street corners.

The first and second shops were fully stocked, and I hurried to buy what I had to get. Everything was going so smoothly that, as I made my way to the third shop, I allowed my mind to wander to what I had to make for that day. I didn't have a car back then, so I was carrying my supplies in plastic bags while making my way to the last shop that I needed to go to. I stopped at a traffic light, waiting for it to turn green so that I could go on my merry way. The light turned green fairly quickly, which was my cue to scurry so that I could meet my deadline.

Just as I was about to step into the street, I felt strong arms grabbing me around my chest and yanking me back onto the sidewalk. It happened so suddenly that it took me a few seconds to process what was happening. Once my mind caught up, I realised that the arms had let me go. I looked back to try and see who had grabbed me, but there was nobody near enough that they could have grabbed me. I chalked it up to a mystery that I possibly would never solve. As I was turning my head to face the direction in which I was going once more, a car zoomed by at high speed, exactly where I would have been had I proceeded with crossing the street.

My heart jolted as the reality of what could have happened hit me. If those arms had not grabbed me and pulled me back, this was likely going to be the day that I died. All around me I heard gasps and shocked exclamations from the people who saw the car zoom by.

After a few seconds, I checked, and the traffic light was still green for me. As I was about to step off the curb, arms grabbed me again around my chest and held me in place. Before I could react, a police car sped by, again, exactly where I was going to be had I managed to take a step forward. I quickly looked behind me while I still had the mental fortitude to do so and discovered there was nobody there! I checked, and checked again, sure that my mind was playing tricks on me, but nobody was close enough to touch me.

The arms were still around me — I could feel them — but there was nobody there. After about thirty seconds, I felt the arms release me. I stood there, dazed, trying to understand what had happened. The people around me were marvelling at the speed with which the two cars had been moving. Speculation was thick in the air. I remember hearing someone expressing outrage that someone could have been seriously injured or worse. That someone would have been me if it weren't for those arms that held me fast and kept me out of harm's way.

It turned out that a driver had broken the law, and when the police attempted to arrest him, he took off. The police pursued him, and it ended up being a high-speed chase. I believe without a shadow of a doubt that God answered my prayer that day. He sent an angel to watch over me and keep me safe. I will never forget it.

—Yemurai Nhongo—

The Angel in the Wreckage

Today I choose to live with gratitude for the love that fills my heart, the peace that rests within my spirit, and the voice of hope that says all things are possible.
~Author Unknown

My husband Gerald and I had moved to Nashville, Tennessee, three years earlier. We were Canadian newlyweds pursuing our musical dreams. After years of writing and singing, we had landed a true prize — an actual music job! Every Sunday, we grabbed our guitar and drove west of the city to an exciting new church in Kingston Springs. We'd spend the morning leading our warm and loving congregation in hymns and harmony. It was bliss!

One Sunday started out no different from any other. By noon, we were back in the car, guitar tucked into the back seat, making our way home. It was shaping up to be a beautiful spring afternoon. A light rain had peppered the highway, and the sun was sneaking through the clouds. We were having that easy, post-church conversation. Did you hear the beautiful new soprano in the front row? What did you think of the sermon? Where should we go for lunch?

Suddenly, a tractor-trailer changed lanes and smashed into our little Toyota Corolla. This was no typical truck. Imagine an oversized 18-wheeler, pulling steel girders and dominating the narrow country highway.

He hit us on the driver's side — my side of the car. He banged us so hard that we slid across the lane, hit the right guardrail, and bounced out in front of his truck. We were now sideways, being pushed down the highway at seventy miles an hour. He hit us again, and we spun around to the far side of his truck. We were now trapped between his wheels and the left guardrail, being dragged backward down the highway. I could hear myself screaming but could do nothing to stop it. We smashed and spun again, this time spinning so that the front of our car was underneath the bed of the truck. His massive tires started to climb up the hood of our car. We both thought, *This is it.*

Within seconds, the guardrail ended, so instead of crushing us, the wheels pushed us off the side of the road. We spun, rolled, and flipped several times, finally landing upside down in the ditch on the side of the road. We landed inches from a rock outcropping that could have crushed the roof of our car.

Instead, we were upside down, arms and legs dangling in the air, hanging by our seatbelts.

"Are you okay?"

"I'm okay. Are you okay?"

"I'm okay."

Our minds were spinning. *What had just happened? How were we okay? And what do we do next? How do we get out of this?*

"The cell phone," I said. "Where's the cell phone? We need to call for help."

Just as we were trying to figure out which side was up, we heard a voice.

"Hello, folks! Y'all doing okay in there?"

We looked back and saw a smiling face where our rear window used to be.

"Hi?" we cautiously replied.

"I'm Dave," the smiling man said. "I'm a paramedic. I'm on vacation, just visiting from New Orleans. I thought I'd check in and make sure you folks are okay. Does that sound alright to you?"

"Yes, please," we answered.

"Can you wiggle your fingers and toes for me?"

We both did as we were told. Everything moved. Nothing was paralyzed. Good news.

"Okay, let's see if we can get you out of there."

Step by step, Dave got us to unbuckle our seatbelts. We cautiously maneuvered ourselves out of our suspended state until we were kneeling on the ceiling of the car, which was now our floor. Dave came around to the side of the car and pushed aside the heavy branches. He offered a strong arm and helped us crawl out of the car.

"Wait, I can't leave my guitar!" Gerald exclaimed.

The two men yanked open the back door and pulled our guitar to safety. It was then that we realized the guitar case had jammed itself into the headrests, preventing it from flying into the front seat and smashing into our heads.

Gerald held the guitar in one hand and reached out to me with the other. Together, we helped each other out of the ditch. At the top, traffic had stopped, and a crowd had gathered at the side of the road. We were met by concerned eyes and gentle voices. Someone had already called 911. The state trooper and paramedics were on their way. Witnesses were sticking around to give their statements to the authorities. We were going to be okay.

We turned around to thank Dave for all his help, but he was nowhere to be seen. No one could find him. No one had seen him climb out of the ditch. He didn't give a statement. No one remembered seeing a car from Louisiana.

He had just disappeared.

It took a long time to process all the parts of that day. Trauma does funny things with your memory. There are parts of the accident that only I remember and parts that only Gerald remembers. It took a while to sort out how the whole thing took place.

But we both remember Dave perfectly.

His dark hair and moustache. His blue jacket and ready smile. His perfect timing and cautious guidance.

In the moment, it didn't feel magical at all. It just felt like the practical help we needed.

But what are the odds that a vacationing paramedic from New Orleans would be driving right behind us in the worst moment of our lives? How could his car have disappeared from the scene without anyone noticing? And what kind of paramedic leaves the scene of an accident before giving his official statement?

We can't answer any of those questions. All we know is this: When we needed rescuing, someone named Dave showed up at just the right moment and at just the right time, and then disappeared forever.

There wasn't a halo. There weren't any wings. But on that Sunday morning, there was an angel in the wreckage.

— Allison Lynn —

Chapter 7

Hope and Faith in Action

In Good Hands

*Life is full of moments that only you
and your angels share.*
~Author Unknown

I grew up in a small mountain community in Colorado, seventy miles from Denver. It was not unusual for us to travel that great distance to attend events, go shopping, or simply get away from the mundane rituals of everyday life.

One Sunday, I was elected to drive my mother, sister, and grandmother to the "big city," as it was known, so they could shop for groceries and household supplies at one of the big membership clubs. We wrapped up the day at a buffet restaurant before leaving the city and heading back to our mountain home. Although the weather was beautiful, it was a typical cold February day.

My mother had the heat turned up high as we journeyed home. After she, my sister, and my grandmother fell asleep, I began to feel rather nauseous and lightheaded. As we neared the bottom of the mountain pass, filled with switchbacks and treacherous curves, I began to think the heat was getting to me.

I lowered my car window a bit to let fresh air into the vehicle and reached to turn off the heat. That was the last thing I remember before awakening to the horrific sound of metal being peeled back like a banana. As if in slow motion, I remember feeling glass pelting me in the face as the windshield shattered. The right wheel of the car slammed into a large rock, which propelled the car downward, over the cliff of the mountain before hitting a tree, bringing us to an abrupt stop. The impact launched my grandmother from the back seat, over the hood of my car, and down the mountainside before coming to rest at a tree.

Once I regained my wits, I heard my sister screaming from the back seat. Supernaturally calm and collected, despite what happened, my instincts kicked in to ensure everyone was okay. My sister was extremely shaken and hysterical but was fine, with nothing more than a cut along her wrist. I was unsure where my mother was, but I knew I had to get to my grandmother.

After I jumped out of the car, I began sliding down the snowy slope and had to grab tree limbs to stop myself near my grandma. She was unconscious and lying on her back. As I tried to ensure she was okay, I felt a hand on my right shoulder. I looked to see a gentleman with olive-colored skin, dark curly hair, and light brown eyes looking at me. He wore a white T-shirt and white jeans. Calmly, he said, "I'll take care of her. Go find your mother." I wasn't sure who he was or where he came from because he was there mere seconds after I arrived at my grandmother's side. Yet, I felt assured he was there to help.

I left him with my grandmother and made my way back up the mountainside to find my mother. I looked back and saw the man in white bend over and say something to my grandmother; I felt reassured she was in good hands.

As I focused my attention on locating my mother, a firefighter came down the slope and stopped me, asking, "Are you okay?"

I responded, "Yes. Just go down there and help that man with my grandmother."

Puzzled, he looked at me and asked, "What man? I'm the first to arrive at the scene, and there is no man down there."

I looked and saw my grandmother lying there in the same position where I had left her; the man in white was gone. Without thinking too much about it, I said, "I don't know where he went, but he was wearing white jeans and a white T-shirt. He was helping my grandmother."

Still puzzled, the firefighter said, "Go ahead and get to the top if you can, and I'll tend to your grandma."

I finally made my way to my mother's side. It wasn't long before other EMTs and firefighters arrived, and my sister and I were taken away by ambulance. They suspected we were experiencing unseen internal injuries due to the severity of the car accident and what we later learned was severe trauma to my mother and grandmother's bodies.

As we traveled via ambulance back to Denver, I could not help but wonder if I should have stayed with my mother and grandmother. I felt such guilt for leaving them and I prayed for them. Just moments before our departure in the ambulance, my mother had died in my hands. She was there when I entered the world, and I was there when she exited.

Recently, an off-duty paramedic who had arrived at the scene of our accident and assisted in caring for my mother and grandma located me. He had been searching for me for thirty years. He said that despite working at numerous car accidents, our accident had traumatized him unlike any other. He was haunted by not knowing if my sister and I were okay after that event, and he wanted to know how our lives had turned out.

After I confirmed that we were fine, he shared that he had been with a group of doctors and nurses who were traveling back to Denver after a ski trip, which is why they were among the first to arrive. They began immediately working on my mother and grandmother. He said, "I just wanted you to know that we did everything we could. Your mother and grandmother were in good hands." Like an instant answer to prayer, my heart's burden of guilt vanished, knowing that my prayer in the back of the ambulance had been answered without me knowing it at the time.

While we know that human angels, such as the first responders and all the passersby who helped, are men and women of great courage, bravery, and kindness, God often dispatches heavenly angels to our side when we need them most. I will never forget the face or features of the olive-skinned, dark-haired angel sent to walk my grandmother home and offer me comfort in my hour of need. Knowing she was not alone brings me comfort to this day.

I have a feeling I'll be seeing that dark-haired angel in the white T-shirt and jeans again someday. And I'll know I am in good hands.

—Leo Pacheco—

62

On His Feet

Hope is like the sun, which, as we journey toward it,
casts the shadow of our burden behind us.
~Samuel Smiles

A very good friend of mine grew up in New York State during the Vietnam years. She watched her young neighbors, not much older than herself, get shipped off. Sometimes, they came back. Sometimes, not. When she married a Canadian, they decided to raise their children north of the border, hoping to avoid the possibility of being drafted.

Her daughter and son grew up, and one day her son came home from university to let her know he'd enlisted. He went through basic training and then not so basic, finally going to Halifax for intense reconnaissance training. He was working hard and happy with his decision, and my friend was working hard to accept it. She knew his life was not hers, but, as a mother, she was worried.

As a friend, hundreds of miles away, I worried for her. Yet, what could I do?

At the time, my father was digging a new drainage system in our yard. He dug a perfectly graded ditch around the perimeter of the house. It rained on one of those August days, and we could see the water flowing around. It made me feel as if we were in a castle, surrounded by our own moat. Long pipes went into the ditch, and we covered them with heavy landscaping fabric, and then shoveled in stones, followed by lighter gravel. Finally, we replaced the soil from the heaps set to the sides of the digging.

Thrusting my shovel into the heap and filling it, I started wondering about my friend.

In that house, and in that yard, I had raised three sons, and the family that owned the home before us also had three sons. Often, while gardening, toys would turn up in the soil: old balls, LEGO blocks, crusted old cars, plastic soldiers. Sometimes, digging into my yard felt a bit like a *Toy Story* movie casting call.

On that day, a plastic green soldier turned up in my shovel of dirt. I didn't see him right away. I dropped one shovelful and reached for the next… and then saw him before dumping dirt over him. He was standing perfectly upright on the growing mound.

If you've ever come across a plastic soldier in your yard, you know they rarely land upright. They're cheaply produced, their faces often featureless, with bits of extra plastic where some mold did not quite work. And they are always off-balance. I shoveled him up again and moved him.

Again, he landed upright.

I halted, leaned on my shovel for a moment, and reflected on my friend and her worries — about what was in the future for her grown boy.

Slowly, I repeated: shovel and toss. Again, this soldier landed on his feet. Again and again. I'd never seen one like it.

Finally, I picked him up. Respectfully, I took him into the house, washed him off, and dried him.

I made myself a coffee and rooted around for pen, paper and envelope. I wrote down the story of finding him and sent the soldier and the paper to my friend.

I shared with her my prayer. "Green plastic guardian, may your charge always land on his feet."

My friend wrote in return to let me know that she'd placed him on the windowsill in front of her writing space, standing guard and guardian.

— Alison Acheson —

63

An Otherworldly Lightness

*Make yourself familiar with the angels, and behold
them frequently in spirit; for, without being seen,
they are present with you.*
~St. Francis de Sales

Never had I felt so vulnerable. Sitting on the doctor's exam table that cold winter day, my bare feet dangling, I shivered inside the exam gown. "Come in," I said, responding to the knock on the door.

A nurse entered. Briefly greeting me without giving me her name, she silently wrapped a blood-pressure cuff around my arm, pulled the cuff snug, and pumped it tight. Eying the gauge, she frowned. "Are you always this scared when you go to the doctor?" she asked, removing the cuff.

In my fragile emotional state, it sounded like an accusation, and I burst into tears. "No," I sniveled, "just when I think I'm finally pregnant after twelve years of trying, and I'm about to miscarry."

Her demeanor warmed. "I'm sorry," she said, handing me a tissue. "What makes you think so?"

The question was routine; the answer was not. Between sobs, I described my symptoms. Queasiness in the morning. Extreme fatigue. A monthly cycle that started on time and didn't stop. I had started to measure my life by the number of days I had been losing blood. Day 17.

She nodded and left the room, shortly reappearing alongside a white-haired man with a stethoscope draped around his neck. "I'm Dr. Adams," said the man with the kind eyes who extended his hand to me. "I hear you're a little scared."

"More than a little," I admitted, wiping my eyes.

"Well, let's see how I can help," he replied, gently patting the hand I had given him.

More questions; more answers. "Okay, no exam for you today. I don't want to jiggle anything around, so we'll just do a pregnancy test. Then you go home and go to bed for a week; call me in three days for the results. But no nothing — I mean, no nothing!" said Dr. Adams, raising an eyebrow as he gave me a stern look. "Your husband has already done his thing. All he gets to do now is wait on you."

I smiled at his choice of words, but I knew exactly what he meant.

After the test, I drove home, called in sick to my office, and went to bed. Life crawled. I ate whatever food my husband brought me, watched TV, read, listened to music, worked crossword puzzles, slept fitfully, and prayed. Rising only for trips to the bathroom, I returned to bed each time, disappointed that the red warning sign of pending miscarriage was still present.

Three days later, Day 20. Heart pounding, I phoned Dr. Adams. "Yes, you are pregnant," he said. "Now, listen. There's a medication that uses DES to help prevent miscarriage. But I'm an old country doctor, and I don't prescribe it. I don't know exactly how it works, and I'm afraid of it. You can go to another doctor and get it if you want, but if you stick with me, it'll just be four more days of bed rest. That'll be a week. If you stop bleeding, come back to see me next month. If you don't, get up and go on about your business. And when nature takes its course — and it will if you're carrying an imperfect fetus — go to the hospital and tell them to call me."

Don't take the drug, don't take it, cautioned a small voice inside my head.

"No, if you're afraid to prescribe it, I'm afraid to take it," I said. "I'll stick with you."

Had I been able to see into the future, I would have known that by 1971, research would show that diethylstilbestrol (DES) was not only ineffective at preventing miscarriage, but it increased the risk of cancer in pregnant women who took it and in daughters exposed to it while in the womb.

All I knew in 1969, though, was that I trusted Dr. Adams and the voice inside my head, so I took four more days of bed rest. Day 24: no change. Ever hopeful, I gave myself three extra self-imposed days in bed. Day 27: still no change.

The next morning, I dragged myself out of bed and began my drive to work. With no radio blasting and no distraction, I contemplated my plight. It wasn't right! Twelve frustrating, disappointing, sad years of infertility — and now this. It simply wasn't right! Suddenly, my desperation erupted. With one hand gripping the steering wheel, I raised a fist in the air and heard myself say, "God, I'm going to have this baby or die trying!"

Startled by the fierceness of my own voice, I slowed the car. Impulsively, I had told God I was willing to die to have my baby. Was I? Yes. My husband would take care of our baby if I died. Still, it wasn't my preference.

I eased the car off the road and stopped. Resting my head on the steering wheel, I spoke aloud. "God, take me if you take anybody. But if you give me a healthy baby and let me live, I promise to bring my baby up in your way." Day 28.

Suddenly, the atmosphere shifted. As if gravity had lost its pull, an otherworldly lightness enveloped me, and I seemed to float. Tip, tip, tip — a light, feathery touch flitted across my body from knees to thighs, to belly, torso, shoulders, and down my back — tip, tip, tip — and I knew what I would confirm within the hour. My bleeding had stopped; my baby was safe.

That promise of safety came with a service contract, as I learned a few months later when an eighteen-wheeler rear-ended my stopped car at a traffic light. The slow-rolling truck pushed car and driver across an intersection, into a residential lawn, and up against the porch of a startled homeowner. The whiplash injury that caused a brief loss of consciousness put me in a neck brace for weeks but left my unborn baby unscathed. Some months later, I delivered a healthy baby girl.

The present had kept the promise of the past. I had not been carrying an imperfect fetus; I had been carrying a perfect baby, one I carried with the hope and faith of a feathery touch.

—Carole Harris Barton—

64

Anam Cara

It's our faith that activates the power of God.
~Joel Osteen

Louis lay dying in his hospital bed. He was a handsome man in his late seventies. His neatly trimmed gray mustache, angular face and firm jawline spoke of strength, while the laugh lines around his closed eyes suggested gentleness. His family, which was gathered around him, had requested a chaplain to be with them. It was my privilege to support them during this sacred time.

His wife Dorie caressed his forehead with hands knotted by arthritis, while his grown son Jacob and his brother Sam told me a little about him — how he had raised his children with love and fairness, how he doted on his grandchildren, and how he loved life. He was a devoted husband, father, and grandfather. He would be missed.

Louis's breaths came further apart. The dying process had begun. The family held his hands and were quiet as they waited with him. These are intimate moments, and I stepped away from the bed so they could have their space and time with him. I closed my eyes and entered a state of meditative prayer.

Moments passed, and I felt a presence next to me. I supposed the nurse must have walked in to check on us. I looked, but no one was there. I closed my eyes, and after a few minutes, sensed something again. Another quick look determined that no one was next to me. I closed my eyes again but did not open them when I felt it again.

I had never experienced anything like this before, and I wondered if I was imagining things. I focused my meditative state to sense what was there. The presence felt nonthreatening. In fact, it felt kind and even amiable in a casual way as though we were old friends.

I decided to reach out to whatever or whoever this was next to me. "Who or what are you?" I asked.

"You know who I am, Chaplain," came the warm reply.

I felt goosebumps when I realized this was the companion who would accompany Louis to his afterlife. Some might refer to this presence as the Grim Reaper or the Angel of Death, but the presence was nothing so dramatic. It was as though another chaplain was standing with me, someone who cared about this family and Louis.

There was some commotion at the bed. "Where is she?" Dorie whispered.

"I don't know," I heard Sam say. "She said she was thirty minutes out, and that was fifteen minutes ago."

"She needs to hurry." Their daughter Sally was on the way but might not make it in time. The end was near.

I checked in with this companion.

"Can you wait for a few minutes until she gets here?"

"Sure," came the reply.

Minutes passed in silence, and it seemed like each breath would be Louis's last. Sally rushed into the room and went to the bedside. "I love you, Daddy," she whispered through her tears. I continued to stand in the background as the family loved Louis during his final moments.

"Thanks for waiting," I said internally.

"No problem," came the friendly reply.

Louis took a breath and didn't breathe again. I offered my condolences as the family wept. Dorie asked me to offer a prayer of blessing and sending, which I did, but I was distracted. I wondered what had just happened.

Days went by, and I began to think the experience was just a figment of my imagination, a bit of wishful thinking. I had coffee with a friend who is a hospice chaplain and mentioned my experience. I said it was probably nonsense and expected her to laugh or be dismissive, but she was unfazed.

"I sense them all the time. You spend enough time around death and dying, and you'll experience all kinds of things if you pay attention."

"Seriously?"

She nodded.

"What was it? Death with a capital D? The Grim Reaper?"

She laughed. "I don't know. I've never asked for a name when I've sensed them. I do know that they are friendly and kind. They seem to have a calm about them that lets the dead know they're okay." She thought for a moment. "They're kind of like chaplains in a way. Maybe that's why we sense them. Kindred spirits, in a manner of speaking."

I considered that. "Friends for the soul. *Anam cara*."

She cocked her head.

"*Anam cara*, from Celtic spirituality. It's a person you can trust with your spiritual life, like a confidant or a spiritual director. It sounds like these guides are friends for the soul, too, but in a different way."

She nodded. "Sounds about right."

It made sense. The presence felt like a friend for Louis's soul as it departed his body, a gentle companion to soothe the transition from this plane to the next. I've never felt that presence since then, but the experience brought me a lot of hope, especially when I have supported other families as they have said goodbye to their loved ones. It brings me comfort to know that their departed are being accompanied into the next life by someone kind, generous and welcoming. I feel peaceful knowing that they, and all of us, will be companioned by our soul friend, our *anam cara*.

—John Kevin Allen—

65

Feathers from Heaven

Angels descending, bring from above,
Echoes of mercy, whispers of love.
~Fanny J. Crosby

Winter flakes fell, wet and heavy. It had been snowing all day. Up to eighteen inches had been predicted. I groaned at the thought of clearing the driveway and sidewalks. Shoveling and handling the beast of a snowblower had been my husband's job until I lost him to cancer.

Bruce would have been out there already, getting ahead of the storm, wearing his famous red-and-black woolen hat with the huge bill and earflaps. I'd tease him mercilessly about the plaid monstrosity and then get to work preparing hot cocoa and muffins to warm him after he'd come in red-cheeked and tired.

But he was gone now, and I was left alone in the big, empty house with no reason to fix cocoa and muffins anymore. It wouldn't be the same without him. I missed him more than ever with the anniversary of his passing coming up. "It takes time," my grief counselor told me. *But how much?* I wondered. It felt like God didn't care, almost like He left when Bruce did. They both felt so far from me.

My spirit sagged, heavy with loss and a sense of abandonment. I needed a sign more than ever. For weeks, I'd asked God to give me one, something to let me know that Bruce was okay. But none had come.

I picked up my mug, sipped some coffee and stared out the picture window into the yard. Bruce and I spent many hours by this very same window, sharing our passion for birdwatching, marveling over the vivid sapphire of a blue jay or the eye-popping yellow and orange of a Baltimore oriole. Still, it was the cardinals we loved the most. It seemed one of them was always appearing to mark any occasion in our lives. It could be for something as special as an anniversary or as ordinary as the two of us barbecuing a slab of ribs together.

It was those precious moments that endeared the regal bird to us, and somewhere along the way the intuitive cardinal became our bird. The proud crest, the vivid red — the color of love, our love. I could feel my lips softly curve at the bittersweet memory.

How I wished one would appear now. Despite the winter storm, the yard was a beehive of activity. I'd never seen so many birds. But there wasn't a cardinal in sight; only finches, chickadees and sparrows pecked at the feeders. The moment a perch became empty, a new bird would land to fill it. It was quite a sight to see. Bruce would have run for his camera and snapped a dozen pictures — if he were still here. *Why, God?* I asked for the millionth time. *He should be here with me.*

The snow continued to fall from leaden skies, coating the wooded landscape. I drew my sweater tighter around me, staring out the window, listless and alone. Tiny wrens nestled in the soft, sheltering needles of a weeping blue Atlas cedar, while mourning doves padded underneath. No matter how much I yearned to see the bright flash of red wing, there was no cardinal to cheer me.

I swiped a tear, longing for Bruce. *Lord, please let me know he's okay.* It was no use. What could He even do to assure me? My husband was gone and I had to accept it. But how? It was too hard. Unable to pull myself away from the window, I realized that everything beyond the glass was Bruce. He'd created the sanctuary. He'd planted and nurtured each shrub, chose each rock for the waterfall he made, and hung all those bird feeders. All of them were gifts for me, except the two I'd bought for him.

Just as I reached for a tissue to dab my eyes, a cardinal swooped past the window. Another one landed on the patio, and a third on the branch of our elm tree. I watched in astonishment as the sky opened to release still more. My heart soared. It was raining cardinals!

I swallowed hard and tried to count them all, but there were too many to keep track of.

The cardinals darted and weaved, landing to rest here and there, and then winged in and out of the woods. It was a miraculous display of brilliant red against a backdrop of pure white. I stood rooted to the floor with my nose pressed against the cold windowpane, not wanting it to end, willing them to stay, and smiling through grateful tears.

My heart sank when they lifted off. All but one. He flew over and landed on a sprig of pine right below the window where I was standing. He was so close I could see every detail, the way his little feathers fluffed and then lay in a perfect silken row as if they'd been combed. His deep, dark eyes were looking right at me. Then, he flitted away in a blur of scarlet. A sweet peace settled over me as I watched him fly over the trees.

"Oh, Lord," my voice quivered, piercing the silence of the empty house. The sign had finally come. God had sent His angels, not on wings of white but vibrant Valentine red. He'd sent an entire host of feathery cherubim. My prayer had been answered. My broken heart could finally mend.

— Susan A. Karas —

Buried Alive

While we are sleeping, angels have
conversations with our souls.
~Author Unknown

"Y ou do the honors," Bill said, laying the shiny new
key in the palm of my hand. I let my fingers curl
around the key, feeling a spark of joy as I pushed it
into the lock. I knew it was just the pins turning the
cylinder and not magic opening the door, but at that moment I felt
like a magician unlocking our dreams and opening the door to our
future.

Since the day Bill and I married, we'd dreamed of this day, but
getting here hadn't been easy. For roughly eighteen months, we had
worked two jobs, sometimes putting in twelve-hour days, living pru-
dently, and saving every dollar we could. Like any good entrepreneurs,
we understood that our future success hinged on finding a need and
filling it. We discovered our community had no travel agency and,
thus, needed one.

Although neither of us had any travel-agency experience, we
were confident we could develop the knowledge and skills to meet
travelers' needs. So, we devised what we thought was a sound plan. I
continued working while Bill completed a six-month travel-industry
course. Then we used most of our savings to revamp a retail space,
lease reservation equipment, buy office furniture and supplies, and
register our agency with the Airlines Reporting Corporation.

All that effort culminated in this one magical, unforgettable moment when everything seemed possible. Once we got inside, Bill popped open a bottle of champagne.

"We did it, babe!" he exclaimed, clanking our champagne glasses together.

We downed the champagne, flipped over the OPEN sign, and waited… and waited… and waited. Four days later, our first customer passed through our doors. For the next six months, Bill was our solo travel agent, focusing on leisure travel customers and small-business travelers. When we had more business than he could handle, I quit my job and joined him. In another six months, our business doubled, and we hired two part-time agents. We were elated, believing we were well on our way to being successful entrepreneurs.

Then lightning struck — an economic downturn that brought high unemployment and lower consumer spending. In hindsight, we should've seen it coming, but we didn't. We'd been too busy making airline reservations and booking trips to take note of the little signs: a slow, steady decline in leisure travel customers and noticeably less business travel. Over a six-month period, our business and income dropped in half, forcing us to lay off our part-time agents. We trimmed expenses and even took second jobs, hoping to keep our fledgling business alive. But the economy worsened, and our corrective measures weren't enough. We got behind on our mortgage and lease payments. We maxed out our credit cards to make ends meet, often using one cash advance to pay off another.

"We can't keep borrowing from Peter to pay Paul," Bill said one evening while looking over our finances. "We've tried to keep our business afloat, but we have to face reality." His voice trembled with fear and disappointment.

The reality was harsh. Everything we'd worked and struggled for lay in ruins. We were buried in debt, and there was no easy fix. We tried debt settlement, negotiating with creditors to reduce the amount of debt on our delinquent, unsecured credit accounts. Unfortunately, the job market was stagnant, and we had no permanent job or reliable source of income to offer in our negotiations. Chapter 7 bankruptcy was our only viable option, buying us time while giving us the debt relief we desperately needed, along with a fresh start. Within weeks of filing bankruptcy, we closed our agency, lost our home, and moved into a two-bedroom apartment, ridden with guilt and shame.

Handling the downturn in our fortunes was an uphill task, but the worst part was confronting the emotional pain. Our small business was like a living, breathing child that we'd conceived and nurtured. It was gone. Losing it was painfully brutal and no less traumatic than losing a loved one. I often sat on the couch feeling empty and numb; pulling my knees up to my chest; wrapping my arms around my shins; and curling up into a ball so I wouldn't have to face the heartache and loss. For days, salty tears flowed unchecked from my eyes. I was emotionally bankrupt, buried alive in grief and despondency, convinced there was nothing I could do to get out from under it.

One night, I fell asleep on the couch and dreamed that I woke up with the strong taste of dirt in my mouth. I was six feet underground with no way of digging my way out. I choked on the dirt and gasped for breath, feeling enormous pressure on my body and arms. "Somebody help me!" I yelled. "I've been buried alive. Help me!"

Suddenly, a hand reached into the dirt and gently pulled me out. I blinked and through blurred vision saw a transparent man with a glowing face and flowing golden hair shimmering above me.

"Grieve no more," he said in a soothing voice.

"Who are you?" I muttered, dusting the dirt off my face and arms.

"I'm a messenger angel. You must continue," he added, tenderly wiping the tears from my eyes. Then, in a flash of bright light, he vanished.

I woke with a start, the warmth of the morning sunlight streaming in through the living room window. My heart and lungs expanded, and the burden of despondency miraculously lifted from me. After a few moments, I sat up, wondering if my unconscious had helped me during sleep or if I'd actually experienced an amazing, unexplainable vision with a divinely inspired message. Regardless, hope and strength filled my spirit, and I felt comforted and loved in a way I'd never felt before.

With my despondency gone, my steady stream of tears stopped.

Bill and I began putting our lives back together. We've had many more challenges and setbacks, some more heartbreaking and painful than losing our business and filing bankruptcy. Yet, when those difficulties arose, I always remembered my angel messenger's tender touch, soothing voice, and comforting words. I did as he said and continued on.

—Sara Etgen-Baker—

Prayer Tree

Prayer does not change God,
but it changes him who prays.
~Søren Aabye Kierkegaard

I looked over my shoulder as I tried to walk nonchalantly past an aisle full of spiderwebs, ceramic pumpkins, and scarecrows at the local craft store. Two women deep in conversation walked toward me. As they neared me, I overheard one of them complain, "It's not even Halloween, and they have Christmas stuff out already!" I quickly ducked into the next aisle filled with orange and gold harvest flowers and miniature hay bales. I fingered a plastic bat hanging from a string as the two passed by so they wouldn't know I was eavesdropping on them. Normally, I would agree with the two shoppers, but that year was different.

I didn't see anyone else nearby, so I quickly slipped around the corner into the Christmas aisle. I saw stacks and stacks of glass ornaments in every color imaginable — even turquoise and lime green! Sparkly snowflakes and tiny glistening angels hung from pegs. There were trumpets, nutcrackers and sprigs of holly. Continuing to look over my shoulder from time to time, I kept an eye out for other shoppers. I'm not sure why I felt embarrassed to be shopping for Christmas decorations, except that it really was only mid-October.

That year, for the first time in twelve years, my husband and I would be together for Christmas. Jeff works in the remote Arctic oil fields in Alaska. His normal work schedule of three weeks on and three weeks off meant he would naturally be at work some years on Christmas. In other years, since we did not have children, Jeff often traded shifts with his alternate, allowing him to be home with his small children for the holidays. But that year, Jeff had a new alternate — without small children — and I was excited he would be home with me.

Most years, we lived far away from both our families, so it wasn't really feasible for me to be with them for the holidays. I usually spent Christmas Day with one friend or another, but it was not the same as having Jeff home. I never could see the sense in putting up a tree and decorations just for me. Now, here I was wanting to put up a Christmas tree in the middle of October.

Suddenly, I saw an elderly lady at the other end of the Christmas aisle. "Can you read this?" she asked as she held out a package of fancy ornament hangers. "The print is too little. I can't read how many hangers are in it."

"Twenty-five. I think." I held the package up close. Then, far away. We both began to giggle. "Twenty-five! I'm pretty sure." I handed the package back to her.

"I need fifty. I'm putting up some of my Christmas trees today," she said.

"You are? How many trees do you have?" I handed her another package of hangers.

"Three in the main living and dining area. Only one in each bedroom, though. People call me crazy, but I love Christmas trees. I put up the three big trees in October every year."

"Your husband and family don't mind all the decorations for so long?"

"Oh, honey, I live alone. More than ten years now. It's not really about the trees for me. It's about the praying. As I hang each ornament, I pray for someone. I pray for them again when I take them down. Some are harder to pray for than others." We were giggling again.

"What a lovely thing to do. This will be my first tree in twelve years," I said and told her why.

She started to leave but then turned back. "Never let anyone tell you it's too early to put up your tree," she said. In the blink of an eye, she stepped around the corner and was gone.

How did she know I wanted to put up my tree this early? I tried to catch her before she left the store to tell her she inspired me to have a prayer tree, too. I looked all over but couldn't find her. I went back to the Christmas aisle with purpose this time and without embarrassment. I bought two packages of the fancy ornament hangers and lots of cranberry-red and gold ornaments. And garland, tinsel and matching gift wrap.

As soon as I got home, I ordered one of those nice artificial trees with realistic tips. It arrived on October 25th. I opened the box immediately and put the tree together, carefully adjusting each limb. As I hung the first ornament, I prayed for Jeff. Then, Steve, Missy, Neoma… I prayed for each of our family members and friends.

Belan! I had not prayed for my friend, Belan. We had had a bit of a falling-out. She walked away no longer wanting to be friends. My heart was broken and deeply hurt. I missed her dreadfully. The lady from the craft store was right. Some people are harder to pray for than others. I smiled, thinking of her.

I hung the last ornament. *Please, Lord, bless Belan in every aspect of her life and bring her the peace she seeks.* Belan did not change her mind, but my heart sure felt better having released the hurt and hard feelings.

Now, whether Jeff is home or not, I put up my Christmas prayer tree — on the first day of November. It's not about the tree. It's about the praying.

— Pamela Haskin —

My Escape

*An angel can illuminate the thought and mind of man
by strengthening the power of vision.*
~Saint Thomas Aquinas

My mother was not a well woman and I had a dark childhood. There is no way to sugarcoat it. She was beautiful, with the kind of striking good looks that made strangers stop and turn for a second glance. And during her good spells, she was a wonderful person with a laugh that could warm you from the inside out.

But when she was having an episode, when her mood was dark, it was a scary time in our household. My brother was five years older than me, so he often escaped to his room or to a friend's… or he would stand up to her.

I was quiet, easily frightened, and younger. I felt stuck. And as a child too young to attend school, I had no true way out. I would lie in bed and hear the screaming at night. It would terrify me, whether it was Mom and her boyfriend screaming at each other, or my mom screaming during one of her spells. I got very little sleep.

On one particularly bad night, I was huddled in the corner of my bed, shaking and wishing it would stop.

"Lie down and close your eyes," I heard. It was a man's voice that came out of nowhere. It was not in the room nor in my head. It was just there, clear as day. Instead of being scared, the voice calmed me. I did as he said and lay down.

"That's a good girl. It will be okay. Close your eyes and think about where you want to be. Dream about the family you'd feel safe and loved with."

I dreamed of a family with loving, happy parents who did everything to keep me safe. It was a wonderful night full of this dream, a peaceful night, and I finally got the sleep I needed.

The next night, the voice was back, reassuring and urging me to continue the dream from the other night. I could even picture the parents in this dream and the words they'd say to calm me. They would tuck me in and read to me every night.

The voice would return only on very bad nights, but I continued the dream, my other life with another family.... Somewhere safe and loved. It became a nightly ritual, one that would soothe me to sleep. My mother would joke with everyone that I was the only kid she knew who asked to go to bed.

Once I was old enough to start school, the voice no longer visited me at night. But I remembered it, and I kept up that dream. It helped me sleep through the nights. It gave me hope and something to look forward to. When things got bad during the day, I would just remember that I was going to go to bed at night.

At school, I was devastated when the teacher told us we would not learn to read and write in a day. It would take months. I desperately wanted to read about other worlds, and I wanted to write about my dream world — my "other family." I wanted to write it all down so there would never be a chance that they would be lost to me.

And, oh, when I finally learned to read and write, it opened so many doors for me. I escaped over and over. I was known as a daydreamer, quiet and pensive, always writing in notebooks.

Other kids kept journals, and I never understood that. I did not want to document my living nightmare. I wanted to explore the other world I lived in, the one that kept me feeling safe and loved.

By age fourteen, I had written four books. It never occurred to me to try to publish anything I wrote. These books were my escape, and as I got older, my writing was my therapy. I gave myself that father figure who was never there in real life. I gave myself a mother who may have made mistakes but never hit me or called me a mistake and garbage. A mother who adored me.

It was not until I was in my forties that I felt the stories were not just mine to keep hidden, to heal me. I had healed. I was married with children of my own. Raising my children with the love and stability I had never known seemed to release me from that need to escape. I still wrote, but it was more for the love of creating than for survival or therapy.

I tested the waters by sending out a short story. Then another. And when I reached over one hundred short stories published, I had my first book published. I'm still going strong. There are days when I am hurting, when the world seems cruel, and I hear that deep, comforting voice say, "Close your eyes and think about where you'd rather be." And it is all okay again.

Sometimes, life isn't fair. Sometimes, we are not given the fair shake those around us get. But it is always possible to turn it into something better. I think of that voice almost every day. I remember it as if it were yesterday, not decades ago. I often wonder if it was my guardian angel simply helping a young child go to sleep without fear, or if that guardian angel was helping to direct me to my path. Either way, I am grateful.

— Trisha Ridinger McKee —

Doubting the Dimes

Those we love never truly leave us.
There are things that death cannot touch.
~Jack Thorne

I was a doubter. A big-time doubter. Even though I listened carefully to every word the storyteller shared and I responded with encouraging words, there was something not right about receiving signs from recently deceased loved ones. To me, every detail of these happenings seemed coincidental.

The problem was that all the people receiving these so-called signs were honest, genuine people whom I completely trusted to tell the truth. Even though they were grieving, it wasn't in their nature to lie, exaggerate or make up stories that weren't true.

The three common signs in the stories were cardinals, feathers and coins. These signs appeared in unusual places on a regular basis after a loved one had passed away. The signs meant that the deceased person was fine and was watching over their loved ones left here on Earth. The details of every story lined up with these explanations.

Cardinals would appear around the kitchen windows of grieving family and friends. White feathers were found inside homes or cars. Coins, usually dimes, were found on the ground or the floor. The only thing that I knew for sure was that these signs gave people comfort while they were grieving. It was more important that those experiencing a loss were coping. If telling their stories put a smile on their faces and made them happy, so be it. My doubts were small in comparison to what the storytellers were dealing with.

Then I started finding dimes in the grocery store parking lot and on walking trails that were rarely used. Dimes collected in the cupholder of the car and on the shelf inside the back door of the house. Occasionally, white feathers appeared during a difficult day, in times of financial struggles, or during a serious health issue. I began to wonder if there really was truth to the meanings behind these happenings and that they weren't coincidences.

I was asked to photograph a fiftieth wedding anniversary party for close friends. While waiting for the guests to arrive, I puttered around in the kitchen, helping with last-minute preparations. Arlie, the caterer, stepped out for a few minutes to pick up some extra supplies. She returned with her arms loaded down with paper plates, serviettes and plastic cutlery.

Emptying the supplies onto the counter, she said, "Would you look at that?"

"Look at what?" I asked.

"This dime," Arlie said, holding up a shiny coin.

"Well, lucky you. You're rich."

"Yes, I am."

Then, the biggest smile appeared on Arlie's face, and tears began to well up in her eyes.

"Arlie, what's wrong?"

"This is from Mom."

Arlie's mom, Grandma Kirby to anyone who knew her, had recently passed away at ninety years of age. Over the years, Grandma Kirby had helped Arlie cater events in the community and surrounding area whenever she needed an extra pair of hands.

"What do you mean, 'This is from Mom'?"

"Every time I cater, no matter where or when it is, I always find a dime on the ground. It's a sign from Mom. She is with me every time I cater."

Arlie managed not to cry, but she told the story with such sincerity that tears welled up in my eyes.

"Oh, Arlie! I really don't know what to say."

We hugged each other, wiped the tears from our eyes, and tackled the few remaining jobs on the to-do list before the guests arrived for the celebration.

I didn't give much thought to the dime and what Arlie said until I was driving home later that afternoon. I could hear Arlie saying, "It's a sign from Mom." Could the dime really be a sign from Grandma Kirby? How could Arlie possibly find a dime each time she catered? The more I thought about the dime, the more I couldn't come up with a logical answer to these questions. Deep down, I knew there was something to the dime being a sign. I just needed time to get my head around it.

Dimes continued to show up in unusual places. One turned up in the pocket of a freshly washed pair of shorts. As a rule, I empty all pockets before washing and do not carry change in my pockets. How did the dime get there? On roadsides where foot traffic and vehicle traffic are minimal, I found dimes. How did they get there? I still had doubts and questions.

The incident that stopped the doubting altogether was at a long-awaited medical appointment. Before entering, I checked the changing room to see if it was empty. It was, so I placed the disposable hospital gown, pants, slippers and head covering on the bench and turned around to close the privacy curtain. There on the floor in front of me was a dime. It wasn't there when I entered, and it did not fall out of my pockets because I don't carry money in my pockets.

As I had been a doubter for so long, I didn't associate the dimes with a specific loved one that had passed away. But when I picked up this dime, I knew it was from Lorraine, my friend and hairdresser for many years. She had recently lost her battle with the COVID virus. I said a quiet thank you to Lorraine and told her how much I loved her and missed her.

That was the breaking point for the doubts I had. Knowing that someone really was watching over me gave me great comfort. A peaceful feeling came over me, and I began to relax. The technicians on duty were the recipients of my sign-from-heaven story. I had officially become a believer.

Looking back, it was easy to see that I was shown everything that I needed to stop doubting. A simple coin sent by a loved one who had passed on gives so much comfort and peace during difficult times. Why doubt?

— Caroline Sealey —

A Sunday Ride

Each day offers us the gift of being a special occasion
if we can simply learn that as well as giving, it is blessed
to receive with grace and a grateful heart.
~Sarah Ban Breathnach

Near the end of our Sunday drive, my pastor husband Tom and I saw an elderly man with a half-raised arm and extended thumb hobbling along the graveled shoulder of the Mississippi interstate. His well-worn clothes hung on his frail form.

"Can we give you a ride?" I asked through the open window of our non-airconditioned '66 Plymouth. He seemed surprised at our offer but reached for the door handle. I quickly sent up a short S.O.S. for God to protect our toddler in the back seat and rubbed my pregnant belly.

"Thank you," he said with genuine gratitude and slid in next to the car seat. Musty air followed him.

"We're turning off the highway soon… to go to church… my husband is preaching… he's interesting… want to come with us?" I rambled on, trying to make up for the stranger's silence. Our daughter sat frozen, eyeing him. My husband also kept an eye on him with the rearview mirror.

"You feeling okay?" my husband asked, seeing the traveler's pale, chalky face.

"I've been better."

"Where ya headed?" I wondered why a sickly, aged man would travel on foot alone.

"Trying to get to my daughter's house," he mumbled hopelessly. "It's been a while since I've seen her…." His words faded. "She's real bad sick."

He added a few more details about his quest, and his humble story stirred our hearts. When we reached the turnoff, we stopped to let him out.

"Wait," my husband said. "We'd like to help."

He handed me our checkbook but held onto the edge as if he really did not want to give it to me.

"Write a check for five dollars," Tom whispered.

What? Five dollars! Was he crazy? Did I have to do it? Maybe I could pretend I didn't hear him. No, that wouldn't work. I had the checkbook in my hand.

Five dollars is not a large amount, but that gift left us only $2.50 in our bank account.

"That's 66 percent of all our money, God," I whispered as if God didn't already know.

"Here you go," I said, forcing a smile and handing the traveler the check. "It's not much, but maybe it will help."

As he was getting out, our little girl reached toward him with her fist. She always clutched her church quarter. It was even hard to get her to put it in the offering plate. But she opened her hand and gave him her treasure. Why couldn't I give as cheerfully as she did?

For a moment, my heart lightened, and my mind cleared of the coming pressures. I almost forgot our own monetary needs. At the end of three years of seminary studies, we had school debt. At the end of my second pregnancy, we would have medical bills. At the beginning of our ministry, we had moving expenses. And now we had $2.50 to our names.

During church, I kept thinking about our morning encounter and my daughter's cheerful giving. My money fears continued to fade, and a peace grew within me as the hour passed quickly.

After the service, one of the members asked if we could stop by her house on our way out of town. My husband had been helping her with questions about the Bible and Christianity.

We drove to the humble home on the rural road, turning onto the packed, red-clay driveway. Rusty metal flowers and plaster statues randomly dotted the crabgrass yard.

"Thank you for stopping by," she said. "Come in. I want you to meet my son."

Although her adult son grew up in the church and was officially a member of the small congregation, we had never met. He worked and lived out of town. As we talked, he seemed quite interested in the fact that we would soon be moving from central Mississippi to central Florida to start a church.

"I have something for you," he said. He quickly disappeared into the other room. As he re-entered, he held a long white envelope. "I appreciate all you've done for my mom... and I've been tucking away some money each week in a drawer. I was wanting to pass this along to you."

I couldn't decide if he was just shy or embarrassed because his gift was small. Maybe he was having second thoughts. Giving can be hard. I know.

He reached out, offering us the long white envelope. A smile spread over his ruddy face, and his hazel eyes sparkled.

"Thank you so much," we said in unison. "You are such an answer to prayer and a great blessing to us!" I added. After a few more words, we said goodbye but waited to open the envelope in private. We didn't want to seem overly eager about the gift and ignore the giver.

The package felt thick. Hmmmm. We faced those big expenses. Final school fees. Hospital bills. Moving costs.

"Count it," my husband prompted as we pulled out of the driveway. I lifted the envelope flap to find many bills. Twenty, forty, sixty, eighty — mostly twenty-dollar bills — but a few hundreds. In total, I counted $1,240, just what we needed to pay off everything and start our ministry in 1976 debt-free.

We had given all we could to God, and He had given it back in multiples.

— Dea Irby —

71

Milk Money

Believe in miracles. I have seen so many of them
come when every other indication would say that
hope was lost. Hope is never lost.
~Jeffrey R. Holland

Early in our marriage, my husband George and I had some tough times financially. It was hard to make ends meet on two meager incomes.

When I became pregnant with our first child, my doctor recommended that I take maternity leave six weeks prior to my due date. At that point, budgeting became an exercise in frugality, faith, and fifty ways to use hamburger.

We lived in a second- and third-floor row home apartment in the city and had one car. Each Sunday morning, George and I walked the two and a half blocks to church to save money on gas. Hand in hand, we enjoyed the serenity of the stroll.

I was enthusiastically new to my faith and in the process of instruction in the rites of the Catholic church. Tithing was a concept easily grasped in terms of giving ten percent of what we earned. Earning as little as we did and needing every penny was something George and I had to reconcile. As my faith deepened and I grew spiritually, I trusted God implicitly.

One Sunday morning as we were getting ready for church, we discovered that we only had one dollar between us. Our tithe would have been ten cents. We didn't have a dime on us, and we really didn't have ten cents to spare. We needed milk, too, and my husband wasn't going to get paid for three more days. He balked at my insistence that we tithe our last dollar.

I said, "God will provide for us. Please, George, I believe this with all my heart."

Naturally protective, my husband could only think of his responsibility to me and our unborn child. However, he was in awe of watching my growing faith. Finally, George relented. I put our last dollar into a church envelope and tucked it into my purse before we left the house.

During our walk to church, we marveled at the beautiful fall day. The leaves had turned bright orange, yellow and various shades of red. We walked on a crunchy, multi-colored carpet.

Walking back to our apartment after Mass, I had flashbacks to my childhood. My brother and I used to rake leaves into huge piles and jump into them. Once the pile scattered, we ran around kicking the leaves into the air.

As my husband and I approached our home, I stepped off the curb into the sea of crimson, impulsively kicking my foot into the leaves and sending them into the air.

George held my hand and cautioned me to be careful. I was eight months pregnant and a little clumsy. Suddenly, we saw something odd within the colorful red and orange leaves. Reaching out, George grabbed a single dollar bill from the air.

He waved the bill over his head. "Look, Nance!"

I clapped. "It's milk money! I knew God would provide. All we needed was faith."

— Nancy Emmick Panko —

72

Punchi's Watch

Don't believe in miracles — depend on them.
~Laurence J. Peter

"My darling Punchi" is how I began all the letters and e-mails I wrote to my mother's sister, my aunt Frieda, until she died of metastatic breast cancer in 2012. Punchi lived in America most of her adult life while my family and I lived in the small but beautiful island nation of Sri Lanka.

Punchi was like a second mother to my brothers and me. She loved us as if we were her own, and we adored her in turn. She was our living, breathing guardian angel and the most beautiful "Santa Claus" who gave us wonderful gifts all year round.

The best time of our lives was when Punchi would come to visit us every few years. It was like a never-ending party, a festival of love and laughter lasting for weeks, with friends, family, and neighbors constantly visiting, and my mother's famous chicken curry served for lunch every day.

It was during one of these visits that Punchi called me to her side when we were getting ready to go to church one morning. She handed me a beautiful velvet box. Inside was an even more beautiful and exquisite watch that was made to look like a bejeweled bangle. I had never seen anything like it before, and when Punchi said it was a special gift for me, I couldn't believe it. That morning in church, and every day for many years to come, that watch-bangle adorned my left wrist and was my most prized possession.

When I say I wore it every day, I mean I literally wore it every single hour of every day. I removed it only to take a bath. I wore it to school with my white uniform, maroon tie, white shoes and socks, and pigtails. I wore it when I went to play with my rambunctious group of neighborhood friends, climbing trees and riding our bicycles at full speed over rutted by-roads. And, miraculously, my watch-bangle survived all my shenanigans — except for that one time when it didn't.

It wasn't even a particularly eventful day that I lost my watch-bangle. I remember walking into our house during lunchtime after a wonderful morning playing hide-and-seek with my friends in our garden. My carefree happiness was short-lived, though, when, in a moment of dread, my right hand grasped at my empty left wrist.

Lunch was forgotten as I flew out through the open door and into the garden. I started what soon turned out to be a futile search for my beloved gift from my darling Punchi. Everyone I knew helped me look for my watch-bangle in our sprawling, somewhat overgrown garden. We combed the lawn a hundred times over. We dug in the dirt around the edges of the land and at the foot of trees, thinking it might have gotten buried, but there was absolutely no sign of my treasure anywhere.

With each passing day, the burden I carried in my heart grew heavier. What made matters a million times worse was the fact that Punchi was due to visit in a month's time. I didn't think I could face her without the watch on my wrist because I thought I would hurt her feelings. I feared she would think I was an ungrateful and careless little girl.

I found myself at my wits' end with two weeks left until her visit. The garden was completely overgrown, and my parents had finally decided it was time to call off the search and mow the grass, which had been put off while the search was ongoing. I was devastated, but there was nothing more I could do. In my despair, I ran to the bathroom, shut the door, fell to my knees and turned to the all-powerful God of the universe I had known all my life.

I said, "Dear God, please help me find Punchi's watch. You know that we have looked for it everywhere but have not found it yet. You also know that Punchi is going to come for a visit in two weeks, no? We have time until then. Two weeks is a long time, and I know that you can see where my watch is right now. Won't you please help me find it? My only prayer is that you help me find the watch before Punchi comes, and I will promise to never ask you for anything else ever again. Amen."

And before I could even get up off my knees, I heard God's voice in reply. It was more of a voice I heard in my mind than out loud, but it was clear and unmistakable.

"Why do you not have more faith in me, Annie? Why do you think I need two weeks to help you find your Punchi's watch, when, with a little more faith, we can find your watch today?"

It took me a while to process what I had just heard, and I stayed on my knees for longer than I expected.

Later, that same afternoon, I felt compelled to walk into our garden. My father was already there, and when he saw me, he asked me to go fetch my uncle, who was working in one of his carpentry shops just beyond our house. Dutifully, I obliged. When we returned, he and my father fell into a discussion about something.

I, of course, had a million things running through my mind. I started walking in one section of the garden, tossing the newly mowed grass with my feet mindlessly, almost habitually, from weeks and weeks of going over the same lawn area. My mind was swirling with thoughts of God and what He had said. I had no clue about how He was going to help me find the watch, but I felt strangely optimistic.

After a few minutes, or maybe longer, my uncle fell in step with me. Without any preamble, he asked me about the watch and whether I had found it. I started to say no and had barely gotten the word out of my mouth when he suddenly bent down right where we were standing and picked up something from the ground. He wiped some mud off it, stuck it under my nose, and nonchalantly asked me if this was the watch I was looking for.

There was mud encrusted all over it, and the glass face was cracked on one side, but it was sitting miraculously on my uncle's palm, just like God had promised. After all this time, eluding our search and remarkably surviving the blades of the lawnmower, Punchi's watch gleamed brighter than ever. It was a testament of both my Punchi's love for me and God's.

—Annie Juliana Francis Ismail—

Chapter 8

Comfort from Beyond

A Love Letter from Hope

Because I feel that, in the Heavens above, the angels,
whispering to one another, can find, among their
burning terms of love, none so devotional
as that of "Mother."
~Edgar Allen Poe

My mom was always my phone call, the person whose number I had on speed dial anytime anything big happened in my life. She was the one I called for the small stuff, too. It never mattered what time of day; she always picked up. When I was knee-deep in raising boys, when my heart was broken after my divorce, when I went back to school as a single mom, and when I was down for the count with a miserable cold, she was there. Sometimes, we spoke six or seven times a day.

My mom was my best friend, my compass, my example of what it means to be human. I was her only daughter, and I was her caregiver in the last two years of her life. Losing her was the hardest thing that ever happened to me. At the same time, it gave me courage because I knew that if I could survive that, there was nothing I couldn't do.

So much has happened since she died three and a half years ago. There are days when I just want to pick up the telephone and talk to her. I want to tell her all about the good man who came into my life, a retired police officer named Christopher who treats me the way a woman deserves to be treated. I want to tell her that I finally followed my heart and moved to the beach, and that it wasn't as hard or as scary as I thought it would be. I want her to know that I am okay because I know she was worried about that in her last days. I want her to know that I am happy… and that I miss her with my whole heart!

The other night, I was walking along Moonlight Beach with Chris, the good man who serendipitously walked into my life one year after I lost my mom. We were on our way home from our favorite pizza joint. It was dark, and there was an eerie marine layer creeping in from the western horizon, slowly consuming the constellations, along with the silvery light of the moon that shimmered across the water. We had walked for about a mile without saying a word, simply breathing it all in… with what little room was left for our diaphragms in our snug blue jeans.

The truth was, except for the extra cheese on our pizza and the added carrot cake for dessert, I had no regrets. I was happy… happier than I had been in a long time. As I watched the fog steal the last handful of stars in the sky, I made a wish out loud.

"I wish my mom would have written me a letter before she passed," I said.

Not knowing how to respond, Chris just smiled at me. I wondered if he knew how much his being there meant to me. And I wondered if (somewhere out there) Mom knew how much her love and influence meant to me. Chris and I walked quietly for another fifty yards or so. I ventured toward the water's edge. It was a low tide, and I could feel the salty mist from the waves stinging my face. Suddenly, Chris called out to me.

"Natalie!" he shouted, so to be heard over the rolling tide. "Come here!"

He took out his pocket flashlight. I could see him shining a bright light at his feet. As I approached, I saw the word "Hope" written in the sand and outlined in rock was a heart shape and peace sign. I instantly broke down in tears, and my heart caught in my throat. Chris took me into his arms and held me tight as I sobbed uncontrollably into his chest. It was, indeed, a sand-written love letter from my mom whose name just happened to be Hope. In that moment, in that man's arms and on that beautiful beach, I knew that she knew I was happy. And even though my calls were "long-distance" these days, she would always find a way to pick up.

—Natalie June Reilly—

74

Father Knows Best

There is no expiration date on the love
between a father and his child.
~Jennifer Williamson

My job was beginning to bore me. After achieving all my objectives and targets, I feared I would become complacent and lose motivation if I didn't continue to seek advanced roles with new challenges. What I called the Four-Year Fidget had gripped me once again as it had done regularly throughout my career. By this time, I had been with the same company for nearly twenty-five years, advancing from an entry-level role through various positions to one where I was now manager of my branch with about a dozen employees. It was time to look for a different job, something new.

Management asked me to consider a district leadership role that would require me to move my family to a city about three and a half hours away. As part of this job, I would also need to successfully complete a self-study course that I knew to be extremely difficult. Without the course certification, I could not hold the role. I didn't know if I could do it. I didn't know the person who would be my new supervisor, but I heard he was tough. Did I want that?

At the same time, a competitor was headhunting me for a position. A former boss of mine who had left our business was now looking to recruit me to his new company. I had always enjoyed the autonomy he provided me when I worked for him, and I was flattered to receive his call. The position he asked me to consider was also a district leadership type of role. I would need to learn all new products and computer systems, and adjust to their culture. Like the other job offer, this one also required me to relocate.

I had to consider if I wanted to remain with the same organization where I was comfortable and had a proven performance record or venture out to a new environment with new expectations. Both opportunities held an appeal to me at a point in my career when things had begun to feel mundane. Both offers came at the same time. The following day was decision day, and I was under pressure to make my choice.

At that time, my husband travelled for his job and was not home, so we chatted on the phone that evening. He had always been supportive of my career, and because he could perform his job no matter where we lived, he told me he was open to moving to either city. He said only I could decide which position was the right one for me. Why couldn't he have stated his preference and let me know in which city he preferred us to live? Instead, he left it up to me to decide. My head reeled.

When I got off the phone with my husband, I dialed my mom. I knew she wouldn't tell me what to do, but she was always a good sounding board when I needed to talk things through. She listened as I explained my dilemma, listed the pros and cons of going either way, and ended with a pathetic plea for her help. As always, she was sympathetic and understanding. She empathized with me and was glad she wasn't being called upon to make such a decision for herself. What came out of her mouth next surprised me.

"Talk to your dad," she said calmly.

"What?" I asked incredulously. My dad had died seven years earlier. I began to think my mother was losing it. I laughed feebly.

"I mean it," she insisted. "Whenever I have a hard decision to make, I talk to him through prayer. He always seems to answer me."

We talked a bit more before I ended the call, no closer to a decision than before I had called her.

What was I going to do? Both companies wanted an answer first thing in the morning. I needed to make the right decision, but, at this point, I had no clue what that right decision was.

As I prepared for bed, I knew it would be a long, sleepless night. I was going to bed with this big problem unresolved. True to form, I found myself tossing and turning, trying to find a comfortable position to sleep. I tried to erase all thoughts from my mind, creating a vacuum of sorts. That didn't work. I focused on my breathing in an attempt to enter into a meditative state. No luck. I even tried counting forward and backward. Nothing helped. By 1:00 in the morning, I was exhausted from my attempts. Crying seemed the only answer. As I mopped the tears from my face, I remembered my mom's advice. "Talk to your dad."

I closed my eyes tight and began my solemn appeal, seeking guidance from him. I must have drifted off to sleep.

"Ballen," a voice said.

I was still half-asleep.

"Ballen," the soft voice called again. *Who was that?* I looked around.

And yet, I knew. There was only one person in the world who called me by that childhood nickname.

My father.

I raised myself halfway off the pillow. At the foot of the bed, my father's face floated.

He was just as I remembered him. His full, round face had a gentle expression, and I found myself relaxing.

"Ballen, why is this so difficult for you?" he asked.

Not waiting for my response, he went on to say, "You always make good decisions. You need to trust yourself."

With that, his face faded into the night.

Puzzled, I glanced around the room. I was alone in the dark. I glimpsed the time. It was 3:10 A.M. It gave me an eerie feeling. When he still farmed, 3:10 in the afternoon was when Dad always came to the house for coffee. It was the time we children got to see our father, who worked long and hard in the fields. It was the time of day when we had a chance to talk with our dad about life's problems. It seemed serendipitous that he chose that exact time to appear to me. His voice was calm and soothing as I remembered.

I lay back down in bed and pulled the covers to my chin. An overwhelming feeling of peacefulness washed over me and bathed me in serene tranquility. It was the most incredible feeling I have ever experienced. It was like I didn't have a care in the world, and everything was right as it should be. I literally floated on a cloud.

Sleep captured me and rocked me in its arms until my alarm sounded.

I woke feeling refreshed.

I knew what I would do.

The answer had come to me in a prayer.

— Marilyn Frey —

Uncle Johnny

Brothers and sisters are as close as hands and feet.
~Vietnamese Proverb

I was seven years old when my twenty-nine-year-old mother was stricken with TB and had to be confined to a sanatorium in Portland, Oregon. My two brothers and I weren't allowed to visit her for six months except for the couple of times we got to see her through the window of her room three floors up from where we stood on the hospital grounds.

Thankfully, my aunt and uncle (Mom's sister and brother-in-law) had opened their home and hearts to us. My older brother and I were enrolled in a new school and made many friends, but although I didn't tell anyone, I worried almost every day about my mother.

We'd go home on the weekends to spend time with Dad, but he rarely talked about Mom while we were there. I was fine with that because I didn't want to share my fears with him; perhaps I was afraid of the answers.

What frightened me most was that I knew Mom's brother Johnny had died from the same dreaded disease one year prior to her diagnosis.

Finally, the day my mother came home, I was able to open up about my fears. "Mommy, I was so scared that you wouldn't get better. I'm so happy that you got well. Were you scared, too?"

I have never forgotten Mom's answer to my question: "Honey, I was scared at first. But one night Uncle Johnny came and sat on the edge of my bed in the hospital. He told me that I was going to be fine.

From that night on, I didn't worry anymore. I knew I'd come home."

I asked Mom if Uncle Johnny was an angel, and she told me that he was, but he looked exactly like she remembered. The contented smile on her face as she spoke of him warmed and comforted my young heart.

We have talked many times throughout the years about that angelic encounter, and Mom's version has always remained as steadfast about the visit as it was the first time she shared it with me.

My mother is now 100 and suffering from dementia. Although she is unable to express her thoughts, there are moments when I notice her face bearing that same contented smile, and I wonder if Uncle Johnny is nearby to comfort her as he did when he appeared at her hospital bed so long ago.

— Connie Kaseweter Pullen —

76

The Nurse

Remember that although bodies may pass away, the
energy that connects you to a loved one is everlasting
and can always be felt when you're open to receiving it.
~Doreen Virtue, *Signs from Above*

I grew up in a large, boisterous family. I was the middle child of five. My mother and father married very young with the sole intent of raising a big family in a loving, supportive home. My mother was a stay-at-home mom, and my dad was an uneducated man who labored very hard to provide a decent living for us all.

We never had a lot, often scrambling for money at the end of the month, but we had more than enough love. Our family was the most important priority in my dad's life, and he made sure we all knew how he felt. On the rare occasion he spoke of a time when he might no longer be with us, he always assured us he would contact us from the afterlife if he could.

I eventually married a wonderful man and was blessed with three children of my own. My oldest was very close to both her grandparents, and especially my dad. She was the first grandchild and the light of my dad's life. Unfortunately, my dad passed away in 1999 when she was only eight. My daughter wrote and read a heartfelt letter at his funeral, letting everyone know how dearly she loved him and would miss him.

About six years ago, in one of the most terrifying moments of my life, my twenty-three-year-old daughter started to hemorrhage and was rushed to the hospital for emergency surgery. I was by her side and was told to call my husband, who was working at the time. We were all very scared, and the situation was touch-and-go for a while. My daughter begged to know if she was going to be okay. After I held her hand and assured her that it would all be okay, praying like a madwoman, she was rushed into surgery. After a tension-filled hour and thanks to a very skilled surgeon, the surgery was pronounced a success. She was sent home that evening to begin to recuperate.

Several days later, we were talking about the experience and the terror we all felt during that very emotional time as she was being prepped for surgery. She began talking about the various doctors and nurses who were attending to her, and she asked me about the young, male, redheaded nurse who had been in the room with us, standing by me with his hand on my shoulder. I was confused and told her that her dad and I had only seen female nurses in the room. She insisted that while she had been lying on the examination table, he had been standing by me. We assumed that she had probably been confused as it was a very intense and trying time.

The following week, we were visiting with my mom when my daughter disappeared into the spare bedroom to grab a blanket. She was gone for a while, and when she came out of the room, she had a strange look on her face. We asked her what was going on. She told us that she had been looking through a photo album that she had discovered sitting on the shelf. She asked my mom about the identity of the young, redheaded man in the pictures scattered throughout the album. My mom told her it was her grandfather as a young man. My daughter's eyes welled up, and she tearfully told us that he was the man who had been standing by me with his hand on my shoulder. My dad had passed away fifteen years earlier, and she had only known him as an older man.

We all marveled at the miracle that my father was with me and my daughter at one of the scariest times of our lives, lending his support. He was always such a caring man who loved his family greatly, and there's no doubt in my mind that he was there with us, lending his loving support when we needed him most. He had promised that if there was ever a way for him to contact us after he passed, he would. He kept his promise.

— Christine Cowles —

77

Butterflies and Birds

Angels are the bridge between heaven and earth.
~Megan McKenna

For some reason, my life and my mother's have run parallel in the oddest of ways. Positive milestones in my adult life were met with devastating milestones in my mother's simultaneously. In light of this, maybe I should have been more prepared for what happened.

On December 12, 2012, my husband and I found out we were expecting our first child. I vividly remember telling my family, and the loud scream of pure joy from my mom.

The joy, in all ways, was short-lived. Less than a month later, my mom was diagnosed with thymoma, cancer of the thymus. The next seven months are etched into my memory. They were filled with doctor's appointments, hospital stays, and a roller coaster of emotions, ending in the biggest heartbreak of my life.

After the second round of chemo, we'd known it wasn't working the way my mother's oncologist had hoped. Her tumor was not getting smaller. She had a conversation with my dad in which she told him that he didn't have to worry; she would always be with him. He asked how he would know it was her. She said simply, "I will be the butterfly."

On July 16, 2013, my mom had surgery to remove her tumor. I remember sitting with her in pre-op, joking and smiling. Never in my wildest dreams did I imagine this would be the last time I would see her alive. Her tumor was worse than anticipated, and her left lung had to be removed. While in recovery after surgery, her heart could not stabilize itself. She passed early the next morning.

My mom was extremely spiritual. She believed in angels, visited mediums, had a regression, was trained in reiki, and would meditate. Growing up, I did not understand it. I found it a little weird and was disconnected from all of it. Since my mom's passing, I have found comfort in all the things I didn't understand as a child. I have seen multiple mediums, been to a healer, added meditation into my routine, and have angels throughout our home.

My experiences with mediums have been extremely comforting. I have been lucky to have had my mom come through and tell me all the things I needed to hear. But my most powerful experience with her in the afterlife came two days before my first Mother's Day as a mother. Mother's Day is the hardest time of year for me. What makes this day harder than birthdays, anniversaries, holidays, and any other milestone is that I cannot mourn in private. I am inundated with spam e-mails, commercials, pop-up ads, cards, and displays in stores reminding me what time of year it is.

That day, I stood in the hallway holding my daughter, looking at pictures of my mom and telling stories about her to my daughter. Out of nowhere, I felt my mom's energy. The energy literally hugged me, the way my mom would have. I could feel her love and presence in that instant. As quickly as I felt it, it was gone. It was exactly what I needed from her.

In January 2018, my father was diagnosed with Stage 4 lung cancer. He passed away three months later. The only thing that gave me comfort in his passing was knowing he would be reunited with my mother. I know she was there waiting for him when he passed. One of my biggest regrets in my dad's passing was not having a similar conversation with him like the one he had with my mom about being a butterfly.

A year and a half after my dad passed, I felt a lump in my left breast. My husband and I already had a trip planned to Denver prior to my scheduled OB/GYN appointment. No one, besides the two of us, knew about the lump at this point. We spent a few days hiking and enjoying nature. I remember hiking Pike's Peak and a bird following us along as we hiked. I thought to myself, *I think the bird is my dad.* I knew that sounded crazy, so I did not say anything to my husband at the time.

We returned home, and the flurry of doctor's visits and tests began. The weekend before we received my results, we were at my in-laws' house. It was a warm day in October, so my husband left the windows open in our brand-new minivan. We went inside and spent the afternoon distracting ourselves with laughs and good food. When we went to leave, there was a bird inside the car! It had pooped all over our new car and was flying around endlessly. Our daughters were screaming, I was laughing, and my husband was trying to get it out of the car. In that instant, I told him the bird was my dad. He was with us in Colorado, and he was here now, I said.

A month later, a good friend took me to see a medium. She matter-of-factly told me, "When your parents visit you, your mom is the butterfly, and your dad is the bird." It confirmed what I already knew in my heart of hearts. Now, every time my daughters see a butterfly or cardinal, they say hello to their grandparents and thank them for visiting.

While I wish with all my heart that my parents were here in the physical world, I have comfort in knowing they are our guardian angels watching over me and, more importantly, my daughters.

My older daughter, the one I was pregnant with at the time of my mom's passing, embodies her spirit. She has my mom's heart and pure soul. While my older daughter may be like my mother, my younger one looks just like her, even more so than me. I truly believe each of them has a piece of her inside. She met both of them prior to them entering this world, and she will be their eternal guardian angel in this life.

— Stephanie DeNicola —

78

Our Tradition

A mother and a daughter always share a special bond,
which is engraved on their hearts.
~Author Unknown

At five years old, my youngest daughter Lisette should have been way too young for me to be talking to her about guardian angels. But here I was, standing next to an adult-sized stretcher, as her child-sized body lay draped in a huge white sheet. Just a bit of her pastel animal-print hospital gown peeked out along her neckline. She was about to be wheeled in for her second brain surgery.

Born with hydrocephalus (and another brain abnormality we would discover years later), Lisette had her first brain surgery at seven months old. Little did we know then that this would be the first of many corrective surgeries to come, and that she would spend a lot of time at the Children's Hospital of Philadelphia.

As a parent, let alone a single mother, nothing can prepare you for these moments except faith in the doctors you've chosen, and, more importantly, an unwavering faith in God.

Unless, of course, you were my daughter, looking up at me from that too-large stretcher.

None of the above mattered to her because all her faith was in me. In Lisette's short time here on Earth, she viewed me as more than just her mother. I was her friend, her hero, her safety, and the only one she trusted to be with her.

With this realization, I knew that Lisette and I needed something special to get us through these difficult and scary times. It would have to be something she could believe in and that we could implement in any time of uncertainty. What we needed was our own tradition of sorts to bond us and reaffirm her faith that I would guide her through each surgery. I alone was responsible for bridging the gap between her and God in a way that a five-year-old would comprehend.

Little did I realize that I would need this tradition more than my daughter.

I have always believed in guardian angels, as I have felt their presence around me and called upon them many times when I was in distress. This surgery would be the perfect time to introduce Lisette to her guardian angels. They would serve as the mediums to bring her faith closer to God in the times she needed Him most.

She was moments from being wheeled away by a team of surgeons. To her, they were terrifying. All she saw were total strangers wearing gowns and masks.

This was the moment.

I took hold of Lisette's hands and asked the surgical team to wait an extra moment. As we locked eyes with each other, I squeezed her tiny hands in mine and asked her if she could feel God and her guardian angels around her. With her faith in me unwavering, she looked around as if she could see and feel each angel, and she responded with assuredness, "Yes, I can feel them."

Our new tradition seemed to bring us both peace in that anxious moment. As I had hoped, this became an instrument of faith we could both rely on every time we faced another challenging procedure. We would hold hands, and I would introduce her to her guardian angels. Once she acknowledged their presence, she would be ready to let go and face what came next. Then and only then would I allow them to take her away.

Months after implementing our tradition, Lisette and I stopped by my mother's house for a routine visit. For some unknown reason, as we entered my mother's house, we stopped right in front of the first door in the hallway, which led to my mother's bedroom.

This particular room was usually off-limits to the grandchildren, as there were many breakables on display. Before I could register what she was up to, Lisette made her way quickly and boldly into her grammy's room. As I rushed to usher her out of the bedroom, my mother decided to make an exception since Lisette wasn't touching or disturbing anything.

"Let her be," my mother insisted, and we made ourselves comfortable right there in the doorframe so that we could keep an eye on Lisette while she explored the room.

As my mother and I chatted away about our day, I was distracted by Lisette's little voice in the background. She seemed to be having a discussion. I then realized she was staring up at an ornate, gilded picture frame on the dresser. I wasn't exactly sure who or what was in the frame as there were several of them clustered together, and I could only see the backs from where I stood.

As I neared the dresser, Lisette's eyes continued to focus on whatever was in the frame. As I turned the frame around, I realized it was my grandmother in the photo.

Confused, I asked her, "Sweetheart, who are you talking to?"

She pointed at the photo I had turned and replied simply, "Her."

I will never forget the expression of peace, happiness and sense of familiarity she had on her sweet little face.

I pulled down the photo and brought it closer for her to see, certain she was mistaken in what she was looking at. I said, "No, angel, you don't know her. That's your grammy's mommy."

She responded without hesitation, "I know that, Mama. She's one of the guardian angels I see beside me before I go into surgery."

As my mother and I stood there in disbelief, I knew I would never worry again about Lisette's surgeries.

Not only was God present, but he brought reinforcements.

—Joan Sammons-Fernandez—

79

Save the Last Dance

Deeply, I know this, that love triumphs over death.
My father continues to be loved,
and therefore he remains by my side.
~Jennifer Williamson

My dad passed when I was in my thirties. I was an only child, and we'd had a special bond throughout my life. My mom was sick often, in and out of hospitals before her death, so my father had been the parent who mostly raised me.

A friend of mine who also lost a loved one around the same time heard about a medium who was giving "readings" at an auditorium in El Segundo. She wanted me to go with her. I wasn't a huge fan of these types of things. I'd seen mediums who heard from the dead and then directed the message to a person in the audience on TV. I thought it was kind of cool, but how often does someone actually get chosen? And was it legit?

About a hundred people signed up to be in attendance that Saturday afternoon. We decided to go and see if we could somehow connect with our deceased family members. I thought it would be fun, and we could grab lunch at our favorite restaurant afterward.

We walked into the auditorium. People were chatting excitedly. I quickly became nervous realizing there was a possibility I could be chosen for a reading. I was shy and didn't like public attention.

My friend and I took our seats and talked about who we would like to hear from. She said she'd like to hear from her aunt, whom she'd recently lost and greatly missed. I said I wanted to hear from my mom. I knew I'd said everything I wanted to say to my dad before he passed, but my mom was a different story. I lost her when I was only twenty-three. She'd had Parkinson's and lost her ability to talk toward the end. I really felt a need to hear from her.

The medium walked onto the small stage and introduced himself. His name was Peter Close, and he had just flown in from England. He said he split his time between the States and the U.K. to help as many people as possible connect with their loved ones. The meeting was only an hour long, and he told us several stories about his adventures during his career. I knew there wouldn't be time for many readings, so what were the odds either one of us would be selected?

I thought about both my parents while Mr. Close spoke. My father had always been my rock growing up, and I was thankful to have been raised by such a wonderful, caring man. And even though my mother had been ill, she left me with memories of her great sense of humor and love of reading.

Suddenly, my friend nudged me. I was stunned when I realized Mr. Close was speaking directly to me. After describing who he was looking for, I nodded my confirmation to him.

"I have a man here who wants to let you know you will be okay. Stay strong. You have always been his special little girl, and he is very proud of you." Instantly, I could feel my dad's presence. As Mr. Close continued to speak, he said a few things only my dad and I would know, and I realized I could feel my dad's love — not just hear words but feel his concern and reassurance. My dad's warmth enveloped me with a special familiarity, and I soaked in every moment. I was trying to hold my emotions together and did so until Mr. Close's last message. "And one last thing. He says, 'Save the last dance for me.' Does that make sense?"

I burst into tears.

Two more readings were given, and when it was over, my friend and I left. As we were driving to the restaurant, she handed me some tissues and asked me what "save the last dance" meant. I told her that one of the special things my dad loved to do was to go dancing. My parents and I, about once a month or so, would venture out to dinner at a nice restaurant that had a small band and a dance floor. My dad was a great singer, a lover of music and dancing, and my mom couldn't carry a tune, but she loved dancing with him. I loved watching my parents twirl around the dance floor, enjoying themselves. Then it would be my turn. He would teach me some steps and we always had a wonderful time.

When my junior-high dances came around, he would prepare me by teaching me the fox trot or a four step in case slow music was played. And for my high-school prom, he put on some music, and we practiced some steps in our family room. I even got a chance at slow dancing with my high-school love at my prom, which was held at the Ambassador Hotel. All these years later, I realized my dad hadn't just taught me some dance moves but how to conduct myself with grace and have confidence on the dance floor.

Looking back, Mr. Close's reading only lasted five minutes, but after nearly three decades, I can still remember every second. It was one of the most moving moments of my life, and I thank God I was able to experience it.

Only my father would know of our special memories of dancing together. At that moment, I knew my dad was looking down at me from Heaven and smiling. Perhaps he was waiting for that last spin around the dance floor.

I'm saving the last dance for you, Dad.

— Kimberly Kimmel —

80

Letter from Mom

The probability of a certain set of circumstances
coming together in a meaningful (or tragic)
way is so low that it simply cannot be
considered mere coincidence.
~V.C. King

My mother suffered from Alzheimer's disease for close to ten years before her passing. She did an excellent job of hiding her condition for years prior to her official diagnosis. I was in denial until a series of events that waved red flags. One such event was when Mom was an hour late to my house, which was out of character for her. I worried something had happened.

As soon as she arrived, she confessed that she had been in a minor car accident. It was clear the incident had rattled her nerves, but she was not physically injured. I surveyed the crunched bumper that would need to be repaired. I felt that everything was fine until she forgot all about the accident less than twenty minutes later.

Not long after that, I had to take the car away. It was the hardest thing I've ever had to do. Then she broke her hip, and that's when everything changed. Mom was still able to live in her home but now with a caregiver. The robust woman I had known all my life, filled with vim and vigor, my best friend, was now a shell of the person she used to be.

Mom was always polite and kind to me, but she had no idea who

I was. She often asked, "Do you know my daughter, Leslie?"

"Yes, she's a lovely girl," I would joke.

Mom would smile, always followed by, "Aren't you the girl who took my car away from me?"

I yearned for her to "wake up" and be normal, if even for a moment. I regretted never telling her how much she meant to me, as not just a parent but truly my guide through life. We never finished a conversation without saying "I love you," but we never spoke more truthful words. Now, it was too late. Sometimes, I would hold her hand and look into her eyes.

When Mom passed away, it was, as many say, a relief. It was an end to her suffering. Yet, there was a hole. There were moments when I felt lost and confused. I needed my mother's encouragement with my life challenges, starting with being a single parent to my three children.

Oh, how I wished I could hear her say, "You've got this."

After her passing, there was the arduous task of cleaning out her house. Mom was a bit of a packrat. It took weeks and countless trips to various charities to clear out everything. I went through the pockets of pants, coats, and jackets on the off chance she had hidden some jewelry. Once, I found three crisp hundred-dollar bills stashed in the pages of a book. That only spurred me on, combing through every book, page by page, just in case. But nothing else was ever uncovered.

One charity trip contained the last three boxes of Mom's books. I pulled into the now-familiar parking lot. A nice man met me at my car before I could get out.

"Sorry, but we were full today. You can try our pick-up truck on Foothill."

I thanked him and went to that location. They were full, too.

"I know it's crazy," a kind woman said. "We're never full. I don't know what's going on. Guess people are just spring cleaning. Come back tomorrow. I'm sure we'll be fine then."

I went home, keeping the boxes inside my car to try again. But the next day, I experienced the same thing—still full. *Fine,* I thought. *I'll go to the Women's Center thrift store.* Full. The Salvation Army thrift store. Full. After ten attempts, I drove home, parked in my driveway, and pulled out each box. I had a hunch.

"Alright, Mom, what is it you want me to find in these boxes of books?"

Box One had fifteen books inside. I leafed through them all—nothing unusual. I even read all her penciled notes in the margins, thinking that was what I was supposed to do. My heart raced with the hope of finding more hundred-dollar bills or maybe a bond or stock certificate. After such close examination the first time, how could I have missed anything? With Box Two, I got the same result. I was convinced this was a complete waste of time and felt foolish, but there was one box left. *Might as well,* I thought. The first book I pulled out was a textbook on religious studies. I remembered seeing it before, covered with notes. Immediately, a large, stiff white envelope fell out and landed on the ground.

Inside the envelope was a greeting card by Flavia, a famous artist many years ago that Mom loved. No hundred-dollar bills popped out. Instead, there was something far more valuable. I opened the card and immediately recognized my mother's cursive handwriting. And this is what it said:

Leslie,

If the angels had asked me what qualities I would like in a daughter, I would have said—

"Give her joy and sparkling wit. Let her share her laughter and gaiety freely. Give her imagination and creativity and love and beauty. Give her courage and inner strength. Give her patience and understanding, compassion, and sensitivity to the needs and feelings of others.

"And when I have to take my share of the inevitable trials and punches life gives each of us in our learning and growing, let her hold my hand and give me unquestioning love and friendship."

In short, why not make her a Leslie? And they did.

I love you,
Mom

I read it over and over. Each time, I felt lighter and lighter. I was whole. And the following day there was plenty of space for my mother's books at the charity.

—Leslie Freiberger—

81

Dragonflies

*The dragonfly brings dreams to reality and
is the messenger of wisdom and
enlightenment from other realms.*
~Author Unknown

"**S**end me a dragonfly, honey. You know how I love them." Fifteen minutes later, three dragonflies hovered over the tall golden reeds along the shore of the mountain pond. I smiled, looked up into the beautiful cobalt sky and whispered, "Thank you."

I feel a blend of sorrow and joy when I see dragonflies, especially at the pond by the old pine known as Michael's Tree. It is where my husband played and fished as a child and is across the street from where we lived. His ashes are buried beneath this tree. It is a lovely and peaceful spot. I first saw the dragonflies at the pond six years ago during our private family memorial service.

Michael and I met at a local coffee shop on Valentine's Eve. His long brown hair, sky-blue eyes and sly smile caught my attention from the moment he walked through the door. Obviously, he was attracted to me, too. He bought us a couple of coffees and sat at my table. We talked for three hours. Three weeks later, we were engaged.

We were middle-aged and had been married before. It was out of character for either of us to enter so swiftly into a marriage commitment. Our family and friends didn't know what to think. But we both "knew" that first evening. We got married more than a year later, but we were inseparable from the time we met.

We celebrated our eighteenth wedding anniversary nine days before Michael died. Since he was in the hospital at the time, I planned an impromptu surprise party. I called friends and family, inviting them to come that evening. I arranged with the hospital staff for a private conference room and ran around town picking up balloons, flowers, and a card. A friend kindly bought a cake. Now and then, I'd pop into Michael's room, placating his irritation that I was neglecting him on our special day.

That evening, when the nurse wheeled him through the door of the party room, his face lit up to shouts of "Surprise! Happy anniversary!" The pangs of guilt I'd felt earlier were worth the joy of the occasion. None of us knew it would be the last time most of them would see him alive.

Michael and I loved spending time with one another. We had only been apart a total of six weeks during our nineteen and a half years together. Most of those times were when we'd go visit family. We didn't like being apart, and we finally promised never to leave one another for more than a day or two again. I even stayed with him every night in the hospital, sleeping on a rickety chair or hard cots during the nine months he battled pancreatic cancer.

On the morning of his final day, he assured me that even though he was going Home, he would still be with me and take care of me. He has given me many proofs of that promise. One of those signs is dragonflies. I've always known of Heaven and felt that our spirits go there when we die, but I never really believed the stories I read or heard, even from my grandmother, of visions or signs from departed loved ones. The day of Michael's memorial changed my belief.

One of Michael's favorite hymns was "I Walk in the Garden." His grandmother sang it to him as a child. It held special memories for him. I located the song on a CD and played it after the opening prayer. Within seconds of the song's beginning, more than two dozen iridescent blue dragonflies flew to the shore and hovered over the pond in front of us. Blue was Michael's favorite color, and these ranged in beautiful shades from sky-blue to indigo. Then, as soon as the song ended, they all flew away. We each knew we had received a message from Michael that he was still with us in spirit and would remain in our hearts and memories.

I've heard it said that dragonflies are messengers from Heaven. I don't know if that's true, but I have seen a dragonfly glide beside me as I walk a beach, fly in front of my windshield when a favorite song of his brings tears to my eyes, and hover near me when I'm sitting along a river thinking of him. Many times over the years, blue ones have flown back and forth along the pond while I am at Michael's Tree. During those times, I sense his joy and feel comforted. I smile and say, "Thank you, honey."

—Carmen Myrtis-Garcia—

82

Painted Nails

True healing involves body, mind and Spirit.
~Alison Stormwolf

Three days before my mother died, we had a talk. We were sitting in a small lounge outside her hospital room with the sun streaming in through the windows. I was curled up in a chair, and she was in her nightgown with her swollen legs propped up on a coffee table.

She looked beautiful, as usual. Even on the way to her deathbed, she had taken pains to curl her hair, put on make-up, and apply lipstick.

From the chest up, one would never guess that she was dying. People would assume she was just a fifty-three-year-old woman in the prime of her life.

"Now, Barbara," she said. "I don't want you to cry."

She meant when she died.

"Mom," I said. "Don't talk like that."

"Look at me, Barb," she said very matter-of-factly, gesturing to the tumors painfully stretching her abdomen. "I could be dead any minute here. The doctor says there's a blood clot in my leg that could go to my brain at any time."

She was right. The only reason she was here was to die. We both knew it. She'd had colon cancer for three years. We'd watched it spread to her ovaries, liver, and lungs. Two days ago, when she almost suffocated in her own bed, we decided it was time to go to palliative care.

"Well, Mom, of course I'm going to cry. You're my *mother*, for

God's sake."

"Okay," she sighed. "You can cry a little bit. But I don't want you to let it ruin your life."

We sat there in silence for a bit.

Finally, I whispered, "Are you scared?"

She thought for a minute.

"No," she finally said. "I used to worry about your father, but I taught him to do the laundry, and I took him to IGA and showed him how to grocery shop. So, I think he'll be okay."

That made me laugh. In the thirty-seven years they had been married, my father had never made himself a cup of tea, let alone done laundry.

"The only thing I worry about," she said, "is you and your sister. You don't get along. You should get along."

Oh, dear. This was true. We definitely did not get along. I don't know why, exactly. It had a lot to do with childhood sibling rivalry. My sister, two years older, was the "beautiful" one. I was the homely, "smart" one. We competed for our mother's love. I guess we were still competing for it.

"I don't know why you can't be like your cousins," she sighed.

Oh, yes, our cousins, sisters — Paulette, Donna, Cathy, Marcella, and Gail. The Clarkin girls. They always got along. They were best friends, Mom reminded me. They helped each other out, did the housework for their mother without complaint, and loved each other. Unlike my sister and me, apparently.

"Well, Mom," I said. "Where you're going, maybe you can help us out there. Send down some love vibes from heaven or something."

She laughed and nodded. "Maybe I will," she said.

The next day, a bed became available at the palliative care unit where Mom planned to die.

Before she was transferred there, she gave my sister a shopping list. They were things she needed, she said.

I was jealous that she had given my sister this task and not me. Did she not trust me to fill it for her? Why Lois? Was she thriftier than me? Did she have better taste in drugstore amenities? Typical.

The things on the list, when I saw it later, were so very mundane that I found them jarring.

Deodorant. Razor blades. Toothpaste. Panties.

Panties? Who would think to order up new panties for their deathbed? I realized, though, that she wasn't dead yet. And, as long as you are alive, you don't actually think things like, "Oh, I won't need these panties because I'll be dead shortly." When you need panties, you need panties.

Tucked on the bottom of the list was written "Nail Polish — Pink."

The day she died, she woke up and told the nurse, "I'm going to die today." The nurse told us she said it very matter-of-factly. The nurse helped her to the washroom, and when Mom got back into bed, she began to fade away.

They called the family, and we all arrived at about the same time. It was a big family, and Mom waited until the last person had arrived before she allowed herself to go into a coma. At about noon, she was gone but for the heartbeat.

So, we all milled around her room, unsure of what to do. There was me, my sister, three brothers, my mother's ninety-two-year-old mother, my mother's three sisters, her brother, and various relatives who could not resist a gripping deathbed scene, including one or two of the angelic Clarkin sisters.

Mom was very popular in life and, apparently, just as popular in death.

A priest came in and performed last rites. We all perked up at this and vigorously prayed along with him. When he was done, we stood around her bed, all seventeen to twenty of us, staring expectantly down at her, waiting for her to die on cue.

She did not.

Her heart kept beating.

Her sisters decided to sing to her. So, they rounded up the various relatives and hangers-on and arranged them choir-like about her bedside again. They took part in a joyful and heartfelt round of "Amazing Grace." Then, again, we awaited the last breath. It did not come.

So, we all awkwardly stood around, taking turns feeling her arms and legs and even taking her pulse occasionally, like we were medics or something. We tried talking to her, telling her it was okay to let go, that we were good with it.

Still, she did not go.

"It's her heart," the nurse said. "It's only a fifty-three-year-old heart. It's still strong. It doesn't want to stop beating."

After about five hours of this, people started to feel somewhat dejected. They began to realize that death would come when it came, and we had no control over it.

Slowly, people began to fade away, going to pick up their loved ones at work or school, to check in at the office, wherever they had to go.

At around 5:00 P.M., only the immediate family was left. Dad decided it was time to take Gram down to the cafeteria to get something to eat.

"We'll stay here with her," my sister said. I agreed.

It was dark in the room, only a lamp on for light. My sister pulled up a chair on Mom's right, and I pulled one up on her left.

We sat there, examining her.

"Let's paint her nails," my sister said, lifting up one of Mom's hands.

"Oh, yes," I said. "Let's! She's got new nail polish."

We giggled as we riffled through her drawer, laughing about the various items on her list before we got to "Nail Polish - Pink."

Since Mom got cancer, she was able to have nice nails for the first time in her life. Too sick to work, she could grow her nails and have glamorous hands to match her glamorous face and body. She used to talk about it all the time.

But now, we realized, her nails were a little chipped and in need of a fresh coat.

"We'll paint them so she can have pretty nails in her coffin," my sister said.

So, we went to work, she on the right hand and I on the left, painting her nails for her coffin.

While we were doing it, we were laughing, sharing what we, and only we, knew about our mother's vanity, and giggling about how we were going to preserve it.

We were just finishing up when we both noticed it at the same time.

"She's stopped breathing," my sister said.

"Oh, my God, she has," I said.

We both stood up and leaned over, my sister on the right and I on the left.

"She's gone," we said.

She was. Her heart had finally stopped beating.

She had decided to die when my sister and I were alone with her, enjoying each other's company and painting her nails for her coffin.

"Love vibes from heaven," I whispered.

At her wake, many people noted how glamorous and elegant she looked in the clothes my sister and I had picked out, together, for her to wear.

And everyone commented on how beautiful her nails were.

— Barb McKenna —

Chapter

9

How Did That Happen?

83

A Blessed Encounter

It was possible that a miracle was not something that
happened to you, but rather something that didn't.
~Jodi Picoult, The Tenth Circle

Unlike my soft-hearted wife, I do not give money to panhandlers. But on hot summer days, I offer them bottled water, which, admittedly, is not always well received. In spite of a few choice words being hurled my way for the effort (along with the occasional water bottle), I still do it.

But this day, it was different.

He was standing at the street's edge, near the exit from the grocery store's parking lot, cardboard sign in hand. There was a line of cars ahead of me, and I began steeling myself for the feelings of guilt that would surely arise as I got closer, fumbling for the unopened bottle of water I kept handy in the cup holder for just such an occasion.

But, like I said, this day was different.

First, there was his appearance. He stood erect, projecting an air of confidence. His white shirt was spotless, almost as if it had just been laundered. He was clean-shaven, with his long silver hair pulled back into a ponytail.

And he was smiling.

As the cars before me slowly pulled into the street, I inched forward. When I got close enough, I read the sign he was holding: "As you do to the least of these," it said, written in bold lettering.

While not a regular churchgoer — okay, a seldom-if-ever churchgoer, much to my wife's chagrin—I knew the rest of the saying, my parents having mandated compulsory Sunday school attendance in my youth. "As you do to the least of these, you have done to me."

But there was something else. Two words, below the saying: "*gaz fuite.*"

I was fairly sure the words were French but struggled with their meaning. My two years of high-school French were long behind me.

But there was no time to dwell on this as he was now standing directly next to my car.

I rolled down the window, water bottle in hand, and offered it to him.

"Thank you for your kindness," he said with genuine appreciation, "but someone else may need that more than I do. God bless you."

And that was it. No indignation for being offered water. No plea for money. Nothing.

A car behind me honked, so I pulled into the street and headed home.

I kept thinking about the man, his sign, his refusal of the water and the fact that he hadn't asked for anything. It was almost as if his presence was more for my benefit than for his own.

And those two words.

I pulled into the driveway and approached the side door. That's when it hit me. *Gaz.* It was French for gas. Not petroleum but the liquid kind. The kind that provides heat.

I pulled out my phone and did a quick French-to-English search of the word, which confirmed it for me. But what about the second word? *Fuite.* I did another quick search. When I read the result, a cold, prickly sensation crept up my spine. It translated as "leak."

I had my key out, ready to insert it in the lock, but now I hesitated. Leaning into the slender crack between the door and the door jamb, I sniffed.

The familiar odor of rotten eggs, associated with natural gas, flooded my senses.

"Oh, my God!" I exclaimed to myself. "There's a gas leak!"

I called the emergency number for our gas company and was

assured they'd send someone right out. In the meantime, I found the main shut-off for the natural gas at the meter, located the valve and turned it off. Next, I went around to the back of the house and pried open a tiny window in our bathroom.

The gas company arrived with lights flashing. They surveyed the scene and asked what had tipped me off.

"Well, you won't believe this, but…"

I told them the whole story about the man at the grocery store, the sign, and how I had hesitated when about to unlock the door.

"You're lucky you didn't try to open it," one of the workers commented.

"Why is that?"

"Anything that can cause a spark, even static electricity, could have ignited the gas. Simply putting your key into the lock and turning it could have set off an explosion."

With the house secure, I called my wife and told her what had happened. She listened silently as I recalled the whole story, and when I finished, she said in a quiet, faraway voice, "I know you don't believe in things like this, but I think you've just had an encounter with an angel."

I didn't argue. It was clear that something amazing had happened, and I had no ready explanation for it.

"But why write me a message in French," I posed to my wife, "instead of English?"

"Did the fact that it was written in French make you think about it, wonder about it and hesitate?"

"Yes."

"If it had been written in English," she continued, "you might have simply dismissed it as the musings of an eccentric man in the grocery store parking lot." She paused and then said the words I knew were coming next. "You need to go back to that parking lot."

"I was thinking the same thing."

I parked outside the store and began my search, first starting with the parking lot itself and then circling around the grocery store. I didn't really expect to find the man, and I didn't.

But I found his sign near the spot where he had been standing at street's edge.

And here's the thing — the truly amazing thing. The words "as you do to the least of these" were there, just like they had been before. But the words that I had read below them, "*gaz fuite*," were not.

It only made sense — because those two words weren't meant for anyone else.

The angel had meant them for me.

— Dave Bachmann —

A Fortunate Mishap

Timing in life is everything.
~Leonard Maltin

One quiet afternoon, I was walking home from the library with a half-dozen books nestled securely in my arm. Suddenly, I felt someone bump my arm, and all the books I was holding tumbled to the ground. I looked around, but there was no one within half a block of where I was. I shrugged in bewilderment and tried to tell myself that I must have imagined it. But I wasn't convinced because I definitely felt something bump me, and I knew I had had a firm grip on the books.

I took a few seconds to gather up the books and then continued on my way. I had hardly taken two steps when suddenly, just in front of me, a car jumped the sidewalk and smashed into a storefront — exactly where I would have been if I hadn't dropped the books.

An elderly gentleman had been attempting to park in front of the store, but he got confused and stepped on the gas pedal instead of the brake. The storefront with its new Buick-sized hole was going to require some major reconstruction, and the car was totaled, but no one was injured.

It still gives me chills to realize that at the pace I had been walking, I would have been right in front of the store when the accident happened. My guardian angel was definitely watching out for me that day!

— Teri Tucker —

The Green Balloon

We should pray to the angels,
for they are given to us as guardians.
~St. Ambrose

We started the day near Fisherman's Wharf. The children could not get enough of the sea lions there — their big brown bodies piled on top of one another, rolling over on occasion to take a dip or find a fish, but otherwise lumped together, whisker-to-whisker, incessantly barking. We were regaled by the kids' imitations of the barking for the remainder of the trip and by their endless fits of laughter.

I think back now to how little the three of them were on that trip, ranging from seven to four. Their blond hair was always a mess and created a halo around their heads in the sunshine. There were always vestiges of food on their faces, no matter how hard I tried to keep them clean. Their hands were always dirty because touch was a key way they explored the world. The dry feel of fine sand through tiny fingers, the sting of salt water on a cut, the stickiness of saltwater taffy on tiny mouths, and the soft wisp of a stray feather on chubby cheeks were portals to the heart of San Francisco for them.

They were awestruck by so many simple things in the city, a revelation that still fills my heart, and I try to emulate in my daily life. We spent hours not only watching the sea lions, but also trailing pigeons whose bobbing heads and plump bodies were endlessly enthralling; scarfing down a late breakfast of hot dogs from a cart, which was lauded as the epitome of epicurean delight; and, pressing our noses to the windows of Boudin to watch the bakers knead and create animals from sourdough.

We didn't have to spend much money on entertainment, except when we came across a balloon vendor near the Golden Gate Bridge. Everyone wanted a balloon. They were fabulously overblown and perfectly round, attached to colored string and available in every color of the rainbow. After buying three balloons, we walked away. Shortly thereafter, the older two children let go of theirs. We watched them drift up into the blue sky and disappear. "Someone in heaven will get a balloon now," my youngest said.

Of course, she had no intention of anyone in heaven getting her balloon and held onto it with determination. Her elfin face carried a smile of spectacular proportion as we walked toward the bridge and gaped at its suspended wonder. As we headed back to the wharf, the giant green balloon trailed devotedly behind her. She would periodically look up at it, give it a few tugs, bring it down to her face and kiss it, then punch it at her brother and sister. She was totally enamored.

As the afternoon began to fade, we decided to take a cable car back to our hotel. The sun was mellowing and cast a celestial glow across the city. We huddled together on a crowded platform in the middle of a broad and busy street to wait for the next car's arrival.

My daughter had begun to play with her balloon, tossing it into the air and catching it again in the golden haze of the afternoon. Without warning, the green balloon seemed to break free and was lured into a gentle breeze. It twirled and danced in the air above her head as she jumped and toddled after it. In a moment that was simultaneously in slow motion and at warp speed, the balloon wafted over the street as four lanes of cars started up at a green light. I began to shout, telling my daughter to stop, while pushing my way through to her. The crowd on the platform released a loud, collective gasp as it foresaw tragedy.

But then, as quickly as the balloon had veered into the dangerous territory over the street, it switched direction and was over the middle of the platform again, my daughter pivoting obliviously after it. The crowd emitted a collective sigh that was immediately followed by the melody of my daughter's giggles.

I finally seized her and the balloon, hugging both to my pounding chest. She struggled to get free, pushed my hands away, and said, "Douglas wants to keep playing!" Confused, I looked at her and voiced my concern that she'd almost run into a busy street, but she countered with innocent incredulity, "Douglas knew that and bopped it back to me."

I asked her who Douglas was, and she guilelessly said, "My guardian angel, silly!" And that was that. There was no hesitation in her answer. Douglas had been there the entire time. We boarded the cable car a few minutes later, all of us safe, some of us relieved, and the youngest of us inspiring a fullness of faith in our unseen protectors.

— Courtney Essary Messenbaugh —

Cosmic Chiropractor

Miracles come in moments. Be ready and willing.
~Dr. Wayne Dyer

During my childhood, my family moved nine times. Our belongings seemed to magically appear in our new house while I was at school. As an adult, I moved thirteen more times. My company sent in a crew that whirled through the house making everything disappear into stacks of crates and wardrobes. Because of a back injury, I was told my job was to stay out of their way. All I had to pack were the clothes and personal items we needed to travel by car the next day.

This time, though, I was in charge of the packing with help from my daughter Valerie. The moving truck was scheduled for Friday, so I had to be ready to drive north on Saturday. Val was staying behind for two weeks to finish the term at the junior college. She was not looking forward to roughing it with a mattress in an empty house.

It was a stressful decision to leave Miami after seventeen years. I had a secure, fulfilling job in the public schools with congenial co-workers and many wonderful friendships. But I was excited about my new position as the first art therapist at a holistic, residential head-injury rehabilitation center in Tennessee. Moving from warm, sunny Florida to living in cold, snowy country again was going to be a challenge.

I sat on the floor packing boxes of memorabilia that reminded me of the wonderful events and experiences I'd shared with so many friends: canoeing in the Everglades, going on spiritual retreats, and volunteering on community art projects with co-workers.

Feeling stress in my back, I got up and poured a cup of tea. I did some stretches and looked out the glass door at a mama duck with her babies passing on the canal. Tears welled up in my eyes thinking about the gathering of friends I was going to see the next evening to say goodbye. We'd been a great team, planning and developing kids' educational peace events together.

After a few hours of packing, physically and emotionally exhausted, I relaxed on the sofa with a glass of wine. Remembering a dream from the night before that kept haunting me, I headed upstairs to record it before going to bed. I reached down to the floor to pick up my dream journal next to my bed and… *Ouch!*

A searing pain flashed from side to side across my lower back. Within seconds, my whole back spasmed and became stiff. I couldn't bend over!

My mind raced through the long list of things that needed to be done the next day. I didn't have time to see my chiropractor.

I shuffled to the bathroom, found my prescription painkiller and, bracing my hands on the nightstand, painfully eased into bed.

I lay awake taking deep breaths to relax my body and give the meds time to kick in. I couldn't stop thinking about my next day's schedule. I knew all I needed was a chiropractic adjustment, but I really didn't have time.

I slept fitfully, waking now and then stiff with pain, agonizing over how I was going to get everything done. I finally fell asleep wondering if the chiropractor could squeeze me in early.

Suddenly, I felt two hands gently grasp my spine and twist, each turning in the opposite direction. Twice!

The creaking sound in my head was so loud that it woke me up. Was I dreaming? Did that really happen? The image of the two hands was vivid in my mind. I was accustomed to having intense and sometimes prophetic dreams. But the physical feeling was new.

I stayed still for several minutes, processing what had happened. Carefully, I moved to a sitting position, stood and inched my way to the bathroom.

No pain! It was entirely gone.

In a daze and completely baffled, I eased back into bed and fell asleep, exhausted.

The next morning, unsure if I'd dreamt the whole thing, I took time moving my legs, then my arms and body.

Oh, my God! Absolutely no pain, even when I bent over very carefully.

I moved with caution while I dressed and walked downstairs for my morning coffee, anxious that one wrong motion would result in pain again. Throughout the day, I struggled to focus on getting things on my to-do list completed, often distracted by lucid images and sounds in my mind of the mystical night visitor's healing hands. I was awed by my miraculous healing.

That night, I relaxed and enjoyed the special time with my friends at the farewell party, not yet ready to tell anyone about my mysterious visitor who I began to think of as my Cosmic Chiropractor.

— Maryann Hamilton —

Wake Up

Our angel friends watch over us when we're asleep
at night and guard us with their gentle wings
until the morning light.
~Author Unknown

My fiancé John and I were taking a long trip by van from St. Louis, Missouri, to Inglewood, California. He had graduated only a month earlier from a junior college with an associate's degree in music.

John and I had attended the same college and formed a band called Axis. All the band members were in the same piano class. We practiced together almost every day and even went to church together.

After graduation, John and I decided we would go to California, break into the music world, and become rich and famous. We were convinced we had what it took to turn music into gold. I had friends in California who said we could stay with them until we found our own apartment. John had already lined up a job to support us until our music careers were established.

"Wow," said John. "It's so hot it's making me sleepy. I think I'll pull over at the next rest stop and take a break."

"Sounds good to me," I said. "I have to go to the bathroom, and maybe we could have a snack. I packed all kinds of goodies for us." We had been driving all day and were entering New Mexico from Texas.

We rested, ate snacks and resumed our trip on the "Yellow Brick Road" to California. The sun was beginning to set as we drove away from the rest stop.

"Oh, my goodness! This sunset is gorgeous! I have never seen anything like it," I exclaimed.

"We'll be seeing sunsets like this all the time now," said John.

We pulled over at the next gas station, which was about ten miles down the road.

As we were leaving the gas station, we saw a hitchhiker. To my astonishment, John pulled over and offered the guy a ride.

"Thank you, man," said the hitchhiker to John. "You're a lifesaver. My car broke down, and I don't have the money to repair it. I decided hitchhiking as far as I can was my only option."

"You're quite welcome," said John. "My name is John, and this is my fiancée, Alice. We're headed to California. Where are you going?"

"My name's David. I'm also going to California. I'm taking a vacation to see my parents," said the hitchhiker as he got into the back of the van.

"Where do your parents live in California?" asked John, yawning loudly.

"They live in Palm Springs," said David.

"We're going to Inglewood," said John. "We're musicians and are hoping to find gigs in California. We've traveled all the way from St. Louis."

The two guys talked back and forth for a while. The hitchhiker looked harmless and seemed very nice. He wore a bandana, jeans and a T-shirt. His hair was not too long, and he had a friendly smile. Yet, I was still leery of picking up a stranger. John, on the other hand, seemed at ease. He was very kindhearted and a free spirit. He was also very good at karate. I always felt safe with him. I finally relaxed and began to doze off. It was now twilight. The sun had gone down completely.

"Hey, man, you want me to drive?" asked David.

"Okay," said John. "I could use a fifteen-minute power nap!" John pulled over and switched places with the hitchhiker. I was not quite awake and not quite asleep when this switcheroo happened.

Sometime later, I dozed off completely. Suddenly, I heard a loud voice saying to me, "Wake up, wake up, wake up!" I awakened as we were skidding off the side of the road at a high speed. Instinctively, I reached over and grabbed the wheel and guided the van back onto the road. If I had not been awakened at that time by the loud, insistent voice, I'm not sure if I would be alive to tell this story. The hitchhiker had fallen asleep at the wheel! John had been asleep in the back seat when the near catastrophe occurred.

"Oh, my God!" said the hitchhiker as he awakened, visibly shaken. He brought the vehicle to a stop and parked it on the side of the road. "I am so sorry. I must have dozed off, too. That was some quick reaction time on your part!"

"I heard someone saying very loudly, 'Wake up, wake up, wake up!'" I said, shaking uncontrollably from fright.

"I didn't hear anyone say anything," said John from the back seat.

"I didn't hear anyone either," said David.

"Well, I did. It was a very loud voice clearly saying, 'Wake up, wake up, wake up!' If I hadn't heard that voice, I'm sure we'd all be dead or injured," I said.

And that was my first angel encounter.

— Alice Potts —

Angel Boy

*And, when you want something, all the universe
conspires in helping you to achieve it.*
~Paulo Coelho, The Alchemist

When my daughter was two years old, we brought her to one birthday party after another for all the little children in a moms' group I was in. Many of the moms were newly pregnant with their second babies, but I was still getting used to being a parent to my little girl. I loved spending time with her, and I couldn't imagine anything or anyone interfering with that time. I had had a hard time getting pregnant. I had also had a hard time staying pregnant, and my pregnancy was challenging. I wasn't ready to face any of that again. I was still soaking in the miracle that I had a child at all.

We did want our daughter to have a sibling; it just took me a while to be ready to try again. When we finally did decide to try, I anticipated it taking a while. We were pleasantly surprised to conceive on our first try. I began to imagine this little being growing inside me and wondered what it would be like to walk around hand in hand with not one but two children. I fantasized about strapping them both into car seats, taking them on trips together, and singing songs loudly on the way.

Around six weeks along, though, I started to feel the way I did with my daughter's pregnancy. When I told the doctor, they suggested a new medicine to try. I wanted to give it a bit more time to see how

I felt. At the nine-week appointment, we heard the baby's heartbeat and saw the cute little body growing. But since I wasn't feeling any better, we decided to give the medication a try.

It worked right away in that I felt much better. I was excited to be able to feel well enough to be present with my daughter. My enthusiasm was short-lived, though. When I went back for the twelve-week ultrasound, there was no heartbeat. I was devastated. Having a miscarriage is not uncommon, and despite the high number of pregnancies that result in one, it didn't make me feel any less alone. The next morning, as reality began to sink in, I felt fractured, lost, and less than the woman I was the day before. I had felt the identity of being a mother to a baby who would no longer be, so I didn't know how to lay to rest that part of my heart.

When I was pregnant with my daughter, my husband and I didn't know her gender until she was born. We had come up with the name Gabriel if it was a boy, and although I loved the name, my husband wasn't convinced it was for us. We didn't have any number-two choices, though. The night I went into labor, in the middle of a contraction, my husband said, "I don't love the boy's name." I reminded him that I couldn't talk about it at that moment. We never needed to revisit the conversation, though, because we had a girl. Since he never loved the boy's name, I asked him if we could use it for the baby we lost. He agreed. Having a name could help me heal, and saying goodbye to Gabriel was not easy, but I made peace with it knowing we could try again.

A few months later, my husband asked me if I liked the name Rafael. He had met someone through work with the name, and since he liked the name and the person he worked with, he wondered what I thought of it. I loved it. When I got pregnant again, we waited to find out the gender. We kept Rafael a secret from anyone other than each other.

One day, while I was parked outside my daughter's preschool waiting to pick her up, a friend whom I hadn't talked to in a while called to catch up. I told her I had had a miscarriage, that I had named the baby Gabriel, and that I was pregnant again. She wished me well for the pregnancy but also wished for healing from my loss. She has always been a very spiritual person, so she asked if she could pull some cards from a deck that had spiritual messages on them. I was curious, so I had her read them to me over the phone. They were a deck of angel cards. She read me a bit about the angel Gabriel. She used the words guardian and strength. I thought about my Gabriel and imagined the words to be describing him, and it made me smile. Then, without me saying a word, she began to read me another card. This time, it was about the angel Rafael. She went on to say that he is the angel who heals — and the angel who comes after Gabriel.

She knew nothing about the name we had picked if we had a boy. She also had no idea if our baby would even be a boy, but the words she read left me in awe. I lifted my hand to my belly to acknowledge the healing the baby had already provided me with. I didn't tell her that Rafael was the name we had chosen for a boy. I just thanked her because the message meant a lot to me.

A few months later, when I gave birth to a healthy baby boy, we named him Rafael. My daughter held him in her arms for the first time and sang his name over and over. "Rafael, Rafael, Rafael." She took his tiny hand in hers and continued singing to him. Our family was finally complete. It was not an easy journey, but I was so relieved we had arrived. I was thrilled to let my friend know that when she had read my cards months before, we had already picked out the name Rafael. And she was right: He was the healing angel.

— Shea Bart Andreone —

The Palm Tree

When you live your life with an appreciation of
coincidences and their meanings, you connect
with the underlying field of infinite possibilities.
~Deepak Chopra

We all heard her screaming for help, and the six of us turned to see where the screams were coming from. But that part of the Florida Everglades was so thick with jungle-like vegetation that seeing anything beyond thirty or forty feet was almost impossible.

It was late December 1972. While working with the police in Virginia, right outside of Washington, D.C., I had been attending a law-enforcement training program in Miami with four colleagues, just days after Christmas. We were planning to return to Virginia the next day, right before New Year's Eve.

But there were loud knocks on our hotel-room doors as the Miami police requested assistance in their recovery efforts due to an Eastern Airlines airplane crashing right into the heart of the nearby alligator-infested waters of the Everglades.

Within minutes, the five of us were dressed and running for the waiting patrol cars of the Miami Police Department. Not long afterward, we were assigned to a large airboat located in a staging area several miles within that endless swamp. The driver quickly started the motor, and the enormous propeller began spinning invisibly in the dark night.

We traveled at breakneck speed in and around countless tributaries, soon arriving at the smoldering wreckage of the enormous airliner. It seemed to cover a very large area of the swamp, perhaps a half-mile across, but it was still dark out and impossible to be sure. There were several fires still burning, and, with our motor turned off, we started to hear the shouts of survivors, some barely clinging to life.

Most of the passengers and crew had tragically perished in that awful crash, but, after almost twenty-four hours of searching, we and countless other airboat police officers had rescued more than sixty people, and we weren't about to stop looking. Rescue helicopters had been hovering above us for almost the entire time and airlifted countless survivors to area hospitals. But now, as it grew dark again, the numerous helicopters couldn't safely be flown in and out of the area.

Using our spotlights to see in the dark, we slowly scanned the entire area at one end of that enormous crash site, but we couldn't find anyone else. The police radio did confirm that a few other survivors had been rescued, and many bodies had been recovered. Our motor was shut off again, and we slowly drifted around in circles, hoping against hope that we would see or hear someone. The only sounds we heard came from countless insects, and we smelled the occasional odor of burning materials. As we approached the thirty-hour mark, and as almost all our cans of gasoline had been used up, we received a call over the police radio to cease our search and return to the staging area. Reluctantly, we did as ordered and were soon speeding back.

But then, when we were more than a mile from the crash site, we heard those screams for help. Her voice was so high-pitched! Our airboat driver instantly shut off the motor, and we drifted to a stop. The six of us turned to see where the screams were coming from. Using the spotlights again, we looked all around but only saw the thick vegetation.

"Hello!" one of my associates shouted, but there was no reply.

Using two oars, we silently drifted around but didn't hear anything else. Yet we had heard a woman's frantic cry for help, so someone was obviously alive, and we weren't about to give up.

"Hello!" the officer shouted again, but there was still nothing.

About twenty minutes later, as we drifted in increasingly large circles with our spotlights shining through the pitch-black darkness of the night, we came upon a tiny, raised mound of earth, almost like a small island no larger than twenty feet in diameter. And it contained one severely bent-over palm tree, the top of it almost touching back down to the water's edge.

On the upper half of the palm tree's limb was a young woman, maybe thirty years of age, and her arms were tightly wrapped around the trunk of that tree. Several alligators were in the dark waters close to the base of that tree.

"Help me," she said in almost a whisper. "Please, help me."

The driver stayed in the airboat, but two of us were quickly up that tree. While the other three stood underneath, we gently lowered her into their waiting arms. Within minutes, we had her safely in the boat with us as we sped back to the staging area.

We then helped the rescue squad carry her to one of the waiting ambulances.

"Were they still there?" she asked in a quiet voice.

"Was who there?" I replied.

She touched my left forearm and said, "The angels… the ones who put me up in that tree."

I was stunned, unable to say anything. She smiled at us as they closed the rear doors to the ambulance.

Several days after our New Year's Eve celebrations back in Virginia, we learned that the young woman had fully recovered and was uninjured, aside from being dehydrated. And I, to this day, believe that, for whatever reasons, she was carried by angels for over a mile from the smoldering wreckage of that airliner and placed safely up in that palm tree. And I also have to believe that the six of us in that airboat were placed there at that exact moment in time. I can't explain any of it, but I do believe it.

— John Elliott —

90

Angelic GPS

Alone is impossible in a world inhabited by angels.
~Author Unknown

I was twenty-three years old, visiting my younger cousin in Mexico City. After a night out partying, my cousin decided to head home early because she had school in the morning.

"Stay!" my cousin insisted. "You're on vacation. Have fun!"

She didn't have a hard time convincing me. I was having a good time and not ready to call it a night. She left. I stayed. After all, I had made friends at the club.

At some point during the midnight hours, I was buzzed and decided it was time to leave. At that point, I had a big problem. I remembered I had stashed my phone and money in my cousin's bag. Also, I had no clue what her address was.

For some weird reason, I didn't panic. I was full of alcohol… and full of myself. My mind was made up. There I was, on my own, no cash, no phone, no address, in a city I barely knew, climbing into a taxicab in the dead of night in a dress and high heels. Thankfully, I could speak Spanish.

I hesitantly greeted the driver. "Um, hello."

"Where to, señorita?"

He had a friendly demeanor. Frowning, I told him I didn't have an answer. Not a real one anyway. I explained my cousin lived in a particular neighborhood in the city.

That was all I knew.

The driver looked at me, puzzled.

It was a long drive, and I didn't exactly give him any way of knowing where I was going, except the name of the district where my cousin lived. *What a horrible position to put a cab driver in,* I thought to myself. *Who gets in a cab without knowing where they're going?* I had no doubt he would pull over and put me out by the side of the road. I didn't really give him much of a choice. This was completely my fault.

The taxi driver could've easily asked me to exit his vehicle. I expected that. I was wasting his time. Cabbies in Mexico work for extremely little as it is.

"Don't worry, señorita," he said with a smile. "We'll figure it out together."

Despite the warning flags, I trusted my life to a stranger. I trusted this strange man to drive me around a strange city and get me safely to my cousin's house.

"That's where my cousin lives!" I shouted as we randomly drove past one street.

How in the world did I find my cousin's house in a sprawling metropolis with over twenty-one million people? I don't know. A miracle. It didn't make sense.

My cousin was shocked to see me at her door. "Oh, my God! I forgot I had your things. I went back to the club to look for you! Are you okay? Where have you been? How did you get here?"

I shrugged.

My cousin lent me some money, and I proceeded to thank and pay the taxi driver.

Ten years later, I think about that day often. It's the day my guardian angel swooped in and guided the taxicab like an invisible hand. There's no other explanation. I put myself in a dangerous situation, and something horrible could have happened to me. But my guardian angel always looks out for me. I will always believe that.

— Mariely Lares —

91

The Little Angel

Goodbyes are only for those who love with their eyes.
Because for those who love with heart and soul
there is no such thing as separation.
~Rumi

My passion for photography took on a new intensity when we found out my husband's cancer was terminal. I wanted to capture every moment of the time we had left so that I could relive those precious final days forever.

Larry was very patient with me. Many days, he was sick from chemotherapy or in pain from the devastating disease, but that never stopped him from helping me with my need to preserve memories.

Even our visitors were subjected to flashes going off in their faces as I carefully captured their interactions with Larry. The grandkids would stop in their tracks and robotically paste on smiles when I was snapping away.

We'd moved our bed into the living room since Larry could no longer manage the stairs to and from the bedroom. I wanted him to continue to be included in our everyday family life. I took photos of the grandkids sitting on the bed next to Grandpa, telling him about their day.

This was before I'd switched to a digital camera, so I was still sending out film to be developed. I recorded when each photo was taken on a calendar so I could put them in chronological order and print the dates beneath the pictures in the album.

On the day Larry began to slip into unconsciousness and we knew his time was short, I chose not to take any more pictures. He deserved to die with relative privacy in the home he loved without the intrusion of a camera's constant flashing. I promised myself that I wouldn't load another roll of film, and the camera was put away.

Our five children were with us on the afternoon that Larry passed. During those powerful moments as he transitioned from his earthly life, I watched our children comfort Larry and each other. Although the scene was priceless, I kept my promise not to take another photo.

Following Larry's death, I began to regret my decision to forgo picture-taking on our last day together. The photos would have helped give me closure.

Several months later, while cleaning the bedroom upstairs that our two preteen grandsons shared, I found a roll of film under the bed, trapped between the wall and the bedpost. Assuming the boys must have thought it was lost and had forgotten about it, I wanted to surprise them by getting it developed.

While running some errands a few days later, my daughter and I stopped by to pick up the pictures. Back in the car, we couldn't resist taking a quick peek.

Stunned is not a strong enough word to describe what we felt upon seeing the photos! Tears rolled down Jacqui's cheeks as she stared at the photo of her and her father together in those cherished last moments.

There were five photos in the envelope, each capturing a precious memory of Larry with one or more of our five kids and me on that final day. When I looked at the negatives, all the rest were blank.

The mystery remains unsolved as to how the photos appeared on that roll of film. I know without a doubt that none of us in the room during that time had access to a camera, and my grandsons were not at the house on that final day. Everyone agreed it had to be some type of divine intervention.

I recalled Larry speaking often of a little girl frolicking gaily about the living room, peeking out from behind the furniture or from under the large dining room table. He wanted me to take a photo of her, but when I told him I couldn't see her, he didn't seem surprised. I've always pictured her to look like one of those whimsical, delicate-winged fairy figurines.

As I added the new photos to my album and reminisced about those final days, I felt blessed to have captured (with a little help) and forever preserved a bittersweet moment in time filled with unconditional love and smiles.

Larry would be proud and happy to know that I was able to complete the album with no regrets about the conclusion. As for me, I have to smile every time I wonder, "How did that sweet little angel pull off this priceless miracle?"

— Connie Kaseweter Pullen —

92

A Daughter by Another Name

Being a daddy's girl is like having permanent armor
for the rest of your life.
~Marinela Reka

"That's my Toots," Dad would say with a proud smile. It usually came when I did something to excite him — like performing well at a track meet or standing up for myself at work. It was only when I was in trouble that he'd use my real name. Otherwise, I was his Toots.

In May 2014, he was diagnosed with colon cancer. It came after months of worsening indigestion and nausea, what we thought then might have been food poisoning or the flu. It would be nearly a year later that cancer would take his life.

The day started with a rush of phone calls and ended in a haze of hurried decisions. That morning, he was hardly speaking, slipping somewhere between the now and the ever after as nurses urged us to say our goodbyes. If someone shouted, he'd rouse momentarily, but as I stood there pleading quietly to him, wishing only for some response that I wouldn't get, I wondered if he'd heard me at all.

In the months he fought, he didn't consider defeat, but it gave us time to explore his wishes, which he would divulge with a joke, but also with enough sincerity for us to know that he meant it. Most importantly, he wanted to be cremated, and for us to put some of his ashes in the floorboards of his favorite venue so he could still be part of the fun.

That place was in a town on a small island off the coast of Ohio where we'd spent our summers growing up. We'd take boat trips there as a family. It was our version of camping, sleeping tightly in the cabin under the stars at sea, falling asleep to the soft lap of water against the hull as we floated in the marina. Each summer, we'd travel with friends from port to port. We'd make a stop at Cedar Point amusement park for us kids to ride roller coasters, spend a few days at Maumee to relax and take in the nature trails, and finally visit Put-in-Bay where we would swim at the yacht-club pool and get ice cream while our parents watched live bands at their favorite haunts along the perimeter of the park.

Two years after I lost my father, my best friend invited me to go with her family back to that island. We had spent those summers boating from place to place with them, and the branches of our family trees had long since intertwined. I still felt steeped in my grief, and I agonized over going for the first time without my mom and brother along to deliver Dad's ashes. But, beneath that, there was an aching pull to connect with somewhere that contained so many happy memories.

It wasn't until we got to the island, and were seated at a restaurant, that the conversation turned to Dad. We reminisced about the many summers we spent there grilling burgers on the docks as the sun melted into Lake Erie, racing each other in golf carts across the island as we'd head out to explore its caves, and sitting on the boardwalk, enveloped in heat, eating lobster bisque. We recalled our trips across the water where he'd hammer the throttle with a childish grin, or the time the engine stalled and we bobbed beneath a storm while he was bent over banging around in the engine hatch.

I thought about how I couldn't set foot in the place he loved, and how hard it would be to come back to honor his last wish, despite how crazy it was. The hurt expanded inside me and left room for little else except the painful longing to know if he was still proud of me.

Finishing our drinks, I looked around. I could see the same horizon I remembered as a child stretching out through the windows, framed now by years of dollars pinned to the walls and ceiling that fluttered in the breeze. Over time, the owners encouraged guests to sign a dollar and leave a message — mark their time there — and left cups of magic markers and staple guns across the counter for anyone who wanted to add theirs.

There were thousands, perhaps tens of thousands, throughout the room — so much so that we could hardly see the worn wood paneling peek through.

I turned to my friend as she rummaged through her purse and pulled out a crisp dollar bill. We grabbed the markers and wrote it for my dad, for Keith, for him to always have a place here. We signed our names lovingly on the edges.

"Where should we put it?" she asked, handing the bill to me.

I leaned back, and as I looked up above my seat, one dollar hung free from the others with a single word in big block letters: TOOTS.

—Erin Hall—

Chapter 10

Miraculous Connections

You Are Important

Be thou the rainbow in the storms of life.
The evening beam that smiles the clouds away,
and tints tomorrow with prophetic ray.
~Lord Byron

I was sitting in the drive-through waiting to order my cup of motivation early one morning when I noticed a car in the parking lot. All the stores were closed and would be for hours. Maybe that's why it looked so strange there.

As I examined the little red car, I noticed the driver was reclined in the front seat, asleep. I assumed he was a traveler who had pulled off the nearby interstate for a nap.

A few days later, he was back. I resolved to bring him breakfast one morning. A few days later, I spotted his little red car and decided it was time. I drove across the street and ordered a bag of breakfast items. When I returned, the man was awake and sitting up in the front seat.

I was nervous. I felt my heart speeding up with each step I took toward his door. I noticed his car was full from floorboard to ceiling with clothing, blankets, trash and all kinds of things. He was a young man, maybe in his twenties. He had dark hair, dark features, and kind eyes.

"Good morning! I brought you some breakfast," I said. I extended the bag and cup holder toward him.

"Thank you so much! You are so kind. What made you want to do this today?"

The honest answer was guilt. I felt guilty sitting in that drive-through every day, waiting for my coffee while he slept in his car. I felt guilty for having the luxury of my latte habit and the job that afforded me a life that did not necessitate things like sleeping in my car in a well-lit parking lot.

Probably, this stemmed from my deeper guilt of leaving my family behind in rural Michigan to make a better life for myself, and being mostly absent from their daily struggles. I could've been the one sleeping in my car, but by some miracle, I wasn't. I had more than I needed and felt compelled to share my good fortune with this young stranger.

Instead, I said, "I want you to know that you are important, and your life matters. People care about you — even some you've never met. So, you have to take good care of yourself. Okay?"

"I don't know how to thank you…."

"Just pay it forward."

"I will. Thank you." He nodded.

"Have a great day," I said, turning to get back in my car.

I felt the lump in my throat growing. Where did that come from? By the time I closed my car door, tears were rolling down my cheeks. I was sure something bigger than me had spoken those words.

I repeated the message, "You are important. Your life matters. People care about you. Take good care of yourself."

After that day, I looked for my friend in the little red car every time I stopped for coffee, but I never saw him again. I never had the opportunity to bring him another hot breakfast, but our relationship was far from over.

For the next several weeks, I had to drive by a large construction site on my way to work each day. A sign went up advertising a new mega church. I Googled the church and found that it came with a price tag of $22 million. Less than two miles away from that church was the parking lot where the young man in the red car slept. The juxtaposition of these things infuriated me so much that I had to write about it.

In the article, I broke down $22 million into the number of meals our local homeless shelter could provide. I talked about how the big business of churches has all but negated the message of Christ, and how greed has gotten in the way of serving others.

I had been flirting with the idea of sending my work to publications for some time. Before clicking the Publish button on my WordPress site, I went to *Elephant Journal*'s homepage to read their submission requirements again. Something told me it was time to tiptoe out of my comfort zone.

Elephant Journal is an online magazine that I read voraciously while navigating a painful divorce and trying to figure out who I was. It was full of real stories written by real people who were going through their own struggles and sharing the wisdom gleaned from their experiences. I hoped that I would be the next real person with real questions about the world to join their ranks as a real, grown-up blogger.

A toned-down-a-bit version of my piece, "What Mega Churches Are Missing," became my first published article on *Elephant Journal*. When the editor sent me my published link, she said, "This is great writing. I can't wait to see more from you. Congratulations!"

I cried tears of joy for about three days after the article went live as people read it, sent me notes, commented, and shared it all over social media. The article was read over five thousand times, and even people who identified as Christian reached out to tell me how much my words had resonated with them.

This opened the door to my writing career.

Over the next three years, I would go on to publish more than one hundred articles. My face was added to the *Elephant Journal* homepage as a Featured Author, and it stayed there until I decided to branch out and send my work to other publications like *The Urban Howl* and *Medium*. I self-published my first book on Amazon, *Dysfunction Diaries* — a collection of short stories from my first blog.

That first article about the man in the red car changed my life in ways I never imagined. It gave me the opportunity to write about mental illness, sexual abuse, feminism, parenting, relationships, my marriage to a closeted gay man, and all kinds of current events. I was amazed at the ripple effect that happened as I shared my story. It healed me and so many others around me. It was a miracle.

Sometimes, I wonder if the man in the little red car was an angel sent here to help me find my voice, purpose and power. Sometimes, I wish I could share with him how my life changed after meeting him. Sometimes, I wonder what became of him, and I send love into the universe with wishes for his comfort, peace and prosperity.

I thought I was delivering a gift to someone in need that morning. Now, I understand I was the one receiving a gift. I still honor the man in the red car by making kindness kits for the homeless. Each bag includes some snacks, personal-care items, and a note that reads, "You Are Important." Grown men will see the words, place a hand to their chest, and ask, "Me?"

It brings me to tears every time.

— Renee Dubeau —

The Mug

Coincidence is God's way of remaining anonymous.
~Albert Einstein

At the end of 2020 — already a hard year — all three of our grown children moved away. My daughter and her husband relocated to a city only about four hours from us, but my two sons moved overseas to join a refugee-aid organization. We were proud of them, but it was very difficult.

It got harder in January when my younger son contracted COVID. During his illness — when he was constantly on my mind and in my prayers, when I couldn't be with him to take care of him, when I didn't know what quality of medical care he was receiving or even whether he was managing to make himself understood across the language barrier, when our other son might fall sick, too — my husband and I went out one day to do some shopping. We bought groceries and got gas. Then, in Dollar Tree, we split up, wandering around separately, lost in our own thoughts.

Something caught my eye. It was a mug — nothing fancy, nothing particularly unusual, nothing that matched my dishes or my decor or anything like that. It was just a random mug. But it called to me. I wanted it.

I didn't need it. We had plenty of mugs already — and fewer people living in our house — and I'm not much given to impulse purchases. But it only cost a dollar, and I'd been having such a hard time, worrying and trying not to worry, and the sight of that mug lifted my spirits.

When I saw my husband coming toward me, I figured he'd glance in my basket and remark that we didn't need another mug. Maybe I'd put it back, or maybe I'd get it anyway, though some of the fun would be gone. But when my husband reached me, he said, "I know we don't need more mugs, but I saw this and liked it, and I thought you might want to get it."

He was holding the same mug.

Fast forward two weeks to a long-awaited video call.

Though we'd had text updates, it had been quite some time since our last video call with our sons. Before our younger son had fully recovered from COVID, they'd had to move across the city to an unfurnished apartment that required complete outfitting. This involved buying and arranging delivery of a refrigerator, microwave and furniture — all in a foreign language. Then there was the Internet to sort out. Now, finally, we were able to see their faces and hear their voices. The relief I felt told me just how anxious I'd been.

Partway through the video call, our younger son — still a bit pale and thin — walked off screen to get a drink of water. He came back drinking from an item they'd bought while furnishing their new apartment.

It was the exact same mug.

Seven thousand miles apart, an ocean and a pandemic between us. A dollar store, a foreign market. But the song is true.

He really does have the whole world in his hands.

— Amanda W. —

95

The Little Girl

When you open your mind to the impossible,
sometimes you find the truth.
~From the television show, Fringe

"Mommy." The little voice rang through the house. "Mommy, come help me," the voice said. The plea came from the back of the house. "It's okay, honey," I said, just like I did a dozen times a day.

I folded the kitchen towel, shut off the light and headed to the bedroom.

"It's okay, honey," I said. "I'll be right there."

My husband looked up from where he sat, reading the paper on the living-room couch. Nicholas, our little boy, played with his toys on the hardwood floor while our Golden Retriever mix watched over him adoringly.

"Who are you talking to?" my husband asked.

I stopped on my way down the hallway. I was not sure how to answer that question.

"She is going to make sure that the little girl who lives here is okay," Nicholas explained in a matter-of-fact tone that only a four-year old could use to describe a ghost.

Jason looked from Nicholas to me. He shrugged and went back to reading the paper. I walked down the hallway and sat on the bed.

"It's okay, sweetheart," I crooned. "It's okay. I'm here."

The little voice stopped like it always did, and I felt peace roll back over our house. I sat there for a few minutes singing a lullaby that my grandma had always sung to me.

We were living in a little house in a subdivision not far from the Army base where my husband was stationed. It was just me, my husband, our little boy, and our dog. It did not take long before I started hearing the little voice. The first time it happened, I ran outside. I looked all around the house and yard, and looked up and down the street, but there was no little girl anywhere. There were no little girls who lived in the rented houses around us. When I stepped back inside, I could hear the little girl.

At first, I ignored the voice. But I realized quickly that if I answered the frightened little girl, the voice would stop. If I ignored the voice, the little girl would beg for her mother for hours, becoming more and more distraught. I would tell her everything was alright or sing her a lullaby and, somehow, some way, the voice would stop.

Nicholas could see and hear her. He would play with her and tell me if she was having a bad day. He said that she really liked it when I sang to her. Daisy could sense her presence, too. She would take her favorite toys to empty spots in the room, lay them down on the floor and then ask to be played with. Sometimes, she would wag her tail and stare intently at seemingly empty space.

It wasn't long before living with the little girl seemed normal.

To my husband, the situation seemed as if it was getting out of control.

One night, as we were getting ready for bed, he brought up the subject.

"I don't know if pretending there is a ghost in the house is very healthy for Nicholas," he said.

"We're not pretending," I replied.

Jason was a very factual person. He was a lifer in the Army and followed orders. To him, there was not anything he believed in if he couldn't see it.

He loved me and adored Nicholas, but that didn't mean he always understood us or believed the same things we did.

"You believe there is a ghost haunting this house?" he asked. "And only you, our toddler and our dog can see or hear it?"

I shrugged.

"It's not a ghost," I explained. "It is a little girl, and she needs us."

I may not have been able to explain everything that was going on, but I knew that was the truth.

One night, after spending most of the day outside, we were all tired. Nicholas was asleep on the couch, and Jason was helping to clean up a few dishes. He was washing, and I was drying. I reached over to take a plate from him.

"Mommy, can you come here?" I heard the little voice from the back of the house.

Jason suddenly looked at me in surprise.

"You heard her," I said.

"No," he denied too quickly. "I heard something."

"Mommy," the voice called again.

His eyes met mine at the exact same minute.

"Mommy," the little girl called.

Jason nodded and gestured toward the back of the house.

I hurried to the bedroom, sat on the bed and spoke with the little girl until she calmed down.

By the time I made it back into the living room, Jason was snuggling with Nick on the couch.

"I don't want to talk about it," he said.

But it didn't matter because we both knew he had heard something.

We lived happily in the little house for years. Eventually we had another little boy. Before he was two, the Army had assigned Jason to a new base. We would be moving in a couple of months. The move would put us closer to our families and help my husband's career, but what about the little girl?

I did not really know how all of this worked, but I guessed that the little girl was somehow attached to either this house or the land it was built on. My friend and I had tried to research something about the land the subdivision was built on or if there had ever been a little girl who had died here, but we never came up with anything.

The landlord had never had any of the tenants talk about a little girl haunting the house when they rented it, and neither had the previous owners. Maybe she could only connect with us. I could not bear the thought of leaving her.

I didn't know how to solve the problem, so I prayed. The more I prayed, the more I thought about my grandma. My dad's mom had lived with us when we were growing up. She had raised four boys, but she had always wished for a daughter. I started telling the little girl all about my grandma who was in heaven now and how maybe she could stay with her since we were moving.

About a week before we were scheduled to leave, the little girl's voice was silent. The house felt strangely different. Nicholas and Daisy were no longer playing with her. I asked Nicholas if he knew where the little girl was.

"She went to stay with Grandma just like you wanted," he said.

I had never mentioned to anyone what I had been praying for.

A few years later, I had another baby boy to complete our family, and I accepted wholeheartedly my identification as a boy mom.

People sometimes ask me if I had wanted a girl. I just shake my head, smile and say that my family was perfect just the way it is. In my heart, I did have a little girl, a little angel who is in heaven with my grandma.

— Theresa Brandt —

96

Love You, Brother

Angels live among us. Sometimes they hide their wings,
but there is no disguising the peace
and hope they bring.
~Author Unknown

I heard a voice saying to me, "John, we just woke you up. We are going to remove your ventilator. Relax; I promise it will be quick. You will have thirty seconds to breathe on your own. After that, if you are not breathing on your own, we will have to insert the ventilator again. We are going to keep your eyes taped closed until after the procedure. If you are able to breathe on your own, we will then remove the tape. You have been in an induced coma for ten days. It will take a while for your eyes to adjust, so don't panic if you can't see right away. Just relax, and I will be back in a few minutes to start."

While I was lying there, someone grabbed my right hand. I heard, "Hello, John. I'm Father John. I'm going to be with you while they remove the ventilator. If you feel any discomfort, just squeeze my hand. I promise it will all be over in a minute."

I remember it being quick and painless. Father John said, "Welcome back, brother. Good job, John. You're breathing on your own now. I'll be back later to check on you."

I remember thinking to myself, *Why do I know that voice?* It sounded so familiar, but I was in no state to try and figure it out.

I remember later I was moved to my own ICU room. I guess it

was because I was still positive with COVID. One of the nurses there recognized me. She began to sing a hymn to me and then prayed over me.

There had to be five or six nurses in the room. If you have never witnessed organized chaos before, it has a beautiful harmony about it. Everyone has their own task that they have to accomplish, and it is done without any hesitation. The timing and the movements are like watching a well-choreographed ballet.

There were vitals being taken, ports being adjusted, needles in my belly and the intravenous doing its thing. While all of this was going on, someone in the hall kept walking back and forth past the room.

He was dressed in regular hospital clothing — a skullcap, goggles and face shield — except he was also wearing a respirator with bright orange filters. He had bright orange gloves on his hands and bright orange booties on his shoes.

At one point, this person began jumping and waving his hands left and right. With whatever energy I had, I chuckled. One of the nurses asked what I was laughing at, so I gestured to the hallway. To my surprise, she didn't see anything.

This mystery person then came to the door of the room, stepped in and then stepped back out of the room. It seemed like he was testing the waters to see if anyone had noticed. Then, without hesitation, he walked into the room. This individual then walked through two nurses, walked around to my right side, and shook my hand.

I thought to myself, *Did I just see this person walk through those nurses?* He then stopped at the foot of my bed, turned around and got closer to me. Because of the bright lights in the room, I could not see his face. Then he said, "I told you I would come back to check on you." He hugged me and said, "Love you, brother," and then walked away. On his way out of the room, he walked through another nurse.

"Love you, brother." There was that voice again, but this time it clicked. It was my friend Vito, whom I had met a few years earlier. Both of us had served in the Marine Corps and became great friends. Every other Saturday, we would have breakfast together. As we left the diner, I would help him into his car, and we would always say, "Love you, brother," to each other.

A few years back, Vito had had a couple of stays in the hospital himself. I remember one time I wasn't sure if he would leave there on his own. Being a pastor, I asked him if he wanted to have confession. That was the fastest "Yes" I ever heard.

Vito was straight to the point and told me everything. He told me things I wasn't sure I wanted to hear, but I felt blessed that he trusted me. Being a World War II veteran, he once had to kill or be killed. That haunted him for decades. We both cried working through that one, and in the end he was able to let it go.

Actually, we laughed and cried through many of his confessions. It was awesome to see him set himself free. I took some anointing oil to restore his strength. It did, and he walked out of the hospital a few days later. We gave each other Communion with a couple of soup crackers and warm orange juice left over from breakfast.

The trust that we shared was very important to me. It is hard to find that today. Our friendship, camaraderie and wholesome fellowship will be cherished forever.

Vito passed a year and a half before I got COVID. I was there with Vito during his darkest hour. And now he had returned the favor—being there to hold my hand when they removed the ventilator and then coming back to check on me.

— Pastor John Esposito —

97

Forever Part of the Sea

*We do not create our destiny; we participate in its
unfolding. Synchronicity works as a catalyst
toward the working out of that destiny.*
~David Richo, The Power of Coincidence

"I sense the presence of a male spirit," the Navajo shaman whispered. "He is not here to do any harm. But he has a story...."

She closed her eyes and began speaking in a language foreign to me. Sitting across from her, I watched as she slowly moved her arms, which she had marked with red sand to protect herself against malevolent spirits that might be around.

I glanced at my living room table, now adorned with many small jars, pouches, and feathers of different sizes and colors that she had taken out of her medicine bag before she began performing the healing ritual.

"He is a man of the sea," she whispered, reclaiming my attention. "But..." She frowned, her eyes still closed. She tilted her head as if puzzled by what she had just learned, perhaps unsure as to what to reveal.

"He's forever part of the sea," she said all in one breath, her eyes now wide open.

I smiled.

"Do you know him?" she asked, surprised by my reaction.

I nodded. I had been feeling his presence for many months now.

"How did you meet him?" she asked.

"That's a long story," I said, looking away into the distance.

Brian and I had never met, but I feel like we are old friends. The first time I learned about him was two days after his sudden and tragic death. It was morning, and as my two children were still dreaming peacefully in their beds, I sat down on the couch in my living room and began sipping my latte, scrolling through my social-media feed, and cherishing the silence I knew would soon vanish. I had just kissed my military husband goodbye on his way to work, and I was enjoying the comforting and reinvigorating feeling of the warm beverage slowly waking up my body when a news report from a military newspaper caught my attention.

I clicked on the link and read about the tragic passing of a U.S. Navy member who was stationed in Hawaii with his wife and two small children. I placed my latte on the end table next to me, sat up straight, and kept reading. I learned that his name was Brian, and he died in a scuba-diving accident. I also read that his wife was six months pregnant with their third baby. My phone fell out of my hand and onto my lap. My fingers were shaking, and my breathing was heavy. Staring into nothing, thoughts started racing through my head.

How could he be gone? He has a family!

They were stationed in Hawaii…. How could something so tragic happen in paradise?

His wife is pregnant….

"Momma." My sleepy three-year-old walked into the living room, carrying her favorite stuffed animal—a white, plush Maltese dog—by the paw. "I'm hungry."

I looked at her, blinked a few times, and shook my head to get myself out of the daze I'd been in. Then, I proceeded with my day. But I couldn't focus. An unsettling darkness had fallen deep inside my soul, and I couldn't explain why.

Three months later, I received a business proposition to work on a memoir. (I am a book editor and ghostwriter.) I read the summary of the story, and it sounded familiar, but I couldn't quite put my finger on it. The memoir was going to be about a love story, lots of adventures, and a tragic loss. I agreed to a conference call with the author, who sounded guarded but tentatively positive. I asked a few routine questions — word length, scope of the book, target audience — and then she started sharing her story.

"I want to write this book because I never want to forget the way he looked at me, the way his hand felt when he held mine, and the love we had for one another. I want to keep Brian's memory alive, for me and our three children."

Brian?

"We had recently moved to Hawaii," she added.

Hawaii?

"He loved the ocean, and he loved scuba diving," she said, her voice breaking.

It can't be....

But it was. I was speaking to the woman I had read about. The woman my heart ached for. The woman who had lost the love of her life. I was speaking to Ashley.

Together, we began working on her memoir. We spent many hours on the phone, during which she told me of the unconditional love that she and Brian shared, the countless funny memories that made us both laugh out loud, the many adventures they embarked on together, and the time she received a phone call from the scuba-diving instructor letting her know there had been an accident that morning in the ocean, and Brian had been rushed to the ER. I listened to her sobbing as I bit my lower lip, trying not to let her hear I was crying, too.

Later, I began talking to him.

"Brian, hi…" I whispered one day when I was home alone. I was sitting at my desk, in front of my computer with a Word document open. The blank page, titled "Chapter One," stared back at me, waiting. "I don't know if you know this, but I'm working on your wife's memoir. It's about your love story, actually, and I have a big favor to ask you: I need your help because I want to do right by you and your wife." As my words were lost to the empty room, I felt ridiculous. *Am I just talking to myself?*

Months, seasons, and chapters went by. During that time, talking to Brian helped me as much as talking to Ashley.

"And good morning to you," I'd often say to the invisible yet perceivable energy I felt every time I'd sit down to work on Ashley's memoir.

"Brian, I am having trouble with this chapter," I confided in him one day. "I need you to tell me how you felt. Take me back to this scene, please."

In that moment, "Time to Say Goodbye" by Andrea Bocelli began playing in my head, and I found myself humming along.

That's odd.

I contacted Ashley right away to tell her about it, and she told me how important that song was to them, something she had never shared with me before. I couldn't see her, but I could tell she had a big, bright smile on her face.

Well done, Brian! I thought.

I knew Brian was at my house the day the shaman came to visit. I also know he left on the day that Ashley and I finished writing her memoir. What the shaman couldn't have known, however, was that a few days prior to her visit, Ashley had placed a memorial containing Brian's ashes at the bottom of the ocean in Hawaii.

The memorial will eventually turn into a coral reef, forever making Brian part of the sea.

— Brunella Costagliola —

98

Mama

God could not be everywhere, so he created mothers.
~Jewish Proverb

I grew up in a rowhouse in Washington, D.C., with my mother, father, brother, aunt, cousin and grandmother, Mama. Mama ran the house. She started the day by fixing breakfast, putting the first pot of coffee on the stove, and straightening our clothes on the way out the door to school or work. Then she took care of the babies during the day, welcomed everyone home with cookies and milk, guided everyone through the dinner routines, and put us all to bed.

From the time I could hold onto the banister and walk upstairs to the second floor, I fell asleep in Mama's room each night. Her room was warm and wondrous, filled with books and pictures. It smelled of flowers and menthol from the lotion she rubbed on our chests each winter night. When I was very young, she would hold me on her lap and sing quietly, or she'd read stories of a great flood and a huge boat filled with every kind of animal. As I got older, I would fall asleep on the end of her bed. I was safe there. I felt loved and cared for, and I knew she would always be there to love and care for me.

Mama died one night in her sleep. My mom stopped the clock, my aunt pulled the curtains, and my uncle covered the mirrors. I was frightened and wanted to climb into her arms and wake her up. My dad held me and whispered that Mama would always be with me, watching over me and guiding me along my way. For days afterward, they would find me curled up at the end of her bed, smelling the flowers and hearing the soft sound of her voice singing her favorite songs.

As I grew older, I would talk to Mama, believing she was listening. Sometimes, I would lose faith because I never received an answer. Sometimes, I would hold her picture and wonder why I was not hearing or feeling her.

Time went by, and I moved out to the suburbs. I had a husband and two little girls by then, ages two and five. One summer night, the five-year-old was restless, and the ice-cream store was just a few short blocks away. "Let's go for a walk," I suggested, and she jumped at the suggestion. I asked my husband to watch our sleeping baby and headed out the door. Hand in hand, Helen and I started our adventure. When we reached the end of the block, someone called me.

"Dorothy!" I heard. "Dorothy!" I turned around but could see no one.

"Just hearing things," I said. "Let's go get that ice cream."

"Dorothy!" It was louder this time. "Dorothy!"

Again, I turned around and saw nothing. An uneasy feeling came over me. I picked up Helen and started to run back home. Entering the apartment, I heard the baby screaming. She had pushed herself under the bumper pad feet first and slid almost all the way out of the crib and then gotten her arm and head stuck between the slats. After freeing her, I held and rocked her, too frightened to think of anything else. I didn't want to think about what would have happened if I had shown up later.

My husband, thinking the baby was safe and asleep, had gone outside with a friend to smoke a cigarette. He hadn't heard the screams. Who had called out to me? Mama was the only person who had ever called me "Dorothy" with a rolling R. If I had not heard her, if she had not called out to me, my baby might not have survived. Mama had always watched out for me, letting me grow and mature and offering a hand or shoulder when needed. When I needed her the most, she was there.

I have told this story many times to my girls, assuring them that

Mama is still watching over us. Angels come to us in many ways. We just have to believe.

— Dottie Hoover —

99

Anna and Me

And tonight I'll fall asleep with you in my heart.
~Author Unknown

was sitting in a dark auditorium watching a play with my Anna seated on my right side. On a stage six rows ahead of us, the front of a school bus was parked on the left side. The headlights were on. Above the stage were faint lights to give us the feel of a night sky full of stars. Ominous trees with thick trunks and forked branches were scattered around, and a thick blanket of fog lay across the floor of the stage. A bus driver and a few children who appeared to be fifth- or sixth-graders were standing by the bus looking concerned. I remember I liked the girl in the red dress.

Suddenly, there was movement behind one of the trees. A tall, dark, monster-like figure was waiting in the darkness. I looked to the right at Anna, who looked stylish and sophisticated, as she often did. Salt-and-pepper short hair was brushed back from her tanned, aged face, and thin-rimmed glasses framed her kind eyes. She smiled and gave my hand a little squeeze.

When I looked forward again, there was a big movie screen. We were now watching a Benji movie. I loved movies with animals. We watched for a few minutes as Benji went off on an adventure to find his family. The smell of popcorn was in the air. The movie screen slowly started to open in the center like automatic doors. Light began to flood through. Anna and I stood up. She was holding my hand as the opening continued to grow wider. There was bright, warm sunlight coming in to embrace us. We took a step up onto the stage and out onto the beautiful white sand of Sarasota beach.

We slid off our shoes and walked toward the ocean, feeling the soft sand as our bare feet sank in with each step. I smelled the ocean air with the slightly briny scent of salt, heat, seaweed, and coconut suntan lotion. Near the water, I spied some shells and seaweed. Sand dollars and small butterfly shells were my favorite. I enjoyed collecting shells with Anna as we walked along the water's edge. A wave came in, and a layer of warm water flowed over my toes and then receded back toward the ocean.

We walked back toward the white condominium she used to live in. My family and I spent some wonderful vacations there with my grandparents before she moved to a house in a retirement community nearby. We stopped and faced each other on the beach. "It is time to say goodbye," she said softly but firmly. A kind smile lit up her face. I felt overwhelming sadness wash over me. Tears streamed down my face. I loved my Anna, and I did not want to say goodbye. We hugged each other tightly, and she told me it would be all right.

I woke up in my bed at home. It had been a dream. My face and pillow were wet, and I still felt like crying. I looked at the alarm clock on my nightstand. It was almost 5:00 A.M. Across the country, where my father and Gramps were with my Anna, it was almost 8:00 A.M. I felt scared that my dream meant she had passed away. She was in her home in hospice. After the news that her cancer was back, she had decided not to go through treatments again.

I convinced myself she was just on my mind. She could not be gone already. My dream had simply been my subconscious helping me deal with the fact that she was going to die soon. It took some time for me to get back to sleep.

Later that morning, my mother called to tell me that Anna had passed at 8:00 A.M. The overwhelming sadness hit me again. It was a while before I thought of the dream I'd had. When I told my mother about the dream, she told me she had a dream about Anna the morning she passed, too.

That was many years ago now. I still wonder if my dream was my subconscious helping me prepare or if she had indeed come to me in a dream to share some of the special things we had done together. I treasure that dream. I would like to believe she came to say goodbye in the only way she could — in a dream.

— Jennifer G. Lorrekovich —

A Gift from Heaven

*Your spirit guides and angels will never let you down
as you build a rapport with them.*
~Linda Deir

During the great ice storm of December 2013 — the one that rattled central Canada and the United States with frost quakes, downed powerlines across the eastern coast, and left millions of people without power for days — a miracle happened in the rural township of King about an hour's drive north of Toronto.

It was Christmas Eve, and we were into our third day without power. Our home sat on top of a hill overlooking rolling meadows and a kettle lake that jutted out from the forest's edge. Everything was buried beneath a sheet of ice over an inch thick. The world outside our window appeared frozen in time.

Five fireplaces roared for days on end, keeping the home warm and providing light once the sun set. As our family prepared for the Christmas Eve celebrations, I stood in the threshold of the great room and took a moment to enjoy the glass ornaments on the tree as they glistened from the glow of the fire. Our son Nathan, who was nearing two years of age, played with his cars and toy train by the hearth.

With the twenty-eight-foot-tall, vaulted ceiling and three walls of windows displaying the winter wonderland beyond their panes, our home was transformed into a snow globe, and the warmth of the fireplace had made this Nathan's favourite spot since we lost power

Miraculous Connections |

days before.

This is really beautiful, I thought to myself. My heart filled with gratitude for all of life's blessings, the greatest of which was our little one.

Needing an item from upstairs, I left for just a minute while Nathan played quietly with his toys. That was when I heard a horrendous crack, followed by a crash and a scream from the main floor. The tiles beneath my feet shook. The sound echoed through our home, louder than the frost quakes that rumbled through the earth's crust days before.

I ran from my bedroom to the gallery that overlooked the great room. The floor was in disarray. My husband and father were there, frantically heaving at a solid 7'x6' wood panel that lay upon the floor. The toy train peeked out from its edge. Nathan was beneath the rubble.

Racing back down the staircase, I thought the worst and prayed that I was wrong.

By the time I made it to the room, the men had raised the panel that had fallen nearly fifteen feet upon my son. With the extreme cold temperature outside and the continuous heat from the roaring fireplaces inside, the wooden facade had dried out, causing the finishing nails to loosen and weakening the glue. When the panel fell, it carried with it a large Thomas Kinkade painting and oversized candle holders.

The painting was damaged and a candle holder broke, but that was inconsequential. All that mattered was that our son survived that accident and had only the tiniest of bruises on his forehead. It was a miracle! He could have died from the impact.

My mother professed that Nathan's angel was watching over him. At the time, I still questioned the afterlife, so I smiled in reply and simply hugged my son a little tighter. My husband's eyes met mine and, within that stare, we both knew the same thing: Our son had narrowly escaped death. As my hands trembled from the aftershock tears of relief streamed down my cheeks.

Three years later, my family and I moved to a new town, and one of our neighbours invited me to hear a spiritual medium in her home. I had never connected with the spiritual realm before, so I decided to attend for curiosity's sake. Nearly twenty guests gathered that night. Before we began, the medium explained to the neighbours — who were few in comparison to the relatives — that our messages might not be as strong because the energy of the family members might overpower ours. However, that was not the case!

"The spiritual guides are telling me that there was an accident," said the medium to the group about halfway through the evening. "They are showing me a fireplace. I see snow and ice. It is Christmas. They are showing me a chimney. Something happened that day. Something fell, and someone got hurt," she exclaimed.

As she spoke to the room, my eyes teared up. My heart raced and my palms began to sweat. The medium was describing that frightful night from years before in vivid detail. In that moment, I froze, and fear overcame me — fear for the unknown, fear that this could somehow be a hoax, and fear for the almighty truth. Feeling lightheaded, I raised my hand and timidly said, "I think this message is for me."

The spiritual medium looked toward me with a warm smile. "Your spiritual guides want you to know that they intervened that night. They want you to know that they were with you then and are with you now," she said.

It was then that I knew it was time to believe!

Messages continued to pour in that night — not just for me but for all who were present. Tears were shed, and laughter filled the room. We experienced a form of enlightenment.

Since that first encounter with the spiritual world, I have seen other mediums, and each experience was just as rich and empowering. I have received messages from grandparents, friends and cousins who have passed before me. These experiences have taught me to live life with an open heart and mind, to listen to my intuition, and to make the most out of each day because our time here is short and precious.

As I wake up each morning and continue along my personal journey, I take comfort in knowing that I am not alone.

— Catherine C. Miles —

A Special Place

Unable are the loved to die. For love is immortality.
~Emily Dickinson

The sound of my cousin's words resonated in my mind like a mantra. Her mom — my Aunt Bonnie — was dying of kidney failure.

For the last fifteen years since my mother's death, Aunt Bonnie and I had nestled closely like a mother bear and her cub. Aunt Bonnie enjoyed giving me motherly advice, and I enjoyed listening to her wisdom. I called her my "second mother," and she called me her daughter. She would say, "I told your Mama that I would always watch over you."

We talked weekly about everything — me, her, the family, and the crazy events of the world. One evening, I shared with Aunt Bonnie my mother's visit from Heaven.

Before falling asleep, I imagined my mother's laughter. I explained that the touch lamp on my nightstand inexplicably turned on when I pictured my mother's smile. Later that week, I tossed and turned and was unable to sleep. To help overcome my despair and restlessness, I decided to watch a docudrama. In the closing scene, a friend read aloud the last entry of her dead friend's diary. She read, "If you were born, you were meant to die.... I know you're sad, and it's okay to be sad. But don't let sadness rule your life."

I found great comfort in those words that night, after fifteen years of grief and sadness. "I honestly believe that my mother sent those messages to me," I told Aunt Bonnie. "I'm ready to lay my mother's ashes to rest," I added as my voice began to quiver. "Aunt Bonnie, will you help me?"

"Come to visit, and we'll find that special place," she said.

***

Two weeks before her death, in one of our conversations, Aunt Bonnie repeatedly told me how much she loved me, and I responded, "I love you, too."

"You're a wonderful daughter to me, and I love you so much," she said.

After that phone call, I took notice of how overly affectionate she was. After her death, I learned that Aunt Bonnie knew she was dying when we had that call.

As I grieved over Aunt Bonnie's death and made plans to fly to California from Florida to pay my last respects, I lovingly carried my mother's ashes with me. I would have to find that special place for her ashes on my own now.

Before Aunt Bonnie's burial services, I met with a cemetery counselor. I told the counselor that I wanted to lay my mother's ashes in a niche wall — a beautiful marble columbarium wall.

"We have two available walls," the counselor said. "I also have a list of others in nearby cemeteries."

The counselor walked me and my cousin to the first available niche. It was a plain white marble columbarium wall. I shook my head.

We walked to the second niche. It was a bright white-and-brown marble wall with elegant gold lettering memorializing each soul within. Instantly, I knew that was the niche wall suitable for my mother.

"It feels right," I said. I turned and said to my cousin, "It's a beautiful marble wall!"

My cousin looked around as if trying to unscramble the scene. She walked up to the wall, turned, and looked toward the grassy burial ground ten feet in front of her. "Right there," she said as she pointed to the ground. "That's the burial spot where my mom is going to be laid to rest next week!"

A stunned silence fell over us.

The cemetery counselor later confirmed that she had no prior knowledge of my Aunt Bonnie's burial plot location. She showed me the only two marble walls that fit my specifications.

As in life and now in death, my Aunt Bonnie kept her promise. She found the perfect place to lay my mother to rest — a special place surrounded by those who love her and a beautiful parting gift to me.

— N.L. Zuniga —

Meet Our Contributors

Alison Acheson's most recent books are a memoir of caregiving, *Dance Me to the End: Ten Months and Ten Days with ALS*, and a picture book, *A Little House in a Big Place*. She is the founder of The Unschool for Writers.

John Kevin Allen is a minister and chaplain ordained by the United Church of Christ and approved for ministry with the United Church of Canada. He is a contributor to *Broadview* magazine. E-mail him at johnkevinallenwriting@gmail.com.

Teresa Ambord is a full-time author and editor for a global business publisher. That's how she pays the bills. But for fun she writes about her family, friends, and pets. She lives in the rural northeastern corner of California with her posse of small pets. They inspire her writing and decorate her life.

Shea Bart Andreone is a writer finishing her first book, *Carry On*, and has a blog called "Twig-Hugger." She has also been published on *The Next Family*, *Mother Figure*, and *Expressing Motherhood*. Shea lives in Los Angeles, CA with her husband, daughter, son, and Hazel the dog.

E. S. Arnold has been writing her entire life, from fourth grade scribbled stories and illustrations to all sorts of writing today. She loves a good fantasy or sci-fi book and plans to write for middle-grade and young adult audiences in the future.

Elizabeth A. Atwater lives in a small Southern town with her husband Joe. She discovered the joy of reading in first grade and that naturally seemed to evolve into a joy of writing. Writing brings Elizabeth so much pleasure that she cannot imagine ever stopping. She sold her first story to a romance magazine when she was seventeen years old.

Dave Bachmann is a retired teacher who taught English, writing, and reading skills to special needs students in Arizona for forty years. He now lives in California, writing stories for children and grown-ups, with his wife Jay, a retired elementary teacher, along with their fourteen-year-old Lab, Scout.

Kerrie R. Barney is currently a full-time graduate student studying accounting at the University of New Mexico — go Lobos! You can find her book *Life, the Universe, and Houseplants*, all about her humorous adventures growing indoor plants, on Amazon.

Carole Harris Barton is retired after a career in government service. Her stories have appeared in other *Chicken Soup for the Soul* books, Tim Russert's *Wisdom of Our Fathers*, and *Mysterious Ways* magazine. She is a wife and mother who lives with her husband, Paul, in Dunedin, FL.

Hosanna Barton is a wife and homeschooling mom of four living in Southern Colorado. She can often be found in her car, taking her children to ballet, baseball, or heading to the gym. She dreams of having the time to write something truly epic someday, but for now, she's thrilled to make her history come alive by re-telling her memories via short stories.

Lainie Belcastro is blessed to have her seventh story in the *Chicken Soup for the Soul* series! She is a published poet, and writes for children, and for women sharing their life challenges. Lainie and her daughter, Nika, are also creators of Mrs. Terra Cotta Pots, an endearing storyteller for children. Learn more at www.lainiebelcastro.com.

Tamara Bell dreamed of being an author since she was eight years old and would stay inside during recess to fold construction paper and write short stories. She is honored to be featured in her third *Chicken Soup for the Soul* book. She has also co-authored a local history book and has even been featured in *Angels on Earth* magazine.

Theresa Brandt writes, cooks, gardens, crafts and is living happily in mid-Missouri. She shares her life with her three (almost) grown boys, the best boyfriend ever, a pack of furry friends, a wonderful extended family and friends. She writes articles for the local paper, freelance stories, and is working on a novel.

Thomas Brooks received his M.Ed. from Ashland University and recently retired from a communications company where he was a technician and technical educator for many years. He is married to a high school science and math teacher, and enjoys carving, making and flying kites, fixing things, and writing when time allows.

Jill Burns lives in the mountains of West Virginia with her wonderful family. She's a retired piano teacher and performer. She enjoys writing, music, gardening, nature, and spending time with her grandchildren.

Kait Carson is a nationally published author of cozy and traditional mysteries. Learn more at www.kaitcarson.com.

This book is the eighth *Chicken Soup for the Soul* book **Pastor Wanda Christy-Shaner** has been published in. She has also been published in numerous magazines. She is a licensed minister, singer, adrenaline buff and animal rescuer. She is in the process of writing a line of children's books.

Barbara L. Ciccone received her Bachelor of Science degree with honors from Regis University in 1992. She has two daughters and two grandchildren. She loves horses and dogs, playing the piano, and reading.

Shelene Codner received her Bachelor of Science in Psychology with a minor in Sociology from Upper Iowa University and will receive her Master of Arts in Communication from Drake University in spring 2022. Shelene enjoys sewing, crocheting, knitting, gardening, reading, writing, photography and spending time with family.

Kim Cook has been writing and creating since she could hold a pencil. Educated at the University of South Florida, Kim is a fifth-generation native Floridian who takes pride in her family, her home state, and her craft. She enjoys creativity of all sorts, including writing, poetry, baking, cooking, painting, and more!

Brunella Costagliola, born and raised in southern Italy, is the owner and CEO of The Military Editor Agency, a writing and editing agency catering to military authors and military-related manuscripts. She enjoys traveling, writing, and cooking, and lives in Florida with her husband, two children, and three dogs.

Christine Cowles received her Bachelor of Arts in English from Kent State University in 1985. She works in a library where she enjoys having access to all the latest titles. She enjoys spending time with her husband, children and granddaughter as well as tending to her ever-changing menagerie of rescue dogs.

Bluedolphin Crow received her Master of Fine Arts and Graduate Certificate in Professional Writing from Southern New Hampshire University. She is a certified content marketer and certified master mindset coach. Bluedolphin loves helping solo businesspeople thrive and grow, nature walks, cats, museums, and art galleries.

Nancy Curtis is currently on the move, but will always consider her home Oceanside, CA. She is thankful to God for giving her this second chance (mentioned in her story). She loves spending time with her husband, her two daughters, and her grandson... and it's even better if it's happening at Disneyland with food in her hand.

Barbara Davey is an adjunct professor in the English Department at Caldwell University where she challenges undergraduates to stop texting and start writing. She is a graduate of Seton Hall University where she received bachelor's and master's degrees in English and journalism. She and her husband live in Verona, NJ.

Stephanie DeNicola works as a director of human resources for an IT software/hardware company in Fort Washington, PA. She and her husband, Michael, are parents to two amazing girls, Raisa and Korbyn. She loves hiking, yoga, music and traveling. E-mail her at Denicola1818@gmail.com.

Dr. MaryAnn Diorio is a widely published, award-winning author of fiction for children and adults. A former university professor, she has written for *The Saturday Evening Post*, *Human Events*, *The Press of Atlantic City*, and Billy Graham's *Decision Magazine*. Learn more at maryanndiorio.com.

Hayley Dodwell is a freelance writer from the UK. She has written articles for numerous websites and is a published author on Amazon. Hayley is also a professional flute player who has performed up and down England for years! She is a vegetarian and a huge animal lover.

Renee Dubeau lives in Nashville, TN, with her husband and four (mostly) grown children. A healthcare worker by day and writer by compulsion, Renee is obsessed with the human condition and all the reasons why people do what they do. Renee enjoys yoga, hiking, gardening, cooking, baking, and playing with her tuxedo cats.

Corinea Andrews Duzick lives in Alabama with her husband. She grew up in Pennsylvania. She has a son and a daughter. She works in a home-health setting. She began writing in the 1980s, mostly poetry. She published a book of poetry in 2011. She enjoys time with her family, her pets, and going to the beach.

John Elliott was an officer with the Fairfax County Police in Virginia from 1974 to 1983; Police in Florida from 1989 to 1998; Interpol in Lyon, France from 1999 to 2012. He also trained officers for the Royal Canadian Mounted Police and for the London Metropolitan Police.

John Esposito is the pastor of a small church in Connecticut. He and his wife have two awesome sons. John enjoys woodworking, playing guitar, and spending time in Appalachia serving their families.

A teacher's unexpected whisper, "You've got writing talent," ignited **Sara Etgen-Baker's** writing desire. Sara ignored that whisper and pursued a different career; upon retirement, she returned to writing. Her manuscripts have been published in a host of anthologies and magazines including the *Chicken Soup for the Soul* series and *Guideposts*.

Leslie Freiberger is a writer. She enjoys living in California where she is raising her three wonderful children in the same house where she grew up. She writes a humor blog, and her essays have appeared in newspapers and online publications. She is an avid hiker, cook and party hostess. Learn more at waffletude.com.

Marilyn Frey, a retired banker, lives and writes in Saskatchewan, Canada. She published her first novel in 2020. Her short stories appear in several regional and national magazines and anthologies. Marilyn believes the complexities of life are the basis of great stories, ones to be told and shared.

Lorraine Furtner was born with inky fingers, loves exploring writing styles and is a published playwright, poet, journalist, and fiction writer. This is her fifth story published in the *Chicken Soup for the Soul* series. She is currently preparing for her next writing adventure in the world of children's picture books.

Gail Gabrielle's dream of becoming a published author continues to blossom in her fifth contribution to the *Chicken Soup for the Soul* series. Her focus always centers on family and her fabulous children, Danielle, Alexandra and Zack. "In the Mood" is a tribute to her son, Zachary Christopher.

Elizabeth K. Goodine is still traveling a spiritual journey in California. She is originally from Maine and hopes to find herself back there when the perfect woodsy cabin or seaside cottage in which to write presents itself. In the meantime, she dabbles in architectural photography, design, and outdoor adventures.

This marks **Lacy Gray's** third time being published in the *Chicken Soup for the Soul* series. Poet, author, and aspiring lyricist, Lacy describes herself as just a girl next door living a colorful life. With sights set on becoming a full-time writer, she finds inspiration in life, both current and past. Learn more at lacygray.com.

Erin Hall is a Michigan native currently living in Chicago, IL. By trade, she is a PR and communications professional but moonlights with her first love — writing. She has been previously published in the *Detroit Metro Times* and *Multiplicity Magazine*. Find her at www. arekdgirl.com, on Twitter @ErinHall802 or e-mail her at ehall802@gmail.com.

Native Californian **Laurie Hall** lives in Plymouth, MA with her cat (and chief shreditor), Sam. Laurie's short stories and non-fiction have been published both in the U.S. and the U.K. Her satirical fantasy, *Blood Will Out (With the Proper Solvent)*, was published in July 2021 under the pen name of Lauren Stoker.

Maryann Hamilton is a retired registered art therapist who enjoys pursuing her soul passion for writing and creating art. A sign above her desk reads: I don't believe in Miracles, I EXPECT them. In her leisure time you may find her lunching with friends or fence judging at horse shows with her daughter in Kentucky.

Charles Earl Harrel served as a pastor for thirty years before stepping aside to pursue writing. His stories, devotionals, and articles have appeared in numerous magazines and anthologies. He is also an eight-time contributor to the *Chicken Soup for the Soul* series. Charles enjoys camping, hiking, and is currently writing a novel.

Rob Harshman is a retired geography teacher who lives with his wife in Mississauga. Rob loves spending time with his family including his four grandchildren. He has written a variety of stories and books, including seven stories for the *Chicken Soup for the Soul* series. He is just finishing twenty-five children's mystery stories.

Pamela Haskin is a frequent contributor to the *Guideposts* family of magazines. She wrote the award-winning book, *A Deliberate Life: A Journey into the Alaskan Wilderness*. Pamela now lives in Sulphur Springs, TX, with her recently retired husband. She continues to put up her prayer-tree on November 1st.

Nancy Hoag graduated with honors from the University of Washington in Seattle. She is a wife, mother, grandmother and author of nearly 1,200 stories and four books: *Cooking With Love and Honey*, *Good Morning! Isn't It a Fabulous Day!*, *Storms Pass, So Hang On!* and *The Fingerprints Of God... Seeing His Hand in the Unexpected*.

Dorothy Hoover has lived in the Washington, D.C. area all her life. Her interests include art, comic books and conventions, and the teaching of art to children. She loves writing stories about her three daughters and three grandsons.

Rosemary Collins Horning received her degree in Journalism from SUNY Morrisville, NY. She lives in Upstate New York where she enjoys hiking, biking, walking, painting, and writing. She also spends time in Virginia with her children and grandchildren.

Georgia A. Hubley retired after twenty years from the money world in Silicon Valley to write about her world. Twenty-one of her stories appear in the *Chicken Soup for the Soul* series. Vignettes of her life also appear in numerous other magazines and anthologies.

Zaquynn Phoenix Iamati always wanted to write a book based on the experiences documented in her journals, which she refers to as her X-files. A few years ago, she joined a writing group and began turning each unusual, factual entry into a short story. This is one of them.

A Southerner who has lived throughout the South, **Dea Irby** moved north to North Carolina in 2012 with her husband and the last of eight children. As an author, she has contributed to two *Chicken*

Soup for the Soul books. Dea, a TEDx speaker, presents on parenting, leadership, and building belonging. Learn more at deairby.com.

Annie Juliana Francis Ismail currently lives with her husband in Colombo, Sri Lanka. She was a music and English teacher for four years at a local private school and is now focusing on being a full-time music tutor. During her free time, she enjoys reading, writing, traveling, and playing the piano.

Ready for her fifth career, **Lydia Jackson** recently graduated from a Culinary Arts program in Ontario. She is passionate about the benefits of healthy eating and nourishing the mind, body and soul, and hopes to be of service through her knowledge and various skills.

Julia Johnson was blessed with living life in a military family and was able to travel to some wonderful places. She has a daughter and a son who were both born in Italy. Her grandchildren bring her much love and laughter.

During retirement, **D. Lincoln Jones** turned to writing to fulfill his creative needs. He's authored two books of historical fiction, with a third nearing completion. He also wrote a short story entitled "The Popsicle Kids" which appeared in *Chicken Soup for the Soul: Age Is Just a Number*.

Susan A. Karas has spent years perfecting her craft, graduating proudly from many writing programs. She won the national Guideposts Writing Contest and has gone on to be published many times in the magazine, as well as in the *Chicken Soup for the Soul* series and various other publications. She is currently working on her first novel.

Kathryn Kemp received her Bachelor of Arts degree, with honors, from Arizona State University in 1971. She and her husband enjoy their lake forest home in Elk, WA with their pets and the daily parade of wildlife. Her greatest loves are God, her husband, and writing Christian children's books.

Jennifer Kennedy is thrilled to have her fifth story published in the *Chicken Soup for the Soul* series and dedicates this special one to the wonderful family Nanny created and the memories they shared on Durham Street. She lives in the Philadelphia suburbs with her husband, sons, and dogs. E-mail her at jenniferkennedypr@gmail.com.

Kimberly Kimmel has 500 articles and short stories to her credit. She also authored, along with an actor friend, a non-fiction book about how to get work in TV and movies as an extra. She grew up in Los Angeles and was a music major in college. Her passions are reading, music, and writing her Western historical romances.

The daughter of Mexican parents, **Mariely Lares** holds a bachelor's degree in computer science engineering. When not writing books, Mariely can be found doing everything from the mundane to the magical all the while trying to unravel the mysteries of the universe.

Corrie Lopez is a teacher and a worship leader who believes in God answering our prayers through our own prayers and those that love us and pray for us. Corrie is surrounded by a biological family, church family, and school family that she thanks God for every single day.

Jennifer G. Lorrekovich is a moderator for Storybird.com. As figment68 she loves to write stories on the site. Jennifer lives with her husband and has two grown children in Washington State. She loves reading, writing, arts and crafts. Her plans are to continue writing creative and inspiring books for young readers.

Singer, songwriter and worship leader, **Allison Lynn**, is drawn to the power of story to grow hearts and communities. Allison and her husband, Gerald Flemming, form the award-winning duo, Infinitely More. Their ninth album of original music will release in 2022. Learn more at www.InfinitelyMore.ca.

Mary Beth Magee's faith leads her to explore God's world and write about it. She writes novels, short fiction, poetry, non-fiction and devotions, as well as recollections in several anthologies. She speaks on a variety of topics. Learn more at www.LOL4.net.

Yashna Malik is a twenty-two-year-old depression survivor from Delhi, India. She is completing her graduation in English and aspires to become a teacher. She has published a book of her poems as well as having her poems published in various anthologies. Her life motto is, live and let live.

Amannda G. Maphies received a B.A. in Sociology, with an emphasis in Human Resources, from MSSU in Joplin, MO in 2002. She has two sons: William, eleven, and Waylan, nine. Manndi works at the UMKC School of Pharmacy at MSU. She enjoys reading, travel, and mountain biking, with a passion for writing her adventures for others to enjoy.

Joshua J. Mark is an editor/director and writer for the online site World History Encyclopedia. His non-fiction stories have also appeared in *Timeless Travels* and *History Ireland* magazines. His wife, Betsy Mark, passed over to the other side on 4 August 2018 but continues to live on with him and their daughter Emily in spirit.

Trisha Ridinger McKee is a multi-genre writer who resides in Pennsylvania with her husband, daughter, and Bulldogs. She works at a university and is an award-winning author of over 100 short stories and seven novels.

Barb McKenna has been a writer since she was six years old. She spent thirty-five years as a journalist for newspapers, television, and radio. She's also been published across Canada in various newspapers and magazines. She has a passion for memoir writing.

Courtney Essary Messenbaugh is a writer who lives in Colorado with her husband, three children, and a very silly dog. She's written about parenting and health and wellness for various magazines and has had a few poems published in journals like *High Shelf* and *Glitchwords*. When she's not writing, you can find her outside.

Catherine C. Miles has a master's degree in communications, plus degrees in psychology and TV production. Learning is a lifelong passion and writing stories is her favorite form of creative expression. She thanks her family for their unconditional love and support and is grateful for everyone who is a part of this literary journey.

Marya Morin is a freelance writer. Her stories and poems have appeared in publications such as *Woman's World* and Hallmark. Marya also penned a weekly humorous column for an online newsletter and writes custom poetry on request. She lives in the country with her husband. E-mail her at Akushla514@hotmail.com.

Carmen Myrtis-Garcia is a retired college teacher and published writer. She founded the Facebook group, Hope for the Widow's Journey and hosts a podcast interviewing widows. She and her husband lived their dream on a small island in Belize. She has a gypsy soul but resides in Colorado. She is writing a devotional for widows.

Yemurai Nhongo completed her bachelor's degree in 2007 and then pursued a career in education. She is passionate about sharing her interests and showing others that they can make money from their interests too.

Leonora Rita V. Obed is a West Trenton, NJ-based fine artist and freelance writer. Her painting, Wichita Gothika, was featured in the exhibition Creative Minds and Unique Voices at Princeton University, Winter 2020. Her poem "Nocturne in E Flat" was accepted into the Aspects Ekphrastic Challenge, Northern Ireland.

Leo Pacheco is an entrepreneur, licensed Realtor, coach, inspirational speaker, and author. He and his wife live near Orlando, FL, along with their two teenage boys. He enjoys traveling, rafting, and serving as a board member for several non-profit organizations. He inspires others to create a "revolutionary life."

Nancy Emmick Panko is a retired pediatric RN and frequent contributor to the *Chicken Soup for the Soul* series. An award-winning author of *Guiding Missal*, *Sheltering Angels*, and *Blueberry Moose*, Nancy is mother of two, grandma to four. She loves to be in, on, or near the water of Lake Gaston, NC with her family. Learn more at www.nancypanko.com.

Sue Pasztor is a retired nurse living in Florida with her husband of forty-six years. She loves to read, and occasionally write short stories of interest. Sue loves traveling and enjoying retirement in a great community of friends.

Donna Paulson has four children and lives on Martha's Vineyard. She enjoys the ocean and hunting for sea glass with her dog, Odie. Donna's novel, *The Curse of the Rum Runners*, is set to be published soon.

Alice Potts enjoys reading and writing. Alice has been reading *Chicken Soup for the Soul* books for many years. After retiring in 2016, she began her writing career. When Alice is not writing, she spends time singing, playing the guitar and piano, and traveling.

Cheryl Potts is a native Californian with fifteen grandchildren. She loves reading and writing historical fiction, gardening, and camping with her husband, Richard, and their cattle dog, Katie. She is currently working on a novel based on her Irish great-grandmother.

Connie Kaseweter Pullen lives in rural Sandy, OR, near her five children and several grandchildren. She earned a B.A. degree, with honors, at the University of Portland in 2006, with a double major in Psychology and Sociology. Connie enjoys writing, photography and exploring nature. E-mail her at MyGrandmaPullen@aol.com.

Natalie June Reilly is a writer living out her days in sunny Southern California. She is a social influencer who founded the movement Nothing but Love Notes on the premise that a handwritten love note can save the day. Gratitude changes everything.

Mark Rickerby is an owner and lead writer at Temple Gate Films, with several shows in development. He has had over twenty-five stories published in the *Chicken Soup for the Soul* series. He loves travel, singing, and old movies. He says, "No matter what I accomplish in this world, my daughters Emma and Marli will always be my greatest sources of pride and joy."

Patricia Ann Rossi is an avid writer, reader and runner. Patricia volunteers as a facilitator at creative writing workshops for cancer survivors. She is active in her community, and serves on local not-for-profit boards as well as her college alumni board.

A recent transplant to Florida, **Joan Sammons-Fernandez** will always consider herself a Jersey girl at heart. Most often you can find her in her office educating and inspiring her many clients as a wellness coach. A few days a week she can be found watching her two beautiful granddaughters. This is Joan's first published piece, but she has many more short stories that she's excited to share in the future.

Caroline Sealey is blessed to be a mum, farm gramma, author, and freelance writer. Her life consists of the four Fs — faith, family, farming, and friends. Thrilled to be a four-time contributor to the *Chicken Soup for the Soul* series, Caroline also has had stories and articles published in magazines and newspapers.

Faye Shannon received her Bachelor of Science, magna cum laude, from Northern Michigan University in 1979 and her master's degree in Social Work from Michigan State University in 1981. She has two grown sons and is a retired clinical social worker. Faye enjoys reading, gardening, baking, and walking her Terrier, Amber.

Ann Sharon Siweck is a published author living in Florida. She loves to read, write, swim, and enjoys her dog. Sharon is a Personality Plus consultant who travels and speaks to women's groups across the U.S. She is a widow of thirty-one years with a desire to minister to other hurting people and widows.

For sixty years, **Judy Stengel's** passion for writing has ignited her soul and brought joy to her and others. A retired reading teacher with a master's degree, Judy has led writing workshops up north and now in Florida, where you can find her meditating, exploring nature with her husband, and expanding her creativity and spirituality.

Jean Haynie Stewart lives in Rancho Mission Viejo, CA, is from Decatur, GA, attended Agnes Scott College, and is married to pilot husband, Bill, for sixty-one years. Freelance writer and editor, her stories are about family, including their twin daughters, two grandchildren, and family pets.

Christine Trollinger is a retired insurance agent. Widowed with three children, she writes for pleasure in her spare time. Christine has been published in several books in the *Chicken Soup for the Soul* series.

Teri Tucker has an MS in Vedic Studies. She is the author of *Enjoying India: The Essential Handbook* and *Travel Fearlessly in India: What Every Woman Should Know About Personal Safety* published under the name of J.D. Viharini, an epithet of Ganga that means "one who wanders around enjoying India."

Amanda W. homeschooled her children and, now that they have flown the nest, tends to the pets, plants, and books they left behind. She also writes, edits, and occasionally teaches.

Dorann Weber is a freelance photographer who has a passion for writing, especially for the *Chicken Soup for the Soul* series. She is a contributor for Getty Images and worked as a photojournalist. Her photos have appeared in magazines and Hallmark cards. She loves reading, hiking, and spending time with her family.

Robin Weber is a wife of forty-seven years and mother of two with five grandchildren. She lives in Dunedin, FL and has worked as a hairdresser at a senior living facility for over thirty-five years. She loves gardening, sewing, and people in general.

Jamie Williams is native-born to Hawaii. Several years ago, Jamie and her family traded life on the island to explore the Rocky Mountains of Colorado. She is a wife to her soulmate, mother of four adult kiddos, and five amazing grandbabies. Her passion for writing started a blog, Ontheseaofhisgrace.com.

Cynthia Zayn lives outside of Atlanta, GA and is a frequent contributor to the *Chicken Soup for the Soul* series. Her other works include the first and second editions of *Narcissistic Lovers: How to Cope, Recover and Move On*; *Finding the Rest: A Guide to Discovering Emotional Peace Amid the Turmoil*; and *To Have and to Hold til Rest Do You Part*.

Alisa Tapia, writing as **N.L. Zuniga** is an aviation administrative law judge for a federal agency and a freelance writer. Her articles have been published in *The Federal Lawyer* magazine. She has served as a contest judge for Ageless Authors, Omega Writers and Women's Fiction Writers Association. She plans to pursue her MFA degree in 2023.

Meet Amy Newmark

Amy Newmark is the bestselling author, editor-in-chief, and publisher of the *Chicken Soup for the Soul* book series. Since 2008, she has published 179 new books, most of them national bestsellers in the U.S. and Canada, more than doubling the number of Chicken Soup for the Soul titles in print today. She is also the author of *Simply Happy*, a crash course in Chicken Soup for the Soul advice and wisdom that is filled with easy-to-implement, practical tips for enjoying a better life.

Amy is credited with revitalizing the Chicken Soup for the Soul brand, which has been a publishing industry phenomenon since the first book came out in 1993. By compiling inspirational and aspirational true stories curated from ordinary people who have had extraordinary experiences, Amy has kept the twenty-eight-year-old Chicken Soup for the Soul brand fresh and relevant.

Amy graduated *magna cum laude* from Harvard University where she majored in Portuguese and minored in French. She then embarked on a three-decade career as a Wall Street analyst, a hedge fund manager, and a corporate executive in the technology field. She is a Chartered Financial Analyst.

Her return to literary pursuits was inevitable, as her honors thesis in college involved traveling throughout Brazil's impoverished northeast region, collecting stories from regular people. She is delighted to have come full circle in her writing career — from collecting stories "from the people" in Brazil as a twenty-year-old to, three decades later, collecting stories "from the people" for Chicken Soup for the Soul.

When Amy and her husband Bill, the CEO of Chicken Soup for the Soul, are not working, they are visiting their four grown children and their four grandchildren.

Follow Amy on Twitter @amynewmark. Listen to her free podcast — Chicken Soup for the Soul with Amy Newmark — on Apple, Google, or by using your favorite podcast app on your phone.

Thank You

We owe huge thanks to all our contributors and fans. We received thousands of submissions for this popular topic, and we spent months reading all of them. Our editor Laura Dean read all of them and narrowed down the selection for Associate Publisher D'ette Corona and Publisher and Editor-in-Chief Amy Newmark.

Susan Heim did the first round of editing, D'ette chose the perfect quotations to put at the beginning of each story, and Amy edited the stories and shaped the final manuscript.

As we finished our work, D'ette Corona continued to be Amy's right-hand woman in working with all our wonderful writers. Barbara LoMonaco, Kristiana Pastir and Elaine Kimbler jumped in to proof, proof, proof. And yes, there will always be typos anyway, so please feel free to let us know about them at webmaster@chickensoupforthesoul. com, and we will correct them in future printings.

The whole publishing team deserves a hand, including our Senior Director of Marketing Maureen Peltier, our Vice President of Production Victor Cataldo, Executive Assistant Mary Fisher, and our graphic designer Daniel Zaccari, who turned our manuscript into this beautiful, inspirational book.

Sharing Happiness, Inspiration, and Hope

Real people sharing real stories, every day, all over the world. In 2007, *USA Today* named *Chicken Soup for the Soul* one of the five most memorable books in the last quarter-century. With over 100 million books sold to date in the U.S. and Canada alone, more than 250 titles in print, and translations into nearly fifty languages, "chicken soup for the soul®" is one of the world's best-known phrases.

Today, twenty-nine years after we first began sharing happiness, inspiration and hope through our books, we continue to delight our readers with new titles, but have also evolved beyond the bookshelves with super premium pet food, television shows, a podcast, video journalism from aplus.com, licensed products, and free movies and TV shows on our Popcornflix and Crackle apps. We are busy "changing your world one story at a time®." Thanks for reading!

Share with Us

We all have had Chicken Soup for the Soul moments in our lives. If you would like to share your story or poem with millions of people around the world, go to chickensoup.com and click on Submit Your Story. You may be able to help another reader and become a published author at the same time. Some of our past contributors have launched writing and speaking careers from the publication of their stories in our books!

We only accept story submissions via our website. They are no longer accepted via mail or fax. Visit our website, www.chickensoup. com, and click on Submit Your Story for our writing guidelines and a list of topics we are working on.

To contact us regarding other matters, please send us an e-mail through webmaster@chickensoupforthesoul.com, or fax or write us at:

Chicken Soup for the Soul
P.O. Box 700
Cos Cob, CT 06807-0700
Fax: 203-861-7194

One more note from your friends at Chicken Soup for the Soul: Occasionally, we receive an unsolicited book manuscript from one of our readers, and we would like to respectfully inform you that we do not accept unsolicited manuscripts, and we must discard the ones that appear.

Changing lives one story at a time®
www.chickensoup.com